1962

ENGLISH SPIRITUAL WRITERS

ENGLISH SPIRITUAL WRITERS

Edited by
CHARLES DAVIS, S.T.L.

With a Foreword by
HIS EMINENCE CARDINAL GODFREY
Archbishop of Westminster

SHEED AND WARD • NEW YORK

NIHIL OBSTAT: JOANNES M. T. BARTON, S.T.D., L.S.S.
CENSOR DEPUTATUS
IMPRIMATUR: E. MORROGH BERNARD
VICARIUS GENERALIS
WESTMONASTERII: DIE 21a JUNII 1961

The Nihil obstat *and* Imprimatur *are a declaration that a book or pamphlet is considered to be free from doctrinal or moral error. It is not implied that those who have granted the* Nihil obstat *and* Imprimatur *agree with the contents, opinions or statements expressed.*

LIBRARY OF CONGRESS CATALOG CARD NUMBER 62-9110

MANUFACTURED IN THE UNITED STATES OF AMERICA

FOREWORD

English spiritual writers have their own peculiar characteristics, as will be seen by the readers of this volume. The publishers and contributors have done a useful and timely work. For we may have become so used to reading the spiritual writings or classics of other nations that we could overlook or give scant attention to our own treasury. This is made quite accessible to us by the efforts of our Catholic publishers to whose enterprise we owe many volumes now available.

Of the particular qualities of older English piety we might say that two are outstanding: first, a lively devotion to Jesus the Incarnate Word; and, second, a tender love of the Passion of Our Lord. These characteristics are clearly seen in the writings of Richard Rolle and in *The Cloud of Unknowing*. In Julian of Norwich we see these traits combined with a certain homeliness of approach to the divine Majesty: such devotions led them up that ladder of perfection described in the classical work of Walter Hilton.

The sturdiness of our nation and its sense of humour are manifest in the life and prayer of St Thomas More, while English grit and doggedness are exemplified in St John Fisher and all the gallant company who followed the Lord Chancellor and the Bishop of Rochester to the gallows or the block. The tender piety of Father Faber, nourished by his keen imagination, will help many: and the robust devotion of Cardinal Manning certainly has a powerful appeal.

We see in their writing and preaching the health and strength of English piety. Doughty champions these and strong defenders of the faith of our fathers. Such reading as we find here will help to keep our faith, as we so often sing, living still.

This book will urge us to pray. We learn to pray by praying, just as we learn to swim by swimming and to skate by skating. From these our fellow-countrymen we can learn much about the kind of prayer that is suited to our own national character. We are grateful for this interesting volume and warmly welcome and commend it.

✠ WILLIAM CARDINAL GODFREY
Archbishop of Westminster

8th December, 1960

EDITOR'S NOTE

THE debt that English Catholics owe in theology and spirituality to Continental Catholic writing is immense; and, to judge from the many translations on publishers' lists, our debit balance is steadily mounting. All to the good in some respects: a narrow nationalism should have no place in the Catholic Church, and it becomes simply ridiculous in theology and spirituality. But the mark of an adult is that he gives and not merely receives, that he makes a contribution to the common endeavour and is not merely supported by it; and so, if the Church in England is to reach maturity once more, it must learn to offer again a distinctive contribution to the thought and work of the universal Church.

The English Catholic tradition is discernible most easily in our spiritual writers. The intangible components of such a tradition are more readily felt in the concrete than analysed in the abstract. The present collection is intended to help such a concrete perception by providing an introduction to our principal spiritual writers. Having taken stock of our heritage, we can go forward and enlarge it with the new insights being granted to the Church of today. The biblical and liturgical movements, the new understanding of the Church and the apostolate, are not destroying but enriching the traditions of the German and French Churches. They can do the same to our own tradition, which developed in this way will introduce fresh notes into the harmony of the present revival, thus adapting it to the temperament of our people while at the same time benefiting the rest of the Church by our national contribution.

This series of essays on English spiritual writers appeared as articles in *The Clergy Review* from November 1958 to July 1961. There were twenty-five articles in the original series, but it was not possible to include them all in this volume. A selection has been made, determined by the enduring quality and significance of the writers studied.

CHARLES DAVIS

CONTENTS

ENGLISH SPIRITUAL WRITERS

I

AELFRIC OF EYNSHAM

BY A BENEDICTINE OF STANBROOK (D.S.H.)

ALTHOUGH overshadowed by the more eminent names of St Bede the Venerable and King Alfred the Great, Aelfric of Eynsham was the greatest of the late Old English scholars. Not much is known of his personal history. Born about A.D. 955, he was educated as a monk at Winchester under St Ethelwold, of whom he afterwards wrote a Latin biography, and thus came under the influence of the monastic revival associated with the names of St Dunstan and his friends. He became Abbot of Cerne Abbas, Dorset, in 987, of Eynsham near Oxford in 1005, and died probably between 1020 and 1025. Throughout this most troublous period in his country's story, his life was devoted to the study and exposition of spiritual doctrine, with the singlehearted aim of promoting sound religion among his fellow-countrymen.

He wrote during the reign of Ethelred the Unready, that worst period of the Danish invasions, of political and military disaster and confusion. The first volume of his Homilies dates from 991, the year of the Battle of Maldon; the second from 944, for which we find the following entry in the Anglo-Saxon Chronicle:

> In this year came Anlaf and Swegen to London on the Nativity of St Mary with four and ninety ships. And they were fighting hard against the town, and sought to set it on fire. But there they suffered more harm and evil than they ever weened that the citizens of any town could have done to them. Yea, the Holy Mother of God showed on that day to the citizens the gentleness of her heart, and saved them from their foes.[1]

But to all these things the homilist makes but one solitary allusion in his letter to Archbishop Sigeric: "And although terrified by the

[1] Retain our Lady's birthday; for the year read 1940; double the number of vessels, not from the sea but from the air; for Olaf Tryggvason and Sweyn Forkbeard substitute Hitler and Goering.

many violent deeds of the hostile raiders, after we had sent your Holiness the aforesaid book, yet, not wishing to be found lying promisers, we have completed this work in a sorrowing spirit." Not even the onslaughts of the wild Norsemen should turn him from his task.

Aelfric's importance in the history of English spirituality is less as an original thinker than as a providential and very capable agent in continuing and popularizing in English the type of work St Bede had done in Latin. His literary achievement is not so much brilliant as practical, evoked by the necessities of the time, executed with conscientious care and in fact comparable with that of Bishop Challoner some eight centuries later. Both men were labouring to bring Christian instruction within the reach of people who sorely needed it but who for one reason or another could not have recourse to such sources as the Fathers and the hagiographers; their influence in either case was not merely defensive but also formative, establishing a recognizable quality in English piety which persisted for long after their own day.

Aelfric's writings were designed expressly for the lower clergy and the people at large, and it was just those classes whose religious instruction and spiritual life would presumably have suffered even more seriously than they actually did from ignorance and neglect after the Norman Conquest and the consequent eclipse of English learning, had it not been for the survival of such aids as his solid, practical and easily intelligible doctrinal instructions.

But like King Alfred himself, Aelfric never for a moment considered that the ability to read translations in English was an adequate substitute for a Latin education. Hence in later years he set to work to compile the first formal Latin grammar in the English language together with a *Colloquium*—a charming little series of Latin-English dialogues for the help of young scholars—"to get both languages into your heads," he says, "before you can advance to higher studies". There was nothing novel in the idea that young Englishmen should learn Latin; they had been doing so, after one fashion or another, for four centuries. The innovation lay in producing an English textbook to make the business easier for all concerned. This laborious elementary undertaking was simply an exercise of apostolic zeal.

> Whence [he asks in the Preface to the Grammar] shall there come wise teachers among God's people, unless they learn in youth? and can the faith prosper, if learning and teachers perish? Therefore God's servants and ecclesiastics must earnestly be warned, for fear that in our days sacred learning should grow cold or perish, as it happened among the English people a few years ago, so that no English cleric could write or understand a letter in Latin, until Archbishop Dunstan and Bishop Ethelwold restored learning in the monasteries.

To his mind, the scholar's duty is obvious:

> It behoves every man who possesses any accomplishment to utilize it for other men, and entrust to some other man the pound that God has entrusted to him, so that God's treasure may not lie idle, and he may not be called a worthless servant and be bound and thrown into darkness, as the holy gospel says. It becomes young men to learn wisdom and it becomes the old to teach knowledge to their juniors, because through learning is the faith made fast. And every man who loves wisdom is happy, and if he who can do so will neither learn nor teach, then his understanding grows cold in regard to holy lore, and so by little and little he departs from God.

That the Grammar met a real need is shown by the fact that it continued to be copied and presumably used until at least the end of the twelfth century.

Aelfric, in other words, was a born teacher—one of the race of English schoolmasters—with the highest conception of his vocation and responsibility. The boy-pupils represented the hope of the future. As first aid, so to speak, for the urgent necessities of the present, he had already, as stated, translated "two books in eighty sections", for whose understanding "grammar" he considers "is the key".

Not only did he summarize the *Regularis Concordia*, translate into English the Heptateuch and various other portions of the Old Testament, and write pastoral letters for bishops and scriptural commentaries for intellectually minded lay friends, but he also compiled in his native tongue a volume of *Lives of the Saints* (some time before A.D. 998) and two sets of *Catholic Homilies* or sermons suitable for delivery on the Sundays and chief feasts of the liturgical year. It is upon these last that his claim to a place among

English spiritual writers mainly rests. Although not the first in the field, his work has thrown that of other homilists into the shade through sheer superiority of matter and style.

"Very many I know in this country", he says simply, "more learned than I am, but God manifests His wonders through whom He will."

In a dedicatory epistle to Archbishop Sigeric (couched as a matter of course, in contrast with the usage of our enlightened age, in careful Latin), he states that the task of translating from Latin writers into our everyday tongue has been undertaken for the edification of the simple who know only their own language (*simplicem Anglicam*), the more easily to reach their hearts, for the good of their souls. He has hastened to compile the book not with garrulous wordiness and unfamiliar terms but "*puris et apertis verbis linguae hujus gentis*", desiring rather to profit the hearers by straightforward speech than to be praised for the composition of elaborate discourses, which in his ignorance he had never learnt. He submits the work to the Archbishop's authority, begging him not to spare correction if needed (*quia malo apud Benignitatem tuam reprehendi quam incauta seductione apud inscios laudari*), but to read it carefully through and decide whether it is fit to be given to the Catholic faithful or merely to be thrown away.

His purpose is explained in English prefaces to each volume:

> I Aelfric, monk and mass-priest, although more weakly than is fitting for such orders, was sent, in King Ethelred's day, from Bishop Aelfeage, Ethelwold's successor, to a minster which is called Cernel, at the prayer of Aethelmaere the thane, whose birth and goodness are known everywhere. Then it occurred to my mind, I trust through God's grace, that I would turn this book from the Latin language into the English tongue; not from confidence of great learning, but because I have seen and heard of much error in many English books, which unlearned men, through their simplicity, have esteemed as great wisdom : and I regretted that they knew not nor had not the evangelical doctrines among their writings, those men only excepted who knew Latin, and those books excepted which King Alfred wisely turned from Latin into English, which are to be had. For this cause I presumed, trusting in God, to undertake this task, and also because men have need of good instruction, especially at this time, which is the ending of the world.

The scope and use of the series is duly set forth. He has taken his materials, he tells us, from highly venerable doctors whose authority is gladly accepted by all Catholics, namely from Augustine of Hippo, Jerome, Bede, Gregory, Smaragdus and sometimes Haymo. Occasionally he has abridged and rewritten:

> We have expounded not only treatises on the Gospels, but also the Passions or Lives of the Saints, for the profit of the unlearned of this people....
>
> I have set down the matter which I have translated in two books, because I thought it were less tedious to hear, if the one book were read in the course of one year and the other in the year following. In each of these books there are forty discourses, without the preface, but they are not all taken from the Gospels, but are very many of them gathered from the life or passion of God's Saints, of those only whom the English nation honours with feast days. Before each discourse we have set the argument in Latin....

Faced with a thousand-year-old collection of homilies in an unfamiliar and unclassical tongue, one's first impulse probably is to dismiss the whole thing as merely a museum piece, a literary curiosity, quaint and outlandish, possibly interesting to specialists but certainly of no profitable application in the world today. Bygone sermons can be so very dull. It is to be noted, however, that this particular work continued to be used and copied, up and down the country, for about two centuries, and therefore presumably had some real usefulness or some popular appeal.

The *Catholic Homilies*, written in the pure Late West Saxon which was the King's English of his time, have been termed "the classic example of Anglo-Saxon prose". Aelfric's prose style, disciplined but never distorted by his training in Latin grammar, is easy, cultured, straightforward and readily intelligible. Occasionally he blossoms into elaborately rhythmed passages heightened by alliteration (a device which still has power to rouse an English ear), though even then the sense is never made to suffer for the sake of the sound. Otherwise it is laudably devoid of rhetorical flourishes, a thoroughly good unpretentious medium for his message, and at times delightful in its clear and simple phrasing. For instance, John the Baptist, we are told, went before Christ "as the beadle before the judge". In the Christmas scene, "Then saw she

(Mary) the child lying in the bin, where the ox and the ass usually seek food." As for Herodias—"Verily there is no worm-kind nor wild beast-kind like in evilness to an evil woman."

Although the Faith remains ever essentially the same, its external manifestations may vary considerably from age to age, and a modern Catholic would probably find it hard to recapture the religious atmosphere of a thousand years ago. The Mass and the sacraments were there of course, but most of our familiar devotional practices and many of our well-worn theological terms simply did not exist. Nobody had invented the Penny Catechism or discovered the formal Meditation, nor had the master-mind of St Thomas Aquinas reduced to an orderly synthesis the components of Christian doctrine. What help had the average tenth-century Englishman towards learning and practising his faith?

Aelfric's method of tackling the problem is liturgical and patristic, based on the Holy Scriptures, the Missal, and the Divine Office, as explained and interpreted by the Latin Fathers. His outlook in fact has much in common with that of the modern liturgical movement. The people were to be taught by the parish clergy, expounding the materials directly at their disposal. Truths of faith carefully set forth and rightly grasped should of themselves prompt in their hearers devotion and amendment of life.

The two volumes of Homilies are uniform in matter and treatment. Each is arranged according to the liturgical calendar and covers the main requirements of the year's pastoral instruction. In addition to discourses for the greater festivals such as Christmas and Easter, provision is made in each for some fourteen or fifteen Sundays throughout the year, for the principal feasts of our Lady, the feasts of several apostles and other well-known saints, the Finding of the Cross, the Greater Litanies, and sundry liturgical landmarks both major and minor, and for formal teaching on the Creed, the Paternoster, and the general obligations of a Christian. The second volume also includes discourses for a series of Common Offices.

From his own words in the Preface it is clear that although displaying great skill and ingenuity in the choice and arrangement of his materials, Aelfric would have been the last to claim originality for his work. His aim, humbly and faithfully carried out, was to transmit to others what he had himself received. In this as in other ways he was in his own lesser degree directly in the tradition of St Bede—at once thoroughly patristic and thoroughly English. His discourses are permeated with the spirit and teaching of the Latin Fathers, the predominant influence being that of St Gregory the Great, whose Homilies furnish most of the materials for the Sunday sermons. St Bede contributes the story of St Gregory, of St Cuthbert and of Drihthelm's vision, besides several more directly homiletic portions. Traces of St Augustine may be detected here, there and everywhere. St Jerome's *Ecclesiastical History* gives the history of the Holy Cross; and there is even one reference to "a wise doctor named Amalarius, who wrote a book on ecclesiastical customs". Otherwise the sermons for Saints' days (a curious assortment, including not only several of the apostles but also such remote heroes as SS. Alexander, Eventius and Theodulus and the Seven Sleepers of Ephesus) are usually taken from their anonymous legends, with the addition of suitable moral considerations; the life of St Martin is from Sulpicius Severus, that of St Benedict simply an abridgement from St Gregory's *Dialogues,* the account of St Fursey's visions of purgatory and judgement (the first of a series which was to include *The Divine Comedy* and *The Dream of Gerontius*) from a legend now enshrined in the Bollandists (January, vol. II). And so forth.

This list of sources, which illustrates the range of the author's reading in his so-called Dark Age, in no way detracts from the value of his book, which is closely packed with lively narrative and solid orthodox doctrine from one end to the other. In places, indeed, it exhibits an astonishing likeness both to parts of Abbot Guéranger's *Liturgical Year*, compiled by a French Benedictine nearly 900 years later, and to the still more recent *Church's Year of Grace* by Dr Pius Parsch.

The general arrangement affords plenty of scope for lessons in Old as well as New Testament history, Christian doctrine and conduct—the moral theologian is notably in evidence—rites and ceremonies and their practical applications either direct or under the form of allegory. Deceptively casual in appearance, the compilation comprises good clear teaching on the Holy Trinity, the Creation, the Incarnation, Passion, Resurrection and Ascension of our Lord, the Holy Ghost and His seven gifts, the Mass and Holy Eucharist, the Old Testament types of Christ, our Lady and the apostles, the commandments and the deadly sins, the Church and the Mystical Body, the Last Judgement, the duties and responsibilities of a Christian in more or less detail—in short, approximately all that a Christian as such would ordinarily need to know and to do, though *not* in tabular form. Any gaps in the one volume would be supplied in the other and covered in the two years' course; and anybody who took the book thoroughly to heart would certainly be sufficiently instructed in Christian doctrine for everyday purposes. Anyone so minded could find a meditation in every line.

A detailed study of the use to which Aelfric has put the second and third nocturn lessons of the Divine Office and the works from which they are taken would be altogether too lengthy, though it might give a hint of the homiletic potentialities of a source not too frequently drawn upon in modern times. Quite a number of the Sunday Gospels and homilies, especially those from St Gregory, were of course much the same then as now and may readily be recognized in their Old English form.

Perhaps a clearer impression of his best efforts could be gained from the fine discourse on the Nativity with which the second volume opens. After briefly stating the temporal and eternal generation of Christ, the preacher sets forth clearly and simply the theological doctrine of His earthly birth for our redemption of the Virgin Mother, whose perpetual virginity was prefigured by the blossoming of Aaron's rod. Mentioning the four kinds of human generation (i.e. of Adam, of Eve, of mankind in general, and of Christ), he speaks of our Lady's virginity, adding the analogies of the honey-bee and of Holy Church, our virgin-mother through the rite of baptism. He next shows how the Old Testament prophecies of Abraham, Jeremias, Micheas, Isaias, Ezechiel and Daniel are fulfilled in Christ, explains the name Christ, our Lord's anointing, and the Christian's hallowing through oil, and deals in a full and methodical fashion with the prophecies of Christ's life and death to be found in the Scriptures and in connection with the names of Sibylla and of Nabuchodonosor. The story of the three youths in the fiery furnace is recounted and ingeniously applied to complete this section. The whole discourse concludes with a reminder of the faith, love, joy and good works which should be the outcome of such a feast, the dignity of our

Lady and an exhortation to invoke her intercession. Not many Christmas sermons in these days would be so comprehensive and thoroughgoing.

This bald summary, while conveying no idea of the manner of Aelfric's preaching as distinct from its matter, does at least bring out clearly the contrast between his handling and that of the school of eloquence which became popular among preachers later in the Middle Ages. His material is drawn directly from Scripture and tradition; the treatment is almost purely objective and expository; the discourse, though carefully prepared, has seldom a formal symmetrical plan; the tone though earnest is calm, one might say detached, and there is no trace whatever of philosophical subtleties or of the invective, afterwards so common, which makes, for instance, Archbishop Wulfstan's "Sermo ad Anglos" such a blistering castigation of national shortcomings. Nor, despite the imminent approach of the dreaded millennial year, does he resort to the apocalyptic fulminations and threats of impending retribution which take so prominent a place in that prelate's harangues to his erring flock.

Aelfric breathes a different atmosphere; his approach is incomparably more winning and attractive. Not that he was unaware of, or indifferent to, the sins and weaknesses of both clergy and laity and the need for improvement in life and doctrine. On the duty of preaching, for instance, he says:

> Ever should the lay folk desire, and pray to God, that He provide them good teachers, who by salutary instruction may stimulate them to the everlasting life.... If the priest cannot say a homily to the lay folk, he should at least through the innocence of his life set them a good example.... The teacher who undertakes preaching should not busy himself with worldly things and neglect God's service. It befits him to feel anxious how he may gain to God the souls of many men by evangelic lore, not how many he may draw to himself by his power.... A good messenger should not preach in order that he may here receive a temporal reward, but should receive sustenance for his preaching, that he may not faint at his preaching....

And elsewhere:

"Laymen require that teachers should impart to them the

evangelical lore that they have learned in books, so that men should not err through ignorance."

This is sufficiently plain and pointed; and occasionally he deals with certain vices in more detail. But his tone is always gently persuasive rather than peremptory, free from anger, ever anxious to obviate boredom, completely self-effacing, and in fact, for the work of a youngish man, remarkably mature. Never does Aelfric obtrude himself between his message and its hearer, for whom on the contrary he provides every help in the way of explaining unfamiliar terms and difficult doctrines, e.g. "Water-vessels are called hydriae, because in the Greek tongue water is called 'ydor' "; and he proceeds to give the use of the stone pots. Speaking of St Benedict and the multiplication of the oil, he says: "Because they eat oil in that country with their food as we do butter." On the feast of Easter he tells his readers: "This tide is in the Hebrew tongue called PASCHA, that is in Latin *Transitus* and in English Passover (*Faereld*), because on this day God's folk passed from the land of Egypt over the Red Sea, from thraldom to the promised country," and draws the appropriate moral. In narrating the Passion: "Wise men have reckoned a legion at 6000, and twelve legions are 72,000. So many angels might easily have defended Christ against those inhuman ones with heavenly weapons; if He would not voluntarily have suffered for us."

It is probably this very solicitude to convey his lesson intelligibly, coupled with the limitations of the vernacular, that is responsible for some rather strange language in a passage in the Easter homily "On the Sacrifice" which at first sight suggests some haziness, to say the least, in his doctrine on the Holy Eucharist, and has even been hailed by certain Protestant divines as embodying their own views—an idea which would have horrified Aelfric. The crucial sentences run as follows:

> In kind it is corruptible bread and corruptible wine; and according to the power of the divine word it is in sooth Christ's body and His blood; not, however, in bodily guise, but after a ghostly manner. Truly, the body in which Christ suffered was born of the flesh of Mary, with blood and bone, with skin and sinews, with many limbs, and a reasonable soul giving life to it, and His ghostly body, which we call the housel, is gathered of many corns, without blood and bone, limbless and soulless; and therefore we are to

> understand nothing therein after a bodily, but everything is to be understood after a ghostly manner. . . . Many receive that holy body, yet it is whole in every particle by ghostly mystery. . . . In sooth it is, as we have already said, Christ's body and blood, not after a bodily but after a ghostly manner. . . .

The rest is quite plain and orthodox. Lingard, in his *History of the Anglo-Saxon Church* (vol. 2, p. 408), examines this passage and shows that it is in fact capable of a perfectly orthodox interpretation; and other parts of the same sermon, taken with his statements up and down the rest of the work, make it clear that Aelfric was as loyal to tradition on this point of doctrine as on any other. We may reasonably suppose that he was simply endeavouring to state a mystery and set forth a dogma for which the theological and technical terms so familiar today had not yet been defined or even formulated, and to do this moreover so as to convey its sense in a language as yet very weak in abstract terminology, to an unlettered congregation totally unversed in the niceties of philosophical thought and diction. Upon its cardinal importance in the life of the faithful he is clear enough, as an extract from one of his instructions on the Paternoster will show:

> The ghostly bread is also the holy housel, with which we strengthen our faith; and through partaking of the holy housel our sins will be forgiven us and we shall be strengthened against the temptations of the devil. Therefore should we frequently cleanse and confirm our soul with ghostly refection. Yet may not he who is polluted with deadly sins dare to partake of God's housel, unless he first atone for his sins; if he do otherwise, he will partake of it to his own injury. . . .
>
> In this life we require bread, and instruction, and partaking of the holy housel. . . .

As regards other matters of faith which have been questioned in later ages, Aelfric's orthodoxy stands in no need of defence; he is as orthodox as the Fathers themselves. To cite a few examples—On Infant Baptism:

> For the great belief of the mother the devil forsook the daughter. Thereby is given an example for our baptism, that the unspeaking children will be saved by baptism, through the belief of the father and of the mother, and of the responsible godfather, though the child be unconscious.

On Prayers for the Dead:

We in this life may help the departed that are in torment.

On the Primacy of St Peter:

Why should the Almighty Ruler ever allow that His chosen servant, whom He had set as a teacher and guardian over all believing people, should through fear so often deny Him? But the merciful Christ would show him, in his own sin, how he should be merciful to other men for divers sins, now that he fully possesses the key of heaven's kingdom; that he should not be too rigorous towards weak men, but should be merciful to others, as the Almighty was to him.

Long before the coming of the rosary and the Angelus, love of our Lady has always been strong among Catholic Englishmen; and here we find her Divine Motherhood, her sufferings, her Assumption and her intercession, all treated of with tender devotion. Thus on the feast of the Assumption Aelfric tells us:

Of this heavenly queen it is yet said by the same Spirit of God, "I saw the beauteous one as a dove mounting above the streaming rills; and so as in the spring-tide, blossoms of roses and lilies encircled her." The blossoms of roses betoken by their redness martyrdom, and the lilies by their whiteness betoken the shining purity of inviolate maidenhood. All the chosen who have thriven to God through martyrdom or through chastity, they all journeyed with the blessed queen; for she is herself both martyr and maiden. She is as beauteous as a dove, for she loved meekness, which the Holy Ghost betokened, when He appeared in likeness of a dove over Christ at His baptism. Other martyrs suffered martyrdom in their bodies for Christ's faith, but the blessed Mary was not bodily martyred, but her soul was sorely afflicted with great suffering, when she stood in sorrow before Christ's rood, and saw her dear Child fastened with iron nails on the hard tree. Therefore is she more than a martyr, for she suffered that martyrdom in her soul which other martyrs suffered in their bodies. She loved Christ above all other men, and therefore her pain for Him was also greater than other men's, and she made His death as her own death, for His suffering pierced her soul as a sword.

What more shall we say to you of this feast-day, but that Mary, the mother of Christ, was on this day, from this world of toil, taken up to the kingdom of heaven to her dear Son, whom she had borne in life, with whom she rejoices in everlasting mirth to all eternity. . . .

The warmth and feeling of Aelfric's treatment of liturgical anniversaries in general appears, for instance, in a sermon for Septuagesima Sunday on the cessation of the Alleluia, concluding with the words:

Verily these daily services show that from this day till Easter is our mourning-tide, and tide of repentance of our sins, with some strictness. "Alleluia" is a Hebrew word, which in Latin is "Laudate Dominum", and no tongue is so sublime as Hebrew. We now leave that sublime tongue in our Septuagesima, and say in Latin, "Laus tibi, Domine, Rex aeternae gloriae", that is, "Praise be to thee, O Lord, King of eternal glory." By the humble Latin speech we show that we should incline ourselves to a humbler life at this tide. "Alleluia" is, as we have said, a heavenly song, as John the Apostle said that he heard a great voice in heaven, as it were the sound of trumpets, and they sang "Alleluia". Angels sang "Gloria in excelsis Deo" when Christ was born bodily in the world. Now we leave the heavenly hymns at our penitence-tide, and with true humility pray the Almighty that we may see His heavenly Easter-tide, after the universal resurrection, in which we will sing to Him eternally Alleluia without weariness. Amen.

Shrove Sunday likewise brings its own message:

Now is a pure and holy time drawing nigh, in which we should atone for our remissness: let, therefore, every Christian man come to his confessor, and confess his secret sins, and amend by the teaching of his instructor. . . .

Other rites and ceremonies provide their lesson, for instance on Palm Sunday:

In God's church the custom exists, established by its doctors, that everywhere in God's congregation the priest should bless palm-twigs on this day, and distribute them so blessed to the people; and God's servants should then sing the hymn which the Jewish people sang before Christ, when He was approaching to His passion. We imitate the faithful of that people with this deed, for they bore palm-twigs with hymn-singing before Jesus. Now we should hold our palm until the singer begins the offering-song, and then offer to God the palm for its betokening. The palm betokens victory. Christ was victorious when He overcame the great devil and rescued us; and we should also be victorious through God's might, so that we overcome our evil practices, and all sin, and the devil, and adorn ourselves with good works, and at the end of our life deliver to God the palm, that is our victory, and thank Him fervently that through His succour we have overcome the devil, so that he could not deceive us. . . .

Although some anecdotes from the Saints' lives which find a place in Aelfric's homilies do indeed strike us today as more than a little surprising, on the whole he follows St Bede in exercising restraint and caution in the choice of materials, e.g.:

The passion of Thomas we leave unwritten, because it has long since been turned from Latin into English in song-wise; but the wise Augustine, however, has said in some treatise of his that one thing incredible was set out in that narrative. . . . Because of this doubt we would not touch his passion. It is, nevertheless, all quite credible, except that only which Augustine gainsays.

His attitude towards dubious matter in general is probably best stated in the words with which he closes the sermon "On the Assumption of St Mary the Virgin":

If we say more of this feast-day than we read in the holy books that have been composed by the inspiration of God, then we should be like those heretics, who from their own imagination, or from dreams, have recorded many false traditions; but the orthodox teachers, Augustine, Jerome, Gregory, and many others have, through their wisdom, rejected them. These heretical books, nevertheless, yet exist, both in Latin and in English, and ignorant men read them. It is enough for believing men to read and to say that which is true; and few are those men that can perfectly examine all the holy books that have been inspired by God's mouth, or by the Spirit of God. Let everyone cast away the heretical lies that lead the unwary to perdition, and let everyone read, or listen to, the holy lore, which directs to the kingdom of heaven, if we will hear it.

The allegorical method of scriptural interpretation, popularized by St Augustine and St Gregory and general throughout the patristic age, is not very popular among preachers in this matter-of-fact and sophisticated age. Undoubtedly the exaggerations and over-insistence of the great doctors and their lesser disciples must be held partially responsible for the subsequent change of taste. But symbolism in word or act is the natural language of religion, indeed a regular feature in Catholic ritual from baptism to burial; and in due place and measure the argument from visible to invisible things—as employed, for instance, by our Lord in His parables and by St Paul in his Epistles—can be of great value not only in illustrating some important or unfamiliar truth, but in helping to integrate the whole spiritual life.

With Aelfric as with his models, the concrete imagery and its moral application go constantly hand in hand and usually to good purpose. Under the guise of allegorical interpretation he manages to get in a good deal of Old Testament history and also plenty of excellent moral instruction, probably easier for his hearers to absorb and remember as being attached to actual biblical texts and stories. His sermon on the Second Sunday after the Epiphany, for instance (derived from St Bede and thence presumably from St Augustine), is simply a workmanlike piece of exposition on the allegorical meaning of the Gospel relating the marriage at Cana. The water of the Old Testament changed to the wine of the New, the waterpots signifying the six ages of the world, even the three floors of the house (which St John does *not* specify), each is expounded in detail. Mid-Lent Sunday suggests an account of the peregrinations of the Israelites towards the Promised Land, in which the taking of Jericho introduces a good sound lesson on the seven deadly sins. In general it may be noted that Aelfric's frequent quotations from the Old Testament are usually chosen to typify or illustrate some point of Christian faith or practice. The following passage, from the homily on the Twelfth Sunday after Pentecost, is a good example of this allegorical method of conveying a practical lesson; the combination of graphic imagery with shrewd insight would suggest St Gregory as its ultimate source:

> The prophet Ezechiel wrote of the four beasts which appeared to him, that they had eyes on every side. . . . The four beasts had eyes on every side of their bodies because God's chosen should consider their deeds beforehand on every side, so that they ever desire good and guard themselves against evil. But it often hap-

pens, through our weakness, that we neglect some things, while about some we are solicitous; and without doubt we have no eye there where the heedlessness is. So this Pharisee, of whom we before spoke, had open eyes for abstinence, for almsdeeds, for thanking God, but he had no care to hold true lowliness among his virtues.

Enough has been said to show the merits of Aelfric as a sermon-maker, and perhaps also to hint at the gentle charm of personality which shines through his discourses. His own deep piety appears in such passages as the eloquent tribute to the crucified Christ which closes his Passion Sunday sermon :

My brethren, let us behold the crucified Christ, that we may be healed of venomous sins. Verily as the people of Israel looked on the brazen serpent, and were healed of the serpent's bite, so will they now be healed of their sins who with faith behold the death of Christ and His resurrection. They were healed from death to transitory life, and here it is said that we shall have life everlasting; so great is the difference between the apparent likeness and the true thing : the apparent likeness imparted to the torn men transitory life; the true thing, which was betokened by the brazen serpent, that is, the death of Christ, imparts to us life everlasting. Through a tree death came to us, when Adam ate the forbidden apple, and through a tree life came again to us and redemption, when Christ hung on the rood for our redemption. The sign of the holy rood is our blessing, and to the rood we pray, though not to the tree, but to the Almighty Lord, who for us hung on the holy rood. To Him be praise and glory, for His boundless humility, to all eternity. Amen.

To the scholar who devoted his life to composing official documents for prelates, religious instructions for the unlearned, and textbooks for schoolboys, the "secret martyrdom of patience", as he calls it, can have been no empty phrase. We do not know whether or for how long the tradition of learning begun by its first Abbot flourished at Eynsham itself (the house had apparently been transferred and refounded before the father of St Edmund of Canterbury became a monk there some two centuries later). But we do know that Aelfric's Homilies must have been welcomed as a godsend and circulated without delay, for passages from them are incorporated (without acknowledgement of course) in the Wulfstan volume, which was compiled within the next few years.

Similarly his long discourse "On the Beginning of Creation" (which summarizes the whole of biblical history from the creation of the angels to the Passion of Christ, with suitable moral applications) was evidently recognized as just what was needed to complete a compilation made by some lesser man a century later.[1] So the process went on; his writings were copied, pilfered, rewritten, imitated in manuscript after manuscript still extant—and how many more long since perished?—until the rise of a new movement in the thirteenth century. Nothing, probably, would have pleased Aelfric better. Indeed, it is not easy to set limits to his influence. He had accomplished his object in helping to consolidate the good effects of the so-called monastic revival among his countrymen; and he had all unwittingly made provision towards safeguarding both their faith and their native diction through worse times to come.

"My brethren," he had written, "let it not seem too tedious to you that you have heard this evangelical lore. We secure ourselves with the saying, do you secure yourselves with the fulfilling of the precepts, that we may all have the reward which eye of man never saw, nor ear heard."

NOTE. The extracts from Aelfric's *Homilies* are taken, with occasional slight revisions, from Benjamin Thorpe's translation; the passage from the Anglo-Saxon Chronicle is quoted in R. W. Chambers' book *On the Continuity of English Prose*.

[1] British Museum. Cotton MS. Vesp. A22.

II

RICHARD ROLLE

BY CONRAD PEPLER, O.P.

RICHARD ROLLE[1] has been called the "Father of English Mysticism" and as such he might be said to sum up the spirit of the mystical writers of the fourteenth century. The title might well be challenged if we took the whole of English history, for certainly the great saints like the Venerable Bede or Ailred of Rievaulx have a greater claim to the paternity of the high spirituality of England, and Columba, Patrick and David if we include the British Isles—for these men were mystics too. But the "English Mystics" as a title nowadays comprises only the fourteenth-century writers who took their place in what might be called "the mystical century" when men and women all over Europe were called to heights of prayer and union with God, and, what is more, set down on paper their experiences and their considerations arising therefrom.

Among these English fourteenth-century writers Rolle is the first and, in many ways, the inspirer of those who followed him. He is not the greatest, nor does he seem to have reached such heights as, for example, Mother Julian of Norwich, Walter Hilton or the author of the *Cloud of Unknowing*. But as a man he was more spectacular and his influence was far more widespread—indeed some of the later writers considered that his effect on some of his

[1] *The English Writings of Richard Rolle* were edited by Miss Emily Hope Allen and published under that title by the Oxford University Press in 1931. The language is not difficult, but for those who prefer a straightforward modern English version G. C. Heseltine published *Selected Works* with Longmans in 1930. The *English Lyrics* are to be found in *The Life and Lyrics of Richard Rolle* by Frances M. M. Comper (Dent, 1928 and 1933). The longer version of the *Incendium Amoris* and the *Emendatio Vitae* were translated by Richard Mysin in the early fifteenth century, and these have been modernized by Miss Comper and were published by Methuen as *The Fire of Love and the Mending of Life*—an excellent work, as it still preserves some of the strength of the earlier English while remaining easily readable. The shorter version of the *Incendium Amoris* was edited in Latin by Margaret Deansley, and this critical edition was published for Manchester University by Longmans in 1915. In this article use has been made of all these editions but the translation from the shorter version of the *Incendium* is the author's own.

weaker followers was not always wholesome. He was very popular and his reputation for miracles after his death left a mark among those who were enthusiastic for the things of the spirit. An Office was composed in preparation for his canonization.

In order to show that Richard Rolle was representative of the English Mystics of the fourteenth century we should first say a word about mysticism. Although the word itself is closely allied to that of mystery, which sums up the heart of the Christian religion, it is used now more exclusively of a special type of religious experience, when the soul is rapt in God, taken in some way out of itself, and infused with special graces of mind and heart. Undoubtedly there is what we might call a "natural" basis to this experience. There are some people naturally gifted with a character apparently readily subject to experiences of a passive or receptive kind. Even without any outstanding moral virtue they see visions or feel the quietude of spirit engendered by the presence of God. We are not here referring to the question of non-Christian mystics, which is another matter altogether, but to people who at the beginning of their spiritual lives find it easier to remain quiet and passive in their prayer, and very soon hear the voices of angels or see the face of the Crucified Saviour in their mind's eye. This is not necessarily true mystical experience in the supernatural sense, but may well be the preparation for it. It is often the poetic element which plays a large part in the groundwork of the mystic. The true mystical experience is reached after a long period of purification in which the character is cleansed of tarnish coming from original and actual sin. As the love of God reaches a certain perfection in the soul the infused virtues and gifts begin to predominate, so that the Christian grows more passive under the direct influence of the Spirit. The Christian is thus led to a union with God in which he becomes transformed by the Spirit. True mysticism is therefore nothing less than a perfection of love or charity.

All this is pertinent to Rolle and the English Mystics. We find in him as well as in Mother Julian of Norwich, for example, a certain initial set of experiences—Mother Julian's visions surrounding the crucifix, and Rolle's fire of love—which reveal an aptitude for the higher passive states. These may well have been fashioned by God from their poetic genius. All the English Mystics were lyrical in many passages of their writings, but none was such an outstanding poet as Richard. His lyrics were almost as influential as his prose writings and translations. He was constantly singing of his love of Jesus and his desire to live with Him for ever. The poet captures the concrete reality as a whole thing; the scientific thinker, such as the theologian, considers the ideal and analyses it into its abstract parts. The mystic, too, is captured by the all-embracing concrete reality of God and the mystical theologian draws on this experience of the heights of reality to try to establish a pattern of the relation between the soul and God. St John of the Cross wrote his poems and then expounded their meaning. So also Richard Rolle wrote his poems of the love of God and then set forth the pattern in the *Incendium Amoris* or *Fire of Love*.

My song is sighing,
  while I dwell in this way;
My life is longing,
  that binds me night and day.
Till I come to my King,
  that I dwell with him may,
And see his fair shining
  in life that lasts ay.

And later in the same poem :

I sit and sing of love longing
  that in my heart is bred
Jesu, my King and my joying,
  why were I not to thee led?
Full well I wait in all my state
  in joy I should be fed.

This stanza characterizes the mystical aspiration of the Hermit of Hampole, who was well known for his posture in prayer. He was called—and in some quarters sarcastically called—"the sitter". He preferred to sit, a receptive posture, relaxed and quiet; to stand or kneel in prayer suggests action and tension as well as respect. Rolle preferred to sit and wait; he asks to be led and to be fed. This is one of the elements that go to make up the mystic, the poet waiting to be captured by the Lord who is love.

But this in itself, even on the natural plane, is not sufficient to make up the stuff of the mystic. He might in this state fall into the lassitude of Quietism, with the sinews of his spirit turning to jelly through lack of exercise. Rolle was not a passive character; indeed there is evidence that during the first part of his life he had to overcome a powerful and irascible temper. It was not a passive spirit which led him to throw up his studies in Oxford in order to retire to solitude, for that must have required a considerable effort of will power. He was also a little intolerant of his patron, Dalton, in his first chaplaincy in Yorkshire; nor was he apathetic to the criticisms of those who accused him of being a "sitter". The regular clergy were not pleased with his mode of life. And this is his answer :

> They were envious because the magnificent Majesty made me miraculous in mind through music. While I transcended such intemperate ones, the fruitful fame flourished with the flashing one, tempest-tost and terrified they were tormented. Here I argue against the errant saucy ones, who, peradventure spoke from envy unworthily. For they asserted (speaking sophistically) that from the food I swallowed I have sustained the sitting . . .

The poetic muse is linked to passion, and in a true mystic this passion has to be trained and focused on the love of God. This is the ascetic process. The poet passionately seizes on reality, and his love of the concrete brings him in such close affinity with his perception that he can express it in verbal form. But the perception must proceed through the material reality to the Spirit of God beneath and within it all. So Richard at first was captivated by the material experiences of the heat of love and the song of angels; and to a certain extent he seems to have been over-conscious of the great popularity which he early earned for himself. But through hard asceticism, together with the responsibility of guiding the recluses under his care towards holiness, his passion was ruled and fully directed to the final reality of the love of God.

The love of God is the principal theme of all his writing and, like St John of the Cross, his greatest work is concerned with the fire of love, *Incendium Amoris*. In considering his teaching on this and other cognate subjects we should remember that he is writing of what is known as the Illuminative Way rather than the Unitive Way which is the theme of St John of the Cross. I have tried to show elsewhere that his life and teaching are characteristic of this illuminative way rather than of the supreme heights (cf. *The*

English Religious Heritage, London, 1958), so I will here assume this as proven. His experiences, vividly described by himself, have the sensible character which suggests the illuminative rather than the unitive way, though he seems to have thought they indicated the supreme heights.

> In process of time great profit in ghostly joy was given me . . . the opening of the heavenly door, so that the Face being shown, the eyes of the heart might behold and see by what way they might seek my Love, and unto him continually desire. . . . I was sitting forsooth in a chapel, and whiles I was mickle delighted with sweetness of prayer or meditation, suddenly I felt within me a merry and unknown heat. . . . Truly in this unhoped for, sensible and sweet smelling heat (nine months) had out run, until the inshedding and receiving of this heavenly and ghostly sound, the which belongs to the songs of everlasting praise and the sweetness of unseen melody. . . . My thought was forsooth changed to a continual song of mirth, and I had as it were praises in my meditation, and in my prayers and psalm saying I utter the same sound : and henceforth, for plenteousness of inward sweetness, I burst out singing what before I said. . . .

These gifts of heat and song are the special feature of Rolle's spirituality. And although he himself rightly insisted on the relative unimportance of the sensible signs of these experiences, his followers were often misled into seeking the physical heat in their breasts and the sound of heavenly song in their ears. But it is important to realize that this heat of love and song of heavenly praise were gifts, and were not come by through any practices which would seem to engender them. They came to him quite unawares, and the spiritual exercises which preceded them were the normal acts of an exceptionally devoted man who had withdrawn into seclusion. There he had lived an heroically hard life and devoted himself to the recitation of the Psalter and to meditation.

In other words, by a fittingly rigorous and devout life he had made himself ready for the state of infused contemplation, which is passive rather than active, receiving from the Spirit of God a mode of prayer and love rather than making deliberate acts of love or actively engaging in prayer. This was many centuries before the disputes among the mystical theologians as to the exact nature and place of infused contemplation, so that we need not enter into the modern distinctions and sub-distinctions regarding the stage of the spiritual life. His namesake, Richard of St Victor, from whom Rolle may well have derived some of his teaching, had already considered the nature of this infused type of prayer, and Rolle himself often used the word "inshed" or "infusa" to mark its nature.

In the shorter version of the *Incendium Amoris*, edited by Miss Deansley, in which he is constantly proving his spirit against his critics, he describes how the divine gift of love brings with it a knowledge and understanding which are evidently the gifts of the Holy Spirit operating freely in the purified soul.

> Thus the love of vanity disappears, the true love breaks forth in the mind, so that the spirit of the lover far from growing cold persists in a strengthening (or comfortable) heat, and the heart never tires of continuous thought on his most Beloved. In this constancy there comes to the lover the excellence of love, so that carried up into a heavenly fire he is there ineffably set on fire with love and burns within himself beyond description, and the height of all graces is reached. And thus he receives a wisdom and a subtlety to speak among the great and proclaims without fear what he is led to say, although he were formerly accounted unlettered and stupid and may even so be.

He then goes on to attack those who say "Where has he learned all this?" as they have not received this infused wisdom and rely upon their arguments.

In this way all prayer and meditation are inspired by the divine operation of the Spirit. But Rolle is no illuminist; he does not believe that these experiences and gifts come without much preparation. The special form of contemplation is not acquired by human effort, but a great deal depends on the penitential activity which makes ready the ground for the fruitful seed of the Spirit.

> No man may come to such revelation and grace on the first day, but only through long travail and eagerness to love Jesus Christ. . . . He suffers them to be tempted in various ways both waking and sleeping. For ever the more temptations, and the more grievous they are, that they stand against and overcome, the more they shall rejoice in his love when those temptations are passed. (*Form of Living.*)

The one who wants to reach the peaceful yet ardent (in the original sense of that word) state of love must rigidly shun "covetousness, pleasure, occupation and business of worldly things, and of fleshly lust and vain love. So that thy thought, which was ever downward, burrowing in the earth, whilst thou wast in the world, may now be ever upward as fire, seeking the highest place in heaven, right to thy spouse where he sits in his bliss."

It seems that by "prayer" Rolle usually means the active form of raising the mind and heart to God either in psalmody and liturgy or in individual aspiration, which prepare for true contemplation.

> Contemplative life, or contemplation, has three parts : Reading, Prayer, and Meditation. In reading God speaks to us; in prayer we speak to God; in meditation, angels come down to teach us that we err not. In prayer they go up and offer our petitions to God, rejoicing in our progress. . . . Prayer is indeed a devout disposition of the mind directed to God, with which he is pleased when it comes to him. Meditation on God and godly things, wherein is the embrace of Rachel, is to be taken up after prayer and reading. To reading belongs reason and the enquiry after truth, that is a precious light granted to us. To prayer belongs the song of praise, passing into contemplation and wonder : and so contemplative life and contemplation stands on prayer. To meditation belongs the inspiration of God, understanding, wisdom and aspiration.

This passage from the *Amending of Life* (c. 12) sums up Richard Rolle's teaching on prayer and contemplation, showing how the active life of study and prayer leads to the point where the Spirit flows over with His gifts and draws the soul to the quietly burning fire of love. Elsewhere he links meditation with prayer as an active form of the spiritual life, linked with "reading". In this he is in the general tradition of the Middle Ages. St Thomas seems to write of "meditatio" and "oratio" in the same manner. Today the words have often a far more general meaning, including every form of converse with God, however passive the soul may be under the inspiration of the gifts. For Rolle prayer is more or less vocal prayer, the use of words (particularly the Psalter and the Office) which can reach a very high degree of perfection.

> Verily we pray well when we think of nothing else but God,

> and all our mind is directed to heaven and our soul is inflamed with the fire of the Holy Ghost. Thus a marvellous plenty of God's goodness is found in us, for the love of God shall rise from the innermost marrow of our hearts, and all our prayer shall be with proper disposition, so that we do not overrun the words but we shall offer almost every syllable with a great cry and desire to our Lord. (*Amending of Life*, c. 7.)

This is indeed the perfection of psalm-saying and psalm-singing. And it is worth reminding ourselves of this liturgical background to the mysticism of all the fourteenth-century mystical writers in England. They are nurtured from first to last on the Mass and the Divine Office. And one of Rolle's great works was to turn the Psalter into English, so that his unlettered nuns and recluses should understand the words of what they recited and come to mean every syllable in this manner. He begins his Prologue to the translation by stating the great benefit derived from saying or singing the psalms devoutly, and claiming that if they continue in this devotion those who recite the Psalter will be raised by our Lord to the contemplative life. It does away with annoyance and anger in the soul; thus the rhythm of the psalms induces the calm of spirit requisite for true, divine love.

The whole of Rolle's teaching turns on his teaching of the infused love of God which revealed itself in the heat and height of fire in his spirit.

> *Amore langueo*. These two words are written in the book of love, that is called the Song of Love or the Song of Songs. For he that loves much likes to sing often of his love, for the joy that he or she has when they think on that which they love; especially if this lover be true and loving. And this is the English of those two words: "I languish for love." (*Form of Living*, c. 7.)

He gives three degrees of this love, which as the above quotation shows he drew from the usual sources of mystical contemplation; Insuperable, Inseparable and Singular. The first degree is rather of a negative character, in that nothing can remove the soul from this love of God, the penance and prayer of the good Christian has overcome all obstacles—it is a great labour, the labour of complete penance, but "all labour is light to the lover: no man may better overcome labour than by love". Thus established against any contrary movements of the heart, the Christian may rise to the next degree, Inseparable love, when his mind is never away from our Lord. Every waking moment holds our Lord in some way in the mind of the lover. You wake to the thought of His love or of His praise. This is everlasting love.

Finally the highest degree is that of Singular love. There is no other love on the soul's horizon; there is no other subject with which to compare the Beloved. He is no longer the highest among many but the only one. This signifies at least the spiritual solitude in which the soul is alone with Christ in the embrace of His love. And naturally Rolle uses this as an argument for the solitary life of a hermit which he had espoused, since it would be difficult to be so undivided in one's attention to our Lord when mixed in the "busyness" of the world.

> Undoubtedly such solitude is most acceptable which has no association among men. He is the more ravished inwardly to joy as he is less occupied with outward things, or hindered with the heaviness and cares of this life.

And yet both from the example of Rolle's own life, as well as in his teaching, we learn that he did not intend to bind this divine love to the cell of the solitary. From the heights of charity the hermit or anchoress pours forth his divine love on to men, his neighbours. Rolle himself moved about a good deal towards the end of his life assisting by his counsel and direction those who were seeking the same perfection; and tradition has it that he died in 1349 of the plague through assisting the sufferers from the disease. It is a singular but not a selfish love. So he teaches in the *Incendium* :

> Therefore if our love be pure and perfect, whatever our heart loves it is God. . . . Truly in the love of God is the love of my neighbour. Therefore as he that loves God knows not but to love man, so he that truly knows to love Christ is proved to love nothing in himself but God.

The true love of God thus includes the love of man, and when compelled to take on the care of souls the contemplative will give himself to the work in thoroughgoing charity. But Rolle, in his work, is nearly always on the defensive for the solitary life so that he finds no opportunity for elaborating the conclusions to be drawn from the principle that in loving God man also is loved most completely and wholly.

There is one aspect of Rolle's teaching on this wonderful gift of love, an aspect that typifies most of the English writers of the fourteenth century, namely a passionate devotion to our Lord and to the Holy Name of Jesus. We recall how later, when Walter Hilton came to revise his own *Scale of Perfection,* he replaced the name of God in nearly every place with the name of Jesus; and how Mother Julian saw all her revelations of divine love in the figure of the crucified Christ. But Richard stands out above the others in this focusing of all the light and heat of his love on our Lord.

The ascetic life of preparation for infused contemplation and the perfection of love if fed by constant meditations on the sufferings of our Lord.

> It is good to meditate on the Passion of Christ and his death, and to recall often what pain and wretchedness he freely took upon himself for our salvation in wandering and preaching, in hunger, thirst, cold, heat, reproofs, cursings and sufferings, so that it might not appear hard for an unprofitable servant to follow his Lord and Emperor. (*Amending of Life.*)

The meditation overcomes the devil and temptation and kindles love in the soul. There is a beautiful work from Richard's pen simply speaking with our Lord and our Lady on Calvary—he sees the individual pains of the Son and His Mother even more vividly than Mother Julian of Norwich.

And all this leads on towards the love of Jesus in the quietude of the solitary's cell.

> One thing I advise thee : that thou forget not his name—Jesus —but ponder it in thy heart night and day as thy special and dear treasure. Love it more than thy life, root it in thy mind. (*The Commandment.*)

Such sentences remind us of the *Jesus Psalter* which so wonderfully nourished the spirituality of Catholics in Penal Times, or again the Russian *Prayer of Jesus* which eventually fills the entire background of the life of anyone who practises it.

And as this devotion to the Holy Name increases the contemplative is led on to the inshed grace of the heat of love, a love which imprints this name in his heart so that every beat is a prayer of love to Jesus.

> Then thy soul is Jesus-loving, Jesus-thinking, Jesus-desiring, only breathing in the desire for him, singing to him, burning for him, resting in him. Then the song of praise and love is come. Then thy thought turns to song and melody. Then it behoves thee to *sing* psalms that before thou didst *say*. (*Form of Living*, c. 8.)

Or again:

> If thou wilt be well with God and have grace to rule thy life and come to the joy of love, fix the name of Jesus so fast in thy heart that it be never out of thy thought. And when thou speakest to him and sayest "Jesus" through habit, it shall be in thy ear joy, in thy mouth honey, and in thy heart melody.... If thou dost think "Jesus" continually and hold it firmly, it purges thy sin and kindles thy heart, it cleanses thy soul, it removes anger, it does away with sloth. It wounds in love and fulfills in charity. .... It opens heaven and makes a contemplative man. Have "Jesus" in mind, for it puts out all vices and phantoms from the lover. (Ibid., c. 9.)

Here is the concrete source of true mysticism, which avoids too great a reliance on too wide abstract terms and ideas about God and His Absolute Infinity. True Christian mysticism never steps across the humanity of Christ, but relies for its nourishment on the Incarnation. Indeed the purpose of the Word's becoming flesh was indeed to make mystics of us all. This insistence on the concrete reality of Jesus is perhaps the most characteristic sign of the illuminative stage in the ascent towards God. And without it the subsequent Unitive stage of "transformation" may well be suspected of the possibility of Pantheism.

Finally it should be said that Richard Rolle was a hermit and writing for hermits or in their defence, so that taken as a whole his teaching may not be applicable to the great majority of Christians today for whom the solitary life is out of the question. But taken in its various aspects, some of which have been outlined above, his doctrine is full of help and sustenance to Christians, particularly to English Christians.

One final quotation sums up Richard Rolle's character well:

In what state may men most love God? I answer: In whatever state it be that men are in the greatest rest of body and soul and least occupied with the needs or business of this world. For the thought of the love of Jesus Christ and of the joy that last for ever, seeks rest without, that it be not hindered by comers and goers and occupation with worldly things. And it seeks within great silence from the noise of covetings and of vanities and of earthly thoughts. And all those especially that live contemplative life seek rest in body and soul. For a great doctor says that they are God's throne who dwell still in one state and are not running about, but are established in the sweetness of God's love.

And I have loved to sit, not for penance, nor for fancy that I wished men to speak of me, nor for any such thing: but only because I loved God more; the comfort of love lasted longer with me than when going or standing or kneeling. For sitting I am most at rest and my heart is most upward. (*Form of Living*, c. 10.)

III

WALTER HILTON

By Gerard Sitwell, O.S.B.

Walter Hilton died in 1395 as an Augustinian Canon of Thurgarton in Nottinghamshire, but there is reason to suppose that it was only comparatively late in life that he joined this community, and almost nothing is known with certainty about his earlier life. Three works can confidently be attributed to him and several others with great probability, but in this article I propose to confine myself to his spirituality as put forth in his chief work, *The Scale of Perfection*.

There is a certain difficulty for us in approaching the *Scale*, because it was written for an anchoress, a person therefore in a very special way of life, which is far removed from the experience of most people today. But the form which the *Scale* took was dictated not only by the fact that Hilton was writing for someone who was in effect a hermit, but also by the fact that he was writing within a very definite tradition, which had come to the West, principally through the writings of the pseudo-Denis, direct from the Alexandrian writers of the fourth and fifth centuries. The spirituality which these writers represented was primarily that of the early Egyptian monks, but there is no doubt that the intellectual background which they provided for this was coloured by Greek philosophical ideas, and particularly that of contemplation as the end of life. It was a very specialized spirituality with an emphasis on contemplation quite unfamiliar to us.

It would be possible to approach a work of this nature in many ways, but I should like in this essay to point out that, in spite of what might be considered its specialized nature, Hilton's treatise is very valuable and full of practical advice for those who are trying to lead a serious spiritual life but would by no means call themselves contemplatives. Its great merit is that it treats the contemplative life as a natural and continuous development of the life of grace begun at baptism, and not as something esoteric only to be embarked upon self-consciously by the few. His main concern is with contemplation, but Hilton lays his foundations deep, and the *Scale* is in fact a comprehensive treatise on the spiritual life. The foundation on which all has to be built is what he calls the reforming,[1] the re-establishment, of the image of God in us. He treats of this in both of the books into which the *Scale* is divided, in Chapters 42 to 45 of the first, and in Chapters 1 to 20 of the second. When he says that man was made in the image of God, the point that he stresses is not the fundamental likeness to the Trinity in the powers of the soul, but that before the Fall the three powers of man's soul, memory, understanding, and will, were all directed to and occupied with God; in so far as its powers were directed primarily to God the soul could be said to reflect His nature. That this was the sense in which Hilton thought of it as an image of God is brought out by the fact that he goes on to say that as a result of Adam's sin man fell from this state "into forgetfulness and ignorance of God, and into a monstrous love of himself" (p. 64). From this condition he was rescued by Christ, and in the second Book (Chapter 2) he sets out the reasons for the Redemption, following more or less closely St Anselm's *Cur Deus Homo*. As a result of the Passion and death of Christ the image of God, in the sense in which he has used the term, may be restored to man, fully only in heaven, but partially here on earth, and into this partial restoration he introduces a further distinction. It may be in faith only, or in faith and feeling. The meaning of this rather curious distinction is this: the soul that is restored in faith only is simply in a state of grace. The soul that is restored in faith and feeling is also in a state of grace, but this further restoration "by the power of the Holy Ghost makes the soul aware of the workings of grace in it" (p. 154). The soul has attained a degree of grace in which "it apprehends God and spiritual truths in the higher parts of its reason" (p. 175), and this is the contemplative state.

It is characteristic of Hilton's wide view of the spiritual life that writing to instruct an anchoress in the ways of contemplation he nevertheless devotes a number of chapters to those who by the terms of his own definition have not yet attained that

[1] I have thought it better to keep this word as a sort of technical term, as I did in my rendering of the *Scale* into modern English in the Orchard Series. References in this article are to that edition: Burns & Oates, 1953.

state.[1] He begins at the beginning, describing the effects of baptism and the sacrament of Penance. He held, incidentally, an unorthodox view on the latter sacrament, holding that the sin was forgiven by contrition and that the priest's absolution was only declarative. A view put forward by Peter Lombard and held by St Bonaventure and many of the Franciscan school, but later condemned by Trent. He does not underrate this state: "The majority of God's elect lead their lives in this state, reformed only in faith" (p. 163). They strive seriously against sin, "and if they live their lives in this state and are found in it at the hour of their death, they will be saved and will be fully reformed in the happiness of heaven, even though they may never have felt any spiritual consolation or received any special grace of devotion all their lives" (p. 163). He gives practical advice for the struggle against temptation (Chapter 11), and emphasizing his distinction about "feeling" or the absence of it he points out that a man may be in this state without in any way being able to recognize the fact.

> He may indeed, if he has the grace and watches over himself, feel sorrow for his sin, and that his will has turned away from it. But he does not see or experience in any way the reforming of his soul, how it is in a wonderful, but imperceptible, way changed from the hideousness of a devil to the beauty of an angel, through the mysterious power of God. He cannot see that, but he must believe it (p. 160).

He goes on to say that a man may easily fall from this state, and must strive constantly against what he calls the image of sin that is within him.

But it is with the attainment of reform in feeling that he is ultimately concerned, and it is important to realize that when he uses the word feeling he does not imply any sort of emotional, still less a sensible, experience. What he means by it in fact, as will appear abundantly later, is an inward awareness of the life of grace, which at any recognizable level is a definitely mystical experience, the experience of contemplation. In Chapters 1 to 13 of the first Book he gives a summary conspectus of the stages of the contemplative life, and in Chapters 10 to 13 he warns at length against attaching importance to any sort of sensible phenomena. They may, he says, be good or evil in origin, and he gives the sound traditional advice

[1] The greater part of Chapters 1 to 20 of the second Book is devoted to this.

that it is by their fruits they are to be known. The attainment of this reform in feeling, he is careful to point out, must be a gradual process.

> Reform in faith is the lowest state of elect souls, below which they cannot well be, and reform in feeling is the highest state that a soul can come to in this life. But a soul cannot suddenly jump from the lowest to the highest, any more than a man who will climb a high ladder and puts his foot on the lowest rung can at the next moment be on the top one. He must go up them in order till he comes to the highest. So it is spiritually (p. 183).

This ladder is the *Scale*, which gives its title to the book, though he nowhere else refers to it.

It is perhaps the most valuable feature of Hilton's exposition of spirituality in *The Scale of Perfection* that while he recognizes the ascent of the ladder as necessarily a gradual process, he does not attempt to mark off the steps one from another. Any full analysis, such as that eventually achieved by St Teresa and St John of the Cross, must of necessity set out the course of the soul's development in a series of stages, and the fact that those two saints did so detracts nothing from the splendour of their achievement. The human mind can assemble and master the data of a complex experience only by some such method, but the fact remains that spiritual development does not occur in jumps. One step merges into another, and there is fluctuation and eddying, even if a general movement in one direction is discernible. The danger of a too clear definition of states, and particularly of the entry into what is called a contemplative or mystical state in general, is that such a state comes to be regarded as something wholly unusual, the prerogative of very special souls. In its more advanced manifestations it is certainly unusual, and it is true that contemplation properly so-called is beyond the power of man to achieve by himself, but Hilton's merit is that for him, as will appear later, the contemplative state is only one in which the essential sanctifying grace given at baptism has reached a degree at which its effects may be recognized. And the attainment of this is a gradual process. When the soul first acquires grace in baptism, or reacquires it in the sacrament of Penance, it may not be aware of the fact, but it is already on the road which may lead it to the heights of contemplation. In effect, therefore, anyone who is trying to do something more than just keep out of mortal sin—and even such a one—already has his foot on the first rung of the ladder; and Hilton's two stages of reform in fact merge into each other.

With all this in view we may look more closely at what he has to say about this reform in feeling. What is needed as the foundation on which everything else must be built is desire for Jesus, as he puts it; "desire of God, of Jesus—it is all the same", he says (p. 73).[1] It is very important to understand exactly what he means by this. Remembering his term "reform in faith and feeling" and the meaning which he gives to it, there is no doubt that when he says we are to desire Jesus, he means that we are to desire a realization of His presence which amounts to contemplation. In his early summary, in Chapter 13 of the first Book, he says, "But your constant endeavour shall be through much prayer to attain to the experimental knowledge of God in your soul" (p. 19). He quotes St Paul: *In caritate radicati et fundati, ut possitis comprehendere,* etc. (Eph. iii, 17, 18) and expands it as follows:

> Be rooted and grounded in charity, not that you may perceive sounds or a sweet savour or any other sensation, but that you may know and experience with all the saints, what is the extent of the infinite being of God, the breadth of His wonderful charity and goodness, the height of His almighty majesty, and the bottomless depths of His wisdom. It is in the knowledge and experience of these things that the work of a contemplative consists (p. 19).

Many passages could be quoted to illustrate the fact, and indeed it is the explicit aim of the treatise. All that is perfectly natural within the Dionysian tradition. And though it may be true that the idea of making the attainment of contemplation the direct end of our life here on earth owed its origin at least in part to Greek philosophy, there is no doubt that the idea was received and consecrated by the Church. Always in the East, and roughly from the thirteenth to the seventeenth century in the West, it held almost undisputed sway. After the Quietist troubles in the seventeenth century the pursuit of contemplation for the most part ceased to be

[1] The extent to which the *Scale* is Christ-centric is remarkable. Hilton habitually uses the Holy Name Jesus when one might expect him to say simply God, and once he applies it to God in a passage from the Old Testament (p. 151). He excuses himself for the practice (p. 292). See also Book II, Chapter 30 (p. 235 and note).

integrated with the spiritual life—a swing of the pendulum which has perhaps gone too far.

But we can get further light on this idea of contemplation as an awareness of grace. Hilton develops it with some fullness in the second Book. He describes, particularly in Chapters 31 to 33, the increase in the soul's *knowledge* which comes as a result of contemplation, "For then the soul understands something of what it knew before only by faith" (p. 246). In Chapter 34 he says that the soul's happiness lies in this knowledge, and it is the gift of Uncreated Love, that is the Holy Spirit, in the soul which brings this about.

> It is uncreated Love, that is God Himself, who is the cause of all this knowledge. For owing to sin and the weakness of its human nature the poor, blind soul is so far from the clear knowledge of God and the enjoyment of His love that it would never be able to attain them, if it were not for the infinite greatness of God's love. But because He loves us so much, He gives us His love, that is the Holy Ghost. He is both the giver and the gift, and by that gift makes us know and love Him. This is the love that I said you should desire, this uncreated Love that is the Holy Ghost (p. 248).

It is the action of God Himself, then, in the soul, which produces this enlightenment which is contemplation, and he has much to say about the further effects it will produce in the soul, which can easily be identified with the effects we attribute to the Gifts of the Holy Ghost. In Chapter 40 he identifies contemplation with various descriptions given by spiritual writers. It is impossible to identify his sources with any certainty for the phrases were all current in the spiritual literature of the Middle Ages, but among them is the phrase *tasting of the hidden manna, Dabo sibi manna absconditum* (Apoc. ii, 17).

> This tasting of manna is an awareness of the life of grace which comes from the opening of the soul's eyes. And this grace does not differ from the grace that an elect soul feels at the beginning of its conversion; it is the same grace but experienced in another way, because the progress of the soul and grace are interdependent. The purer and more detached from the love of the world the soul is, the stronger is the grace, the more interior and spiritual the experience of the presence of God. So the same grace that first turns men from sin and makes them set out and advance on the spiritual road by the practice of virtues and good works makes

> them perfect, and it is called *an awareness of grace*, for he who has it is conscious of the grace within him (pp. 277-8).

He has a further important comment to make on this when he says, that though "the overwhelming consciousness of it [grace] passes, the effect still remains and keeps the soul calm and makes it desire its return" (p. 278). Today we are shy of seeking "the awareness of grace", and yet the fostering of this divine life within us is the whole business of our spiritual lives, and it is for this reason that we can apply so much of what Hilton says about seeking contemplation to the development of the life of grace, in which for us the sacraments will play a larger part than they did for him.

We can find yet another line of thought converging on the same point. In the second Book he describes the soul's progress under the figure of a pilgrimage to Jerusalem (Chapter 21), a pilgrimage which he envisages as being made on foot. One condition is laid down as the guarantee of success in this adventure, and that is determination. The pilgrim will suffer great harm on his journey, he will be robbed and beaten, but he is to keep on his way nevertheless. Surely we are very mistaken if we think of these difficulties as only coming from without. The difficulties that really beset the spiritual life and cause discouragement come from ourselves. They are our temptations and falls into sin, and it is in face of these that we have to keep our goal before us and keep pressing on. It is no new advice, but it is fundamental. Hilton gives it to his anchoress seeking to attain contemplation, but it is applicable to any stage of a life seriously seeking God. The pilgrim is to encourage himself always by repeating, "I am nothing, I have nothing, I desire only one thing." These words, Hilton says, express what must be his fundamental attitude, namely one of humility and charity. He has rightly stressed the need for these two virtues—the only touchstones of sanctity—before, but his expression of them in this formula is of great significance, for it throws further light on the desire which he talked about in the first Book. "I desire only one thing" the pilgrim is to repeat to himself, and that is to be at Jerusalem, and this Hilton has expressly told us at the beginning of the chapter means to attain reform in feeling, and that, we have seen, means a high degree of grace. Here he explicitly equates this with charity, and the meaning of both words is enhanced by the identification. We must have charity, the love of God, and it is God Himself who gives us this. He is both the giver and the gift, as Hilton has put it.

We may look a little more closely at Hilton's application of his principles. In the first Book, where he is inculcating the need of the soul to reform the image of God in itself, he says that it is to do this by "seeking Jesus". And where is He to be found? "There is no need to go to Rome or to Jerusalem to look for Him, but turn your mind into your own soul, where He is hid, and seek Him there" (p. 79). But the first result of this effort will be disappointing. "What hinders you then that you can neither see nor hear Him? In truth there is so much noise and disturbance in your heart caused by useless thoughts and desires of the flesh that you can neither see Him nor hear Him" (p. 80). That is surely profound spiritual teaching. The first result of turning seriously to God will be an increased awareness of our own sins and imperfections. We shall find, not Jesus whom we seek, "but only the mere remembrance of His name. What more? In truth you will find nothing but an obscure and heavy image of your own soul, which has neither light to know God nor affection to love Him" (p. 83). That is what many who are making a real effort to lead a spiritual life so often feel. They think it is a bad sign, but it is a good one. It means the real work has at least begun. Hilton calls it finding the image of sin in ourselves, the roots of all the seven deadly sins, and he devotes no less than thirty-eight chapters (Book I, ch. 55-92) to describing these roots of sin and how we are to deal with them. Such is the foundation that he lays for the spiritual life of his contemplative.

He makes use of yet another image to describe the soul's progress, the passage through the night. There are two days or lights, he says, a false one and a true one. "The false light is the love of this world that a man has because of the corruption of his human nature; the true light is the perfect love of Jesus felt in the soul through grace" (p. 204). A man may withdraw himself from the false light of this world, that is from attachment to the things of sense and to his own self-will, but he will not immediately come to the perfect love of God. He cannot come suddenly from one light to the other, any more than he can pass from one day to another without going through the night, and indeed as long as he is on this earth he will never reach the full light of God's day, for that is complete reform in feeling, which is only attained in the Beatific Vision. It is a good image, but it is to be noted that Hilton is using it in a wider sense than that in which it was afterwards used by St John of the Cross. For Hilton the night is the whole spiritual life of a man after he has turned seriously from the love of the world and set his heart on the love of God. Sometimes the night will be distressing, for the world will still exercise an attraction, but gradually the soul will come to rest in it, for the grace of God is drawing it, and from time to time it will see glints and gleams of the true day. Hilton's teaching is admirable on this subject. A man who has embarked on this journey through the night may well find habits of sin, the desires of the flesh, and his worldly activities pressing in on him:

> Nevertheless, if you find it so, do not be too depressed, and do not struggle too much, as though you would put these things out of your mind by force, for you cannot do that. Wait till grace comes, be patient and do not let your efforts be too violent: if you can, quietly turn your will and your thoughts to Jesus as though you attached no importance to these feelings (p. 206).

Rightly understood accepting the situation is an important part of the spiritual life. We get impatient, and then we get impatient with ourselves for being impatient. But Hilton's advice presupposes that the desire for God is there, "I desire only one thing," and it is indeed this desire which constitutes the night.

> For its [the soul's] desire and its longing for the love of God, for the vision and the possession of Him, drives out of the heart all worldly interest and all desires of the flesh, and makes the soul recollected and occupied only with how it may come to His love, and so it brings it into this fruitful nothing. And all is not darkness and nothing when it is so occupied.... For Jesus, who is both love and light, is in the darkness whether it is distressing or peaceful (p. 207).

Doubtless Hilton has in mind his anchoress, who is living a life of itself conducive to great recollection, but the teaching again remains valid for anyone trying seriously to serve God. In the saint the desire is overriding, but in the weakest of us, if it is there at all, it produces its effect.

There is still much in *The Scale of Perfection* that might be commented upon, but only the barest mention of a few points can be made here. In the latter part of the second Book Hilton is, of course, directly concerned with contemplation properly so-called, and his teaching on it is thoroughly in accord with tradition. In Chapters 30 and 33 he gives what is the normal teaching for the necessity of transcending the imagination, but it is to be noted that he does not seem to advocate the adoption of a specific exercise in this, a technique, in the way that the author of the *Cloud* does. He has much to say of the effects this contemplative union with God will produce in the soul. There will be a general ease in the practice of virtue, "Love brings all virtues into the soul and makes them agreeable and pleasant . . . for the soul does not struggle to attain them as it did before, but it possesses them easily and rests in them through this gift of Love" (Book II, ch. 36, p. 258). It is the characteristic effect of the Gifts of the Holy Ghost by which the powers of the soul are made in St Thomas's words *bene mobiles a Spiritu Sancto*. Hilton distinguishes very well between the humility and patience that a virtuous soul may acquire by its own efforts aided by ordinary grace and those virtues as they will exist in a man who has come to the knowledge of God in contemplation (Book II, ch. 37 and 38). It is worthy of note that only in the last three chapters of his two lengthy Books does he treat of the experiences such as visions, which are often thought of as constituting the essence of the mystical state. There is neither space nor need to discuss these, but it may be noted that in the prominent part given to angels in the production of these phenomena we may perhaps see traces of the Eastern theology that lay behind his work. This is a point, however, which has not been explored.

He wrote before the days of scientific methods of mental prayer. For him the basis of all prayer is vocal prayer as we know it, and he seems to have regarded everything beyond this as at least to some degree inspired or contemplative, but he has a most consoling chapter on distractions at prayer. (See Book I, ch. 24-33.)

In matters of food and drink and sleep and bodily penance he advocates a wise discretion. "Moderation is best," he says (p. 35), while in the long section dealing with the roots of sin and how we are to destroy them (Book I, ch. 55-92) he has much valuable advice to give. He stresses that spiritual sins are worse than carnal ones, a view which is theologically correct, though the contrary is often thought, and his chapter (83) on how the anchoress is to behave towards visitors could hardly be bettered as advice on the practical application of the virtue of charity.

The Scale of Perfection is a more closely woven piece of writing than might appear at first sight, a tapestry in which the main design can easily be traced, but in which it is surrounded by much elaborate detail, no part of which is unrelated. To us a few strands may appear alien. It would be surprising if it were not so in a work nearly 600 years old, but they are of very minor importance. What may be more of a difficulty is that, because of the spiritual tradition in which he wrote, Hilton ignores completely, save for a few incidental and perfunctory references, the whole of the Church's liturgy. Many today will find that a serious gap in his teaching, but it is to be remembered that right up till a generation ago it would hardly have been noticed. I have tried to show that a more sacramental spirituality would fit with ease into his conception of man's relation to God, and of course his wise understanding of a human nature which does not change is valid for all time.

IV

THE CLOUD OF UNKNOWING

By Gerard Sitwell, o.s.b.

In my essay on Walter Hilton I pointed out that a movement towards a very highly specialized view of the contemplative life, which owed its inspiration to the renewed influence of the Alexandrian schools of spirituality of the third to the sixth centuries, began to spread over Western Europe in the Middle Ages. The movement reached England in the fourteenth century, and the treatise known as *The Cloud of Unknowing* is perhaps its most characteristic product. The identity of the author has never been established, but from linguistic and manuscript evidence it is agreed that the treatise belongs to the second half of the fourteenth century, and probably to the East Midland district.

The charm of the *Cloud* comes from the fact that the author, although he was broaching a subject of deep theological speculation, was evidently a man of wide sympathies. We have no idea who he was, but one can conceive him as a successful and popular lecturer at a high academic level, one who was capable of handling abstruse and difficult matter without sinking into mere abstractions, and who never loses touch with the world of real men and women. Nevertheless he makes it clear in his first chapter that he is writing for the instruction of a disciple who aims at the highest reaches of the spiritual life. "Seest thou not how sweetly and how graciously he hath privily pulled thee to the third degree and manner of living, the which is called singular?" And he goes on significantly:

> In the which solitary form and manner of living thou mayest learn to lift up the foot of thy love, and to step toward that state and degree of living that is *perfect*, and the last state of all (Ch. 1, p. 4[1]).

Always and necessarily the extreme contemplative tradition

1 Page references are to Dom Justin McCann's edition, Burns & Oates (1943).

was something that went with the solitary life. The author is careful to point out in his Prologue that his teaching is only for those who have a genuine vocation to this life, but the fact that he should devote his whole treatise to it is a good example of the influence of the school of contemplative spirituality. Contemplation was for him not just something which may occur in a life devoted to the whole-hearted service of God, but was something to be cultivated, and his whole work is concerned with the way in which this may be done. As has been said, the author is conscious that his work is esoteric. In the Prologue he is insistent that it is only for those who have set themselves to be perfect followers of Christ, and that not merely by the practice of good works but precisely through contemplation, and he is anxious that his book should not even come into the hands of others. But granted that a man feels justified in aiming at contemplation, then this, he says, is the way in which it must be done. The doctrine is that of the unknown writer of the end of the fifth century who chose to go under the name of Denis the Areopagite.

Denis was profoundly impressed by the inadequacy of the human mind to comprehend God. We call God good, beautiful, or true, and our knowledge of these qualities is gained from human experience, but so far does this fall short of the reality in God that it is more exact to say that He is neither good nor beautiful nor true—as we understand those words. We are better advised to recognize our limitations and the transcendence of God, and not to try to comprehend Him by the exercise of our active intellect. Nevertheless union with God is the ultimate end of our existence, and even the immediate end, but it is one which is achieved, not in the intellect as we ordinarily understand the term, but in what he called the highest point of the spirit. A thirteenth-century commentator on Denis, Thomas Gallus, gives perhaps the clearest explanation of this. There is a more profound manner of knowing God, a super-intellectual one. The highest cognitive faculty is not the intellect, but there is one which far excels this, which he calls the higher will (*principalis affectio*) or the spark of conscience (*scintilla synderesis*), and by this alone may man be united to the Divine Spirit. The use of the senses, imagination, reason and intellect are all suspended.

The Victorines, St Bernard, and St Bonaventure were all influenced by this idea, though the interpretation they put upon it was that the union is in fact a union of love, of the will. "Love knocks and enters, but knowledge stands without." It is the so-called mysticism of darkness. The experience of God in contemplation is so far removed from any human experience of knowledge that it is described as "unknowing", and the entry into it is entry into the *cloud of unknowing*. Whatever may be thought of the theory it had important consequences, for it meant in practice that in the attempt to reach God the activity of the intellect must be reduced to the simplest possible form, there must be no use of the discursive reason, no meditation in fact, though there may remain an apprehension, however dark, of the Being of God. This is the cloud of unknowing, and the conscious striving after the attainment of this is what our author calls the cloud of forgetting.

It is to be noted that man cannot actually achieve this union in the *cloud of unknowing* by his own efforts. It is essentially supernatural, the direct work of God in the soul. All man can do is to prepare for it by simplifying the object of his intellectual activity as much as possible, and by directing the acts of his will to this object, by acts of love in other words. All this, of course, applies only to the actual time of the "work", as the author of the *Cloud* calls it, when the soul is actually contemplating or striving after contemplation. As we have seen, no human efforts can command contemplation, but man can prepare himself for it by entering into the cloud of forgetting, and it is with this immediate preparation that the treatise of the *Cloud* is exclusively concerned. It will be an exercise to which the contemplative devotes himself for an hour or several hours a day, but this special effort must be accompanied by a remote preparation which embraces the whole of life, and which may be described in the most general terms as the practice of virtue; it is Cassian's "practical" life.

With all this in mind we may look at some passages in the *Cloud*. He describes the "work".

> Lift up thine heart unto God with a meek stirring of love; and mean himself and none of his goods. And thereto look that thou loathe to think on aught but himself, so that nought work in thy mind nor in thy will but only himself (Ch. 3, p. 5).

It is the undistracted focusing of the attention on the simple Being of God.

And therefore, when thou purposest thee to this work, and feelest by grace that thou art called by God, lift up thine heart unto God with a meek stirring of love. And mean God that made thee, and bought thee, and that graciously hath called thee to thy degree; and receive none other thought of God. And yet not all these, except thou desirest; for a naked intent directed unto God, without any other cause than himself, sufficeth wholly. And if thou desirest to have this intent lapped and folden in one word, so that thou mayest have better hold thereupon, take thee but a little word of one syllable, for so it is better than of two; for the shorter the word, the better it accordeth with the work of the spirit. And such a word is this word GOD or this word LOVE. Choose whichever thou wilt, or another; whatever word thou likest best of one syllable. And fasten this word to thine heart, so that it may never go thence for anything that befalleth (Ch. 7, p. 13).

There is no discursive reasoning, no inward discussion of the subject. Just what this means in practice he has made clear:

As oft as I say "all the creatures that ever be made" [are to be eliminated], so oft do I mean, not only the creatures themselves, but also all the works and conditions of the same creatures. I except not one creature, whether they be bodily creatures or ghostly; nor yet any condition or work of any creature, whether they be good or evil. But, to speak shortly, all should be hid under the *cloud of forgetting* in this case (Ch. 5, p. 11).

Even thoughts about God and the saints are a distraction:

Yea—and if it be courteous and seemly to say—in this work it profiteth little or nought to think of the kindness or worthiness of God, nor on our Lady, nor on the saints or angels in heaven, nor yet on the joys of heaven; that is to say, with a special beholding to them, as thou wouldst by that beholding feed and increase thy purpose. I trow that on nowise it should help in this case and in this work. For although it be good to think on the kindness of God, and to love him and praise him for it; yet it is far better to think on the naked being of him, and to love him and praise him for himself (Ch. 5, p. 11).

He shows how meditation hinders the work. If a man starts thinking even of the Passion of Christ, he will be led to thoughts of his wretched past life, and that will perhaps bring to his mind some place that he has dwelt in. "So that at the last, ere ever thou knowest, thou shalt be scattered thou knowest not where" (Ch. 7, p. 13). And yet meditation must be used.

> And yet, nevertheless, the thing that he [the thought] said was both good and holy. Yea, and so holy, that whatever man or woman weeneth to come to contemplation without many such sweet meditations beforehand of their own wretchedness, the passion, the kindness, the great goodness and the worthiness of God, surely he shall err and fail of his purpose. And yet, a man or woman that hath long time been practised in these meditations, must nevertheless leave them, and put them and hold them far down under the *cloud of forgetting*, if ever he shall pierce the *cloud of unknowing* betwixt him and his God (Ch. 7, p. 13).

Important advice which puts the work in its right perspective. He says again:

> And therefore, although it be good sometime to think on the goodness and the worthiness of God in special, and although it be a light and a part of contemplation; nevertheless in this work it shall be cast down and covered with a *cloud of forgetting* (Ch. 6, p. 12).
>
> The sharp stirring of thine understanding, that will always press upon thee when thou settest thee to this blind work, must always be borne down; and unless thou bear him down, he will bear thee down. Insomuch that when you weenest best to abide in this darkness, and that nought is in thy mind but only God, if thou look wisely thou shalt find thy mind not occupied in this darkness, but in a clear beholding of some thing beneath God (Ch. 9, p. 17).
>
> I say not that such a naked sudden thought of any good and clean ghostly thing under God, pressing against thy will or thy witting, or else wilfully drawn upon thee of set purpose for increasing of thy devotion, although it be a hindrance to this manner of work—that it is therefore evil. Nay, God forbid that thou take it so. But I say that although it be good and holy, yet in this work it hindereth more than it profiteth. I mean for the time of this work. For surely, he that seeketh God perfectly, he will not rest finally in the thought of any angel or saint that is in heaven (Ch. 9, p. 18).

He makes it clear that it is God who is to be sought and not an experience:

> As it is said before, the substance of this work is nought else but a naked intent directed unto God for himself. A *naked intent* I call it. Because in this work a perfect prentice asketh neither releasing of pain, nor increasing of reward, nor (shortly to say) nought but himself. Insomuch, that he neither recketh nor regardeth whether he be in pain or in bliss, but only that his will be fulfilled whom he loveth. And thus it seemeth that in this work God is perfectly loved for himself, and above all creatures (Ch. 24, p. 36).

The character of the experience as a pure gift of God is emphasized:

> And therefore lift up thy love to that cloud. Or rather (if I shall say thee sooth) let God draw thy love up to that cloud; and strive thou through help of his grace to forget all other things (Ch. 9, p. 18).
>
> Although it be hard and strait in the beginning, when thou hast no devotion, nevertheless afterwards, when thou hast devotion, it shall be made full restful and full light unto thee, that before was full hard. And thou shalt have either little travail or none; for then will God work sometimes all by himself. But not always, nor yet a long time together, but when he liketh and as he liketh; and then wilt thou think it merry to let him alone (Ch. 26, p. 39).
>
> ... it is the work of only God specially wrought in whatever soul he liketh, without any merit of the same soul.... It is neither given for innocence, nor withholden for sin (Ch. 34, p. 45).

In just one passage is there any reference to the sort of results that may ensue from this exercise:

> Then will he [God] sometimes peradventure send out a beam of ghostly light, piercing this *cloud of unknowing* that is betwixt thee and him, and show thee some of his secrets, the which man may not and cannot speak. Then shalt thou feel thine affection inflamed with the fire of his love, far more than I can tell thee, or may or will at this time. For of that work that pertaineth only to God dare I not take upon me to speak with my blabbering fleshly tongue: and shortly to say, although I durst I would not. But of that work that pertaineth to man, when he feeleth himself

> stirred and helped by grace, I like well to tell : for therein is the less peril of the two (Ch. 26, p. 39).

It is the peculiarity of the *Cloud* that the author will not pursue this subject but shies away from it. There is, however, another effect which he, in common with Hilton, and indeed all writers on the subject, emphasizes, and that is its effect in producing virtue :

> It [the cloud of unknowing] destroyeth not only the ground and the root of sin, as it may be here, but also it getteth virtues. For if it be truly conceived, all virtues shall be subtly and perfectly conceived, felt, and comprehended in it, without any mingling of thine intent. And have a man never so many virtues without it, all they be mingled with some crooked intent, for the which they be imperfect (Ch. 12, p. 22).

And the two fundamental virtues to which it will lead are humility and charity. It is in Chapter 13 that he speaks in particular of the virtue of humility—meekness—and he treats of it in the most profound sense of that frequently misunderstood virtue. For him it means, as properly taken it should, a true knowledge of oneself in relation to God and to other men, and there are, he says, two ways in which this may be achieved. The first is purely natural. By the ordinary use of his intellect a man may come to a knowledge of his own sinfulness, and more particularly a knowledge of what Hilton called the roots of sin within him, the latent capacity for evil which is in all men. The second way in which a man may acquire humility is supernatural. It comes as an inevitable result of the true mystical experience, for in that experience the soul comes to a knowledge of God which is of an altogether higher kind than any which it had before. It sees something of the super-abundant love and worthiness of God in himself, "in beholding of which all nature quaketh, all clerks be fools, and all saints and angels be blind". Realizing something of what the goodness of God means the soul forgets all else, including itself and its own merits or demerits, "and in this time it is perfectly meeked, for it knoweth and feeleth no cause but the chief". Humility which comes as a result of this experience is of an altogether deeper kind than that which comes as a result of the natural use of man's reason, and it is necessarily something which cannot be acquired at will. Until, or unless, it is given man must work to acquire what he can by his own efforts, and there is no advancing to a higher state except on this foundation.

There are a few more points which may be noticed. Like all this school of writers he advocates a great discretion in the matter of external austerities. Chapter 42 is devoted to this, "that by indiscretion in this work, men shall keep discretion in all other things and surely never else". Contemplation is to be pursued unremittingly by the method which he has taught, and if this is done, a sufficient detachment from the things of sense will follow automatically.

> But peradventure thou askest me how thou shalt govern thee discreetly in meat, and in drink, and in sleep, and in all these other. And hereto I think to answer thee right shortly: "Get what thou canst get" [in the sense of Take what comes]. Do this work [striving for contemplation in the way he has prescribed] evermore without ceasing and without discretion, and thou shalt know well how to begin and to cease in all other works with a great discretion. For I cannot believe that a soul continuing in this work night and day without discretion may err in any of these outward doings; and else methinketh that he should always err (Ch. 42, p. 54).

This teaching is the whole theme of the contemporary *Epistle of Discretion*, which is probably by the same author.

One further piece of advice which he gives is of interest. He warns against an unwise straining after this work in a number of chapters.[1]

> A young man or a woman, newly set to the school of devotion, heareth this sorrow and this desire read and spoken of; how that a man shall lift up his heart unto God, and unceasingly desire to feel the love of his God. And as fast in a curiosity of wit they conceive these words not ghostly, as they be meant, but fleshly and bodily; and travail their fleshly hearts outrageously in their breasts (Ch. 45, p. 58).

The result may be reaction and seeking bodily comfort and recreation. Or it may produce physical phenomena such as unnatural heat in the breast.

[1] 45, 46, 51-57.

> And yet peradventure, they ween that it is the fire of love, gotten and kindled by the grace and the goodness of the Holy Ghost. Truly, from this deceit, and from the branches thereof, spring many mischiefs : much hypocrisy, much heresy, and much error (Ch. 45, p. 58).

It is well to remember that these warnings at the time they were given were not just academic. In England the movement towards mysticism was very real, as the existence of the school of writers to which the *Cloud* belongs testifies, but it seems to have been well controlled. Possibly the national temperament, which is little given to extravagant self-expression, was to a large extent responsible for keeping it within bounds. At any rate we have little evidence for the existence in this country of the more unrestrained varieties of mystic. Margery Kempe was an example, but she is exceptional, and she appears always to have kept within the limits of orthodoxy. On the Continent, however, and particularly in the Low Countries, the contemplative movement was more widespread and in consequence attracted many unsuitable devotees. Whole sects such as the Brethren of the Free Spirit and the Beghards gave themselves up to "enthusiasm" of a most unbridled nature. Mgr Knox in his study of the subject[1] refers to a company of Beghards who "ran from place to place in most singular and fantastic apparel, and begged their bread with wild shouts and clamours, rejecting with horror every kind of industry and labour as an obstacle to divine contemplation" (p. 124). These excesses of behaviour were almost always the accompaniment of perfectionism and antinomianism; the belief that the adept was so perfectly united to God that he was above the ordinary laws of morality, and that what earned damnation in the worldling was inculpable in him. It is these sort of people that the author of the *Cloud* has in mind when he refers to heretics, as for example in Chapter 53.

The subject matter, then, of *The Cloud of Unknowing* is this special "work", as the author calls it, or spiritual exercise. One in which the activity of the intellect though not eliminated is deliberately reduced to a minimum, but in which, nevertheless, the soul is not reduced to a purely passive state. There is an unwonted —and I use the term strictly—activity of the will. The soul is not

[1] R. A. Knox, *Enthusiasm*, Oxford (1950).

seeking nothingness, extinction, but God. Its end is to be united, and ultimately in its cognitive faculties, with the very source of all being, but this can only be achieved by the self-revelation of that Being, a revelation which its own activity can only hinder.

It is of interest that the author of the *Cloud* nowhere refers to this exercise as prayer, though that is what we should call it now, and Father Augustine Baker, when he took up this teaching in the seventeenth century, treated it as a form of prayer. Incidentally, there can be little doubt, I think, that when he addressed himself to prayer in what he called his third Conversion, it was this exercise advocated in the *Cloud* that he adopted, with the very interesting results that he describes.[1] It is to be noted that it did not take him as far as he had got before with much less theory.

Probably few today would be tempted to try and follow the method of the *Cloud* in all its rigour, but it reminds us of many valuable lessons in the spiritual life, and particularly of the desirability at times of just resting in God. The process for most of us will probably not be of long duration, but it is valuable.

[1] *The Confessions of Father Baker*, Chap. V, edited by Dom Justin McCann, London (1922).

V

DAME JULIAN OF NORWICH

By A Benedictine of Stanbrook (D. S. H.)

I

"Then she was bidden by our Lord to go to an anchoress in the same city, named Dame Jelyan . . . for the anchoress was expert in such things and good counsel could give." Thus speaks Margery Kempe in her spiritual autobiography in the first half of the fifteenth century; such was the impression left upon her contemporaries by Dame Julian of Norwich. Nevertheless, it may safely be affirmed that as a spiritual and mystical writer, Julian is more widely known and loved—and certainly more copiously discussed —in these days than ever before. From the very small number of extant manuscripts, not more than five, compared with, say, the fifty of Hilton's *Scale of Perfection,* it seems unlikely that her work had much circulation either in her own day or for centuries afterwards. Possibly the stern moralists of the period, bent on inculcating the fear of God and disapproving of over-confidence in His mercy, found matter for suspicion in the apparent mildness of her teaching, her message of hope and comfort. At all events, like more than one such treasure, it was reserved by Providence for the consolation of a later age. To those engaged in the grim struggle against Jansenism, for instance, the appearance of the first printed edition issued by Dom Serenus Cressy, O.S.B., in 1670, may well have come as a timely reinforcement.

The book, entitled *Revelations of Divine Love*, consists of a methodical recital of sixteen "Shewings" received by its author on 8 May or 14 May 1373 and the following day. It exists in two distinct forms, a shorter and earlier version written soon after the event, surviving in a single copy dated 1413, and a revised and expanded version represented by four MSS. of much later date.

Of the writer herself, just sufficient is known to establish her authentic existence. The scribe of the earliest MS. refers to her as "a devout woman whose name is Julian . . . a recluse at Norwich". According to her own account she was born towards the end of 1342. By 1404 at the latest (possibly several years earlier, if indeed, as has been suggested, the words: "This place is prison; this life is penance" do refer to her physical restrictions), she was in residence as a recluse in the anchorhold adjoining St Julian's Church, then in the gift of Carrow Priory less than a mile away. Until destroyed by enemy bombing in 1942, the south-eastern wall of St Julian's Church in Norwich showed clearly where the anchoress's cell had once stood, with its window through which the high altar would have been visible. The site is now occupied by a chapel, opening by an archway from the restored main building. It was here she received a visit from Margery Kempe about the year 1410. The date of her death is not known; but she was still living in 1416.

Dame Julian refers to herself as "a simple creature unlettered", and the exact meaning of these phrases has been much discussed. Neither her thought nor its expression is that of an uneducated person. Perhaps she knew neither French nor Latin and no more theology than any other woman of her day. This would be in no way surprising, nor would it necessarily imply illiteracy. The knowledge of Latin seems not to have been common even among nuns, and although some acquaintance with French was more usual, fourteenth-century Norfolk notoriously set no great store by that language. It had its own vigorous vernacular culture and was briskly leading a nation-wide return to the official use of English in civil affairs. Certainly Julian was not ignorant of her native language, which she handled with remarkable ease and ability; nor, apparently, was she unable to read an English Bible, for her book is studded with biblical quotations and allusions. It may originally have been dictated, but the method of its revision rather suggests careful personal application.

A formidable array of literary influences, echoes and reminiscences, from St Augustine to Meister Eckhart and from the *Ancrene Riwle* even to St Catherine of Siena, discernible in the *Revelations* and especially in the Longer Version, seems also to belie Dame Julian's estimate of herself. Probably, however, their origin was at least as often oral as written; and in this respect she was definitely a child of her own era.

Medieval Norwich, then the second city in the kingdom, was unusually rich in churches, religious houses, and charitable institutions; St Julian's Church stood within half a mile of the Cathedral Priory and the flourishing Dominican house, and within easy reach of the Franciscans (strongly established in East Anglia), the Carmelites, and the Austin Friars. Margery Kempe's book confirms the impression that the city positively swarmed with ecclesiastics of all kinds, moving freely among the people on friendly and accessible terms. Monks and Mendicants, not always Englishmen, debated in public and in private; spiritual counsel was apparently to be had for the asking, while a mounting wave of church-building zeal bears witness to the practical reality of popular devotion throughout the county.

In our days of divided allegiances, it is hard to realize either the general solidarity of a united Christendom or the immense power and diversity of the spiritual current circulating intimately among its members, and in particular the part played by the spoken word in the fourteenth century. Whatever may have been the state of decadence elsewhere, here in England at least the period was certainly one of great religious activity. It seems clear that the main bulk of religious business, so to speak, was transacted not by way of books but by word of mouth—a method which usually leaves no tangible permanent record.

Similarly vernacular eloquence was not necessarily a literary product. Such devices as alliteration, rhetorical repetition, and the numerical classification of which Julian appears so inordinately fond, were familiar pulpit expedients to rouse the listeners' attention or to impress some important statement on their memory. Hence the search in such books as hers for evidences of literary antecedents and stylistic models, patristic echoes and learned influences in general, may be somewhat misleading. There is more than one way of acquiring a well-stocked mind; Dame Julian may have been technically "unlearned"; she was not an ignoramus.

Was Julian a Benedictine nun of Carrow Priory, and did her great mystical experience take place there? From a practical point of view it would be far more difficult to explain or account for her on any other supposition. It is true that she gives no details of conventual or liturgical life, but then neither does she refer to her life as an anchoress, except possibly in the one inconclusive sentence. Why indeed should she? To provide biographical material is not the primary aim of a writer on spiritual topics. Most of the things we should like to know about her she would have regarded as either obvious or irrelevant. She does not tell us, for instance, that the mysterious illness which preceded her visions of our Lord's Passion began on or about the feast of the Finding of the Holy Cross, nor that St John of Beverley, in whom she displays a special interest, was very popular in England at this period (Henry V attributed the victory of Agincourt to his intercession) and was commemorated on 7 May, perhaps the day before the actual "Shewings". Both these points are manifestly of importance, but nobody in her own day would have needed the reminder. The background is simply taken for granted.

Although the earliest MS. calls Julian merely "a devout woman", and the few references in local wills afford no further clue, Margery Kempe, as we have seen, gives her the title of Dame, which then as now was usual for Benedictine nuns. The one clear non-biblical quotation in her book is a sentence from St Gregory's *Life of St Benedict*: "For to a soul that seeth the Maker of all-things, all that is made seemeth full little"—a thought evidently pondered upon and already well impressed on Julian's mind. The reference to "prime day" has a distinctly monastic ring, and so has the exclamation "*Benedicite, Dominus!*" though the latter may have been merely a customary formula for certain occasions. Canonical enclosure as observed by English Benedictine nuns at this period need not have precluded the presence of an altar-boy in attendance on the priest who visited her, nor that of a mother at what was doubtless assumed to be her daughter's deathbed.

It is obvious from her writings that the author had led a very pure and unworldly life, with a definitely religious bent. She was no beginner in the spiritual art. The impression that her whole mentality—apart from her preternatural experiences—was that of a nun, is, of course, not capable of demonstration. It may be noted, however, that in recounting her petition for "a bodily sickness", she tells us: "This sickness I desired in my youth"—the kind of request a fervent young novice might easily make and, like Dame Julian, forget all about afterwards. Our Lord's words to her: "I thank thee of thy service and of the travel [i.e. labour] of thy youth," and her own allusion a little later—surely a personal one—to "them that wilfully and freely offer their youth to God", might well be taken to denote a nun's vocation, and there is no conclusive evidence to the contrary. But the question perforce remains open.

That she was already a recluse at the time of her "Shewings" seems less probable. Anchorites and anchoresses formed a recognized part of English medieval life, and their curious vocation was evidently not so rare as to be considered abnormal. Often, if not usually, they were already professed and seasoned religious. St Benedict in his Rule mentions with apparent approval "the Anchorites or Hermits, that is those who not in the first fervour of their religious life, but after long probation in a monastery, having learnt in association with many brethren how to fight against the devil, go out well-armed from the ranks of the community to the solitary combat of the desert". Just how solitary in actual practice would depend on circumstances. There would obviously be a better chance of solitude in some remote hamlet than in the midst of a thriving provincial city, upon which all the main roads of its populous county converged like the spokes of a wheel; but there would be corresponding disadvantages. In any location, an anchoress must live next to a church in order to be present at Mass, and being strictly enclosed must have at least one attendant to see to her every-day needs. Two of Julian's servants are, in fact, mentioned together with herself in contemporary documents. The recluse as such evidently enjoyed a certain privileged position, and in all probability would have no difficulty in obtaining any spiritual counsels or books that might be locally available. For this object, at any rate, St Julian's anchorhold could hardly have been better placed. On the other hand, he or she would be expected to give advice on spiritual matters to all and sundry who cared to seek for it—an arrangement convenient enough for the visitor but liable to be somewhat distracting for the would-be solitary. The anchorite at the Preaching Friars at Lynn acted for a while as Margery Kempe's confessor, and must have found the charge no sinecure; while her encounter with the anchorite at the Chapel in the Fields, who accused her on hearsay of a very grave sin and was not to be convinced of her innocence, shows that contact with gossip and scandal was not easily avoided. "From mill and from market, from smithy and from anchor-house, one hears the news," quotes the *Ancrene Riwle*. Hence it was well recognized that any candidate for such a way of life ought to possess not only a strong will and a solid religious formation, but also the "maturity of demeanour and of speech" which the same authority declared "proper in an anchoress". Whether the age of thirty would be considered sufficient for such qualifications in any particular instance is again completely uncertain; even so, it surely would be the very minimum.

II

Of the genuineness of her mystical experience, Julian herself never had any serious doubt. Modern theological scrutiny has endorsed her conviction.[1] It has also analysed her states of prayer and vindicated her essential orthodoxy, although at times her actual expressions may appear exaggerated or inaccurate. For instance, the sentence, "There is no Doer but he", may be an over-simplification of God's omnipotence, but is certainly not meant as a denial of man's freewill. "Sin is behovely" is exactly parallel to the *O felix culpa* of the *Exsultet*, neither more nor less. The statement "that in each soul that shall be safe, is a godly will that never assented to sin, ne never shall" belongs to a similar type of apparent inaccuracy, which must be offset by her more precisely orthodox pronouncements elsewhere.

Like St Teresa, Julian possessed a keen intellect and shrewd common sense, but though well grounded in Christian doctrine was in no way a trained theologian. Both women, too, labour under the same difficulty of conveying through ordinary language, word by word, things sometimes apparently contradictory seen as a simultaneous unity in one intense flash of insight; the result of their efforts remains for themselves hopelessly inadequate and for the reader often incomprehensible.

The *Revelations* themselves did not, of course, impart any new doctrinal truths, but simply a very strong and clear realization of truths already known through the normal channels of instruction

[1] See especially: *Julian of Norwich: The Teaching of a Fourteenth Century English Mystic* by Paul Molinari, S.J. (Longmans, Green & Co., London, 1958).

—"the common teaching of Holy Church, of which I was before enformed and grounded".

Unlike some visionaries, Julian never refers to current events. She has no impassioned denunciations to deliver, no messages for individuals, no personalities of any kind. On the one occasion when she ventured to enquire "concerning a certain person that I love, how it should be with her", she "was not taught in this time" but received a gentle correction: "Take it generally, and behold the courtesy of thy Lord God as He shews it to thee. For it is more worship to God to behold Him in all, than in any special thing." This goes far to account for a certain air of universality and timelessness which is one of her great attractions.

No summary can do justice to either the content or the charm of Dame Julian's book. For anyone wishing to make her acquaintance, the simplest way would probably be to begin with the Shorter Version of the *Revelations* which gives the facts of her experience and the gist of her teaching with a freshness and directness all its own. This version is moreover invaluable as furnishing an earlier and purer text of the portions common to both than any existing MS. of the Longer Version, upon whose development it also sheds some very significant light.[1]

Without questioning the supernatural origin and character of her "Shewings", may it not be suggested that the feast of the Finding of the Holy Cross on 3 May, a few days earlier, was perhaps used by Divine Providence as their immediate preparation?[2]

> How might my pain be greater than to see Him suffer that is all my life, all my bliss and all my joy?

In such a soul as hers, the liturgy of Holy Cross Day, with its solemn veneration of the cross and its refrain of "We adore Thee, O Christ, and we bless Thee, because by Thy cross Thou hast redeemed the world", could well have produced a state of heightened sensibility apt for the reception of extraordinary graces. At any rate, it provides precisely the root-idea underlying the whole

[1] The Shorter Version, first published from the fifteenth-century MS. by the Rev. Dundas Harford, M.A. (*Comfortable Words for Christ's Lovers*. H. R. Allenson, London, 1911), has recently been edited by Sister Anna Maria Reynolds, C.P. (*A Shewing of God's Love*. Longmans, Green & Co., London, 1958).

[2] The exact chronology is uncertain, but does not seriously affect the argument.

series of revelations. In this connection her own statement in the Shorter Version is very much to the point:

> Such pains I saw that all is too little that I can tell or say of them, for it may not be told, unless every soul should feel in himself that which was in Christ Jesus, according to the saying of Saint Paul: "Let that mind be in you which was in Christ Jesus".

—a text which actually occurs in the Office and Mass for Holy Cross Day. Illumined by an intensely loving and penetrating insight into the central mystery of the cross, or rather of the crucified Redeemer, her book is in effect simply a prolonged meditation upon the Passion of Christ, its significance and its implications in regard to God and man.

The author plunges straight into her story:

> I desired three graces by the gift of God:
> The first was, to have mind of Christ's Passion.
> The second was bodily sickness.
> The third was, to have of God's gift three wounds . . . the wound of contrition, the wound of compassion, and the wound of wilful longing for God.

There follows the account of that unique experience which was to be not only the unexpected, unmeritable and overwhelming reward of her long and fervent prayer, but the inspiration for the remainder of her spiritual life.

Julian, at all times refreshingly free from vanity and pose of any kind, possesses far too much supernatural common sense to cherish any illusions about her own worthiness to receive such favours.

> Because of the showing I am not good, but only if I love God the better. . . . I saw it for the profit of many others. For truly it was not showed unto me for that God loves me better than the least soul in grace. . . . For if I look singularly to myself, I am right naught.

But:

> Because I am a woman should I therefore believe that I ought not to tell you about the goodness of God, since I saw at the same time that it is His will that it be known?

With this realization she sets to work to efface herself behind the message for which she is merely the instrument, and to transmit it as fully and clearly as possible to her fellow-Christians. To guard against possible error she relies upon the guidance and authority of the Church to which she repeatedly protests her loyalty.

> All this blessed teaching of our Lord God [she tells us], was shewed me in three parts, that is, by bodily sight, and by word formed in mine understanding, and by ghostly sight.

From corporal visions of the dying Christ, keenly perceived and quietly described, she passes almost naturally to the "ghostly sight" of various truths of faith which suddenly spring to life with startling force and clearness as our Lord brings them before her. God's care for all creation, His infinite goodness and His immanence in all things; the vileness of sin and the malice of the devil; Christ's victory and our Lady's compassion—all these and many other matters come up for consideration. On prayer there is some excellent plain teaching. Above all she is shown our Lord's measureless love for mankind as manifested in His Passion. He tells her:

> It is a joy, and a bliss and an endless liking to me that ever I suffered Passion for thee; for if I might suffer more, I would suffer more.

To which she responds with the most complete and loving confidence in His power and will to "make all things well".

A spell of reaction and trial is followed by a final vision of the indwelling of the Godhead within the soul and the assurance of ultimate triumph:

> Know it well: it was no raving that thou saw today. But take it and believe it, and keep thee thereto, and thou shalt not be overcome.... He said not "Thou shalt not be tempested; thou shalt not be travailed; thou shalt not be distressed." But He said: "Thou shalt not be *overcome*."

III

The longer and more generally known version of Julian's book was not completed until at least twenty years after the actual

"Shewings", possibly even a good deal later. It is based closely upon the text of the Shorter Version, is about three times its length, and bears all the marks of a leisurely and deliberate composition.

A comparison shows that the original text has been carefully revised in the interests of orthodoxy and clearness. Scarcely a page of the earlier part but has some word or phrase added or omitted, qualifying, safeguarding, or merely heightening the effect, as the italicized words in the following quotations show :

> "For in every soul that shall be saved, is a godly will that never *finally* assenteth to sin, nor never shall." "For I trusted in God *of his mercy.*" "I looked thereon *with the eye of my understanding.*" "The wound of *verie* contrition, the wound of *kind* compassion," etc., etc.

Here and there passages have been rearranged and rewritten. A brief list of the "Shewings" is prefixed to the whole volume. St John of Beverley and St Denis, each with his little paragraph, make their first appearance. At the same time there are some notable omissions in the Longer Version. The boy acolyte, the mother's presence, St Cecilia with her three wounds, the apostrophe to sin, the spirited outburst beginning, "But God forbid that ye should say or take it thus, that I am a teacher, for I do not mean that, nor mean I ever so. For I am a woman, unlettered, feeble and frail," and the text from Philippians—all have disappeared. The writer seems bent on suppressing any concrete detail which might divert attention from the message behind which she must efface herself.

Equally characteristic, and far more considerable, are the passages of explanation and commentary, inserted with increasing frequency, which end by transforming what was primarily a meditation on the Passion into a devotional treatise on the scheme of Redemption in general. These are indeed among the most sublime and inspiring as well as the lengthiest portions of the book.

Given such an expansion, there is inevitably a softening of outlines and a shifting of emphasis in the story. Not that less is said about the actual "Shewings"; in fact, the corporal visions of the dying Christ are described in even fuller and more touching detail. But as the work proceeds, each experience so evidently treasured and pondered upon tends to appear mainly as a starting-point for further consideration and analysis of its underlying truths. As she herself observes: "When the shewing which is given for a time is passed and hid, then faith keepeth it by grace of the Holy Ghost unto our life's end." Dialogue, discourse and digression, revelation and reflexion, merge imperceptibly into one another as Julian patiently strives to unfold the doctrinal implications of what she has learnt.

One marked development brought by the years is her increased preoccupation with the Holy Trinity. This is emphasized even at the beginning of the first "Shewing":

> And in the same shewing, suddenly the Trinity fulfilled my heart most of joy; and so I understood it shall be in heaven without end to all that shall come there. For the Trinity is God. . . . For when Jesu appeareth, the blessed Trinity is understood as to my sight

and continues thus at intervals throughout the book.

Realizing so keenly our Lord's love for man, and the pains of His Passion, Dame Julian finds herself confronted with all kinds of problems attendant upon the dark mystery of evil—the reality of sin, freewill and predestination, the salvation of the heathen—which can be neither answered nor ignored. Her only solution, not reached without a struggle, is to entrust the whole question to God's love and mercy and the teaching of Holy Church, and be content not to know what He wills to remain hidden.

Of all the additions to the original text, by far the longest and most difficult to follow is attached to the fourteenth "Shewing", which is primarily concerned with prayer. Chapters 44 to 63 really constitute a separate treatise, amounting to almost one-third of the entire work and expounding at length some of Julian's most characteristic doctrines. Here, too, occurs the time-note: "Twenty years after the time of the shewing, save three months, I had teaching inwardly . . .", which after all is merely a *terminus a quo*; the actual writing may have occupied several years longer. It seems possible that the whole section was composed and inserted after the general revision was more or less complete, perhaps in fulfilment of the desire to say yet more, expressed on the last page of the book: "This book is begun by God's gift and His grace; but it is not yet performed as to my sight."

Chapter 64 resumes abruptly with a return to the Shorter

Version and her usual style of explanatory rewriting. In this section accordingly Julian seems to be resorting to every expedient to bring home to her fellow-Christians something of what she herself has been shown and bidden to proclaim—God's infinite love for man, man's utter dependence upon His grace, and the love and confidence with which he must repay Him. Bound up with this is the doctrine of God's indwelling in the faithful soul, first made clear in the sublime sixteenth revelation (where she had seen our Lord seated in her soul as a king in his royal city) and becoming ever stronger and more insistent in the course of years.

> He made man's soul to be his own city and his dwelling-place.
> Our soul is made to be God's dwelling-place.
> God is never out of the soul in which he shall dwell blessedly without end.

Here, then, we find the allegory of the lord and his servant, set forth in careful detail to show God's loving pity for fallen man, and incidentally illustrating the "courtesy" and "homeliness" so marked in all our Lord's dealings with Dame Julian. More appealing still is the well-known description of Christ as our Mother. This idea, said to be derived from St Anselm, is actually to be found, at least in germ, in St Augustine and St Ambrose; indeed it goes back to the prophet Isaias. It appears no fewer than three times under different guises in the *Ancrene Riwle* and is met with again in the fifteenth-century *Quia Amore Langueo*; in other words it is a familiar theme in medieval devotion. But nowhere can it have been elaborated with more exquisite feeling and expression, or to more consoling effect, than in this passage, which may well be regarded as the culmination of Julian's teaching. The truth she here depicts is simply that which years before, according to her own telling, she had been taught by our Lord Himself:

> And from the time that it was shewed, I desired oftentimes to wit in what was our Lord's meaning: and fifteen years after and more, I was answered in ghostly understanding, saying thus: "What? wouldst thou wit thy Lord's meaning in this thing? Wit it well: love was his meaning. Who sheweth it thee? Love. What sheweth he thee? Love. Wherefore sheweth he it thee? For love. Hold thee therein, thou shalt wit more in the same. But thou shalt never wit therein other without end." Thus was I learned that love is our Lord's meaning.

IV

No survey of Dame Julian as a spiritual influence would be complete without some consideration of her interview with Margery Kempe, who has left an account of it, too characteristic not to be given in full.

> Then she was bidden by our Lord to go to an anchoress in the same city, named Dame Jelyan, and so she did, and shewed her the grace that God put into her soul, of compunction, contrition, sweetness and devotion, compassion with holy meditation and high contemplation, and full many holy speeches and dalliance that our Lord spake to her soul; and many wonderful revelations, which she shewed to the anchoress to find out if there were any deceit in them, for the anchoress was expert in such things, and good counsel could give.
>
> The anchoress, hearing the marvellous goodness of our Lord, highly thanked God with all her heart for His visitation, counselling this creature to be obedient to the will of our Lord God and to fulfil with all her might whatever He put into her soul, if it were not against the worship of God, and profit of her fellow Christians, for if it were, then it were not the moving of a good spirit, but rather of an evil spirit. "The Holy Ghost moveth ne'er a thing against charity, for if He did, He would be contrary to His own self for He is all charity. Also He moveth a soul to all chasteness, for chaste livers are called the Temple of the Holy Ghost, and the Holy Ghost maketh a soul stable and steadfast in the right faith, and the right belief.
>
> And a double man in soul is ever unstable and unsteadfast in all his ways. He that is ever doubting is like the flood of the sea which is moved and borne about with the wind, and that man is not likely to receive the gifts of God.
>
> Any creature that hath these tokens may steadfastly believe that the Holy Ghost dwelleth in his soul. And much more when God visited a creature with tears of contrition, devotion, and compassion, he may and ought to believe that the Holy Ghost is in his soul. Saint Paul saith that the Holy Ghost asketh for us with mourning and weeping unspeakable, that is to say, he maketh us to ask and pray with mourning and weeping so plenteously that the tears may not be numbered. No evil spirit may give these

tokens, for Saint Jerome saith that tears torment more the devil than do the pains of Hell. God and the devil are ever at odds and they shall never dwell together in one place, and the devil hath no power in a man's soul.

Holy Writ saith that the soul of a rightful man is the seat of God, and so I trust, sister, that ye be. I pray God grant you perseverance. Set all your trust in God and fear not the language of the world, for the more despite, shame and reproof that ye have in the world, the more is your merit in the sight of God. Patience is necessary to you, for in that shall ye keep your soul."

Much was the holy dalliance that the anchoress and this creature had by communing in the love of our Lord Jesus Christ the many days that they were together.[1]

The passage will repay careful examination. In the *Revelations*, although her thought ranges through the whole universe, Julian appears only in converse with God; in this unhoped-for page she is seen in contact with a fellow-creature, helping her from the store of her own experience. The well-to-do matron from Lynn, mother of fourteen children, moving in the same orbit of fifteenth-century English life but a complete contrast as regards character and history, was just entering seriously upon the pursuit of perfection, and journeyed to Norwich in search of guidance and encouragement. Unlike the anchoress at York, who flatly refused to see her, Julian welcomed Margery with the greatest patience and sympathy, and the two spent several days conferring together. Thus the anchoress's advice, as quoted, can be only a summary of what she actually said; and a certain terseness of wording suggests that it is closely condensed. It must have left a deep and lasting impression on its recipient, who states elsewhere that none of her recollections were written down by any one at this time or for twenty years after. This is one of the rare instances in which we can in any way test the accuracy of Margery's memory and the fairness of her portraiture, and it redounds highly to her credit as a reliable witness. For here is the authentic Dame Julian, neither blurred nor distorted, her speech and teaching recognizable down to the very turn of a phrase. Whatever misgivings she may have had as to some of Margery's spiritual marvels, her reception is

[1] From *The Book of Margery Kempe*, 1436*: A Modern Version* by W. Butler-Bowdon pp. 72-4; MS. pp. 21a-21b.

gracious and self-effacing, her diagnosis shrewd and kindly, full of quiet good sense; her words, carefully based on the highest authority, are penetrating and enlightening, suffused with a certain calm sweetness as of mellow sunlight. All unconsciously, beneath the discreetly impersonal exterior, they inevitably reflect something of the depth and beauty of her own life in God.

One very noticeable feature in them is Julian's increased use of the words of Holy Scripture, which she cites copiously, with enviable ease and aptness. There are texts from the Epistles of St James and St John, from the Epistles to the Romans, Corinthians, and Hebrews, as well as from the Gospel of St Luke. There is a quotation from St Jerome and a strong suggestion of the doctrine of St Gregory—all chosen with exact reference to the matter in hand.

Her advice, eminently sound and for the most part quite suitable for general application, is thoroughly in line with the teaching of the *Revelations,* and occasionally even verbally reminiscent of the latter part of the Longer Version. The importance of contrition ("We may never leave off mourning and weeping"), of charity, of perseverance in prayer and in following the divine promptings, has already been stated in various terms again and again. Even more typical of her teaching is the emphasis upon God's indwelling in the faithful soul, reinforced as it is with the double reference to the soul of a rightful man as the seat of God and to chaste livers as the temple of the Holy Ghost. (In fact, it raises an unanswerable question: When, exactly, was the Longer Version completed? Perhaps, after all, not so very much earlier than Margery's visit in 1410 or thereabouts. The correspondence is perfect.) Her final sentence: "Patience is necessary for you, for in that shall you keep your soul"—two texts neatly put together—could hardly be bettered; the old anchoress's last words of encouragement to her fellow-Christian are no less telling today.

VI

ST JOHN FISHER

BY E. E. REYNOLDS

ST JOHN FISHER'S writings are so little known that it will be helpful to begin with a list of them. The classification here used must not be applied too rigidly. In the wider sense of the term, all his writings were spiritual, for they concerned the defence and propagation of the Faith; but in the special application of the term as used today—aids to personal sanctification—only a small number of his published works can be so classified.

I. SERMONS

(a) OFFICIAL

1. *Funeral sermon on Henry VII* (1509)
2. *Requiem sermon on Lady Margaret Beaufort* (1509)
3. *Against the pernicious doctrine of Martin Luther* (1521, at St Paul's Cross)
4. *Concerning certain heretics* (1526, at St Paul's Cross)

(b) PASTORAL

5. *The Seven Penitential Psalms* (1509)
6. *Two sermons on the Feast of All Saints* (1520)
7. *Good Friday Sermon* (?)

II. CONTROVERSIES

8. *De unica Magdalena* (1519)
9. *Convulsio calumniarum* ... (1522)
   Defending the presence of St Peter in Rome.
10. *Assertionis Lutheranae* ... (1523)
    An answer to Luther's *Assertion*.
11. *Sacri sacerdotii defensio* ... (1525)
    English translation by Mgr P. E. Hallett (1935).
12. *Defensio Regie* ... (1525)
    In defence of Henry VIII's book.

13. *De veritate corporis . . .* (1527)
Against Oecolampadius.
14. *De causa matrimonii . . .* (1530)
Defence of Catherine of Aragon.

III. SPIRITUAL

15. *De necessitate orandi* (1520?)
16. *A Spiritual Consolation* (1534-5)
17. *The Ways to Perfect Religion* (1534-5)

A collected edition of the Latin works was published in Würzburg in 1597; it also contained Latin translations of Nos. 3, 5, 7 and 17.[1] Three pieces not otherwise known are a sermon (*De Justitia Pharisaeorum*), *Epistola . . . de Charitate Christiana,* and No. 15, none of which had been previously published as far as is known.

De necessitate orandi was translated into English and published in Paris in 1640 as *A Treatise of Prayer*. Only the initials of the translator are given, R.A.B.; it is conjectured that these stand for Robert Anderton, Benedictine. St Edmund's is fortunate in possessing one of the few known copies. I think that it is possible that *De necessitate orandi* is a translation of a lost English original; it is clearly intended for ordinary folk and is not controversial as Fisher's Latin works were. So R.A.B.'s work may be a translation of a translation. It was reprinted, with slight modifications, in 1887.

The only volume of Fisher's writings now in print is in the E.E.T.S. series (1876) which contains Nos. 1, 2, 3, 5, 7, 16 and 17 in our list; the 1935 reprint added No. 4.

It will be noticed that No. 6 has not been reprinted. It was first published in 1532 by William Rastell (St Thomas More's nephew). Only four copies are known, of which three are in the U.S.A., and one in the Bodleian. An account of these sermons is given on pages 80 to 86 of my *Saint John Fisher*.

St John Fisher was a preacher and teacher. This is not to ignore his pastoral work (so unusual in his day) as Bishop of Rochester for thirty years, nor his great influence as Chancellor of Cambridge University during the same long period; in both these capacities

[1] The translations were the work of John Fenn (brother of Blessed James Fenn) who was at New College, Oxford, before he fled to the Low Countries. For forty years before his death in 1615, he was confessor to the English Augustinian nuns at Louvain.

he put emphasis on the need for more good preachers and teachers. When he was Vice-Chancellor of Cambridge in 1502, a Papal Bull was granted at his request for the appointment of twelve preachers of the University to be available for any diocese. Two years later he persuaded the Lady Margaret Beaufort to endow a chantry at the University for a preacher of annual sermons in London and other places. The Lady Margaret Readerships in Divinity in both Universities were also established at his suggestion. His statutes for St John's College (of which he was the effective Founder) show that he regarded the training of priests as its primary purpose. Alas, what he hoped would be a seminary for priests became, after his death, a nursery of Protestants.

He himself was a constant preacher. His earliest and anonymous biographer wrote of "his great and painful diligence in preaching the Word of God, which custom he used not only in his younger days, when health served, but also even in his extreme age, when many times his weary and feeble legs were not able to sustain his weak body standing, but forced him to have a chair, and to teach sitting".

William Rastell, speaking from personal knowledge, wrote: "He was also a very diligent preacher and the notablest in this Realm, both in his time or before or since, for his excellent learning and moving the affections of his hearers to cleave to God and goodness, to embrace virtue and to flee sin."

I have stressed John Fisher's zeal as a preacher because it has a direct bearing on his spiritual writing. His intention was not to dazzle by rhetoric or learning, but to win his hearers' confidence. The style he used was suited to the needs of ordinary folk. His language was therefore simple and the illustrations he used homely. Here is an example:

> If a table be foul and filthy by long continuance, first we scrape it, after when it is scraped we wash it, and last after washing we wipe and make it clean. Our soul is compared unto a table whereon nothing was painted, nevertheless with many misdoings and spots of sin we have defouled and made it deform in the sight of God. Therefore it is needful that it be scraped, washed and wiped. It shall be scraped by the inward sorrow and compunction of the heart when we are sorry for our sin. It shall be washed with the tears of our eyes when we acknowledge and confess our sin. And

last it shall be wiped and made clean when that we be about for to make amends and do satisfaction by good deeds for our sins. These three things that we have spoken of cometh without doubt of the gracious pity of God. Thou art sorry for thy sin, it is a gift of Almighty God. Thou makest knowledge of thy sin weeping and wailing for it, it is a gift of Almighty God. Thou art busy in good works to do satisfaction, which also is a gift of Almighty God.

This extract comes from the sermon on Psalm 50, *Miserere mei Deus*, in the series on the Penitential Psalms. These were preached in 1508 to a congregation that included the Lady Margaret Beaufort, and it was at her request that he wrote them down—not the least of that great lady's good works! The book was published in 1509 and reprinted seven times before the Saint's martyrdom. This popularity was well founded, and, in spite of the classification given above, I would place it at the head of his spiritual writings. It is a great loss that this book is not available in modern spelling.[1] It is one of the forgotten classics of our religious literature.

No one should read these sermons, or meditations, as they may be called, who wants soft speaking. The preacher warned his hearers again and again of the reality of hell:

Of a truth every man and woman shall stand before the throne of Almighty God at the day of Judgement, and at that time such as never would be penitent for their offences in this life shall be punished very sharply and grievously in the eternal pains of hell and with this most sharp and grievous words spoken by Almighty God, "Go ye cursed people into the eternal fire." They shall go away from his face whose beauty cannot be expressed, whereon the angels desire to look and to behold it.

But against that fearful picture, he set the infinite love and mercy of God:

Truly the mercy of our most mighty and best Lord God is great, and so great that it hath all measures of greatness. Sometimes trees be called great for their goodly and great height. Pits be called great for their deepness. Far journeys be called great because

[1] The vocabulary would need some modernization. John Fisher was a northerner and he used words which have dropped out of the language. Thomas More was a southerner and his vocabulary is therefore more like present-day speech, so his books are easier to read.

they are long. Streets and highways be called great for their breadth and wideness. But the mercy of God containeth and is measured by all these measures of greatness, and not only by one of them.

The theme of this series of sermons is the need for contrition, confession, and satisfaction which are called the three parts of penance. We may get the impression, if we read the book from cover to cover, that his theme is over-laboured, but we shall get a different impression if we read the sermons at intervals as they were preached. The variations he gives to his thoughts from sermon to sermon repay study from the point of view of craftsmanship in preaching. His use of everyday similitudes has been illustrated, but he also had the ability of putting his ideas in epigrammatic form to make them the more memorable. One quotation must suffice; he was speaking of Apostolic times: "In that time were no chalices of gold, but there were many golden priests; now be many chalices of gold, and almost no golden priests."

A harsh saying, but it explains his zeal for the training of priests who would be good preachers.

It is tempting to linger over these sermons for there is so much in them for our instruction, but I must hope that the reader will explore their riches for himself.

Two specifically spiritual writings were the fruits of the Saint's imprisonment in the Tower—others may have been lost. While St John Fisher was engaged on this work in one cell, in another cell St Thomas More was composing his finest book *A Dialogue of Comfort*. These testaments, as they may be called, of the two Saints are a precious memorial of them.

A Spiritual Consolation and *The Ways to Perfect Religion* were written by John Fisher for his half-sister, Elizabeth White, a Dominican nun at Dartford.[1] No doubt he visited her there as it lay in his diocese, and perhaps she asked him to write down the instruction he had given her by word of mouth. We can easily imagine how precious these two manuscripts must have been to her in the years of exile and poverty that were before her. They were published in the reign of Queen Mary; this was fortunate as otherwise they might have been lost.

A Spiritual Consolation takes the form of a meditation "made

[1] The little that is known of Elizabeth White and the Dominican nuns is given in *A Hundred Homeless Years* by Godfrey Anstruther, O.P., on pp. 4-14.

in the person of one that was hastily prevented by death". The treatment can be illustrated by an extract. He expresses his regret for having put off so frequently the opportunity "to repent me and amend my life".

> And so, alas, from time to time, that now death in the mean time hath prevented me; my purpose was good, but it lacked execution. My will was straight, but it was not effectual, my mind well intended, but no fruit came thereof. All for because I delayed so often and never put it in effect, that, that I had purposed. And therefore delay it not as I have done, but before all other business put this first in surety, which ought to be chief and principal business. Neither building of Colleges, nor making of sermons, nor giving of alms, neither yet any other manner of business shall help you without this. . . . Be you your own friend, do you these suffrages for your own soul, whether they be prayers or alms or any other penitential painfulness.

When he wrote of colleges and sermons, was he reviewing his own life?

The Ways to Perfect Religion begins with an elaborately worked-out "comparison between the life of hunters and the life of religious persons". One thing is certain; John Fisher knew what he was talking about when he described the coursing of the hare. This may be an unexpected glimpse of him, but one of the all too few sidelights we have on his personal life is a note from Lord Bergavenny inviting him to bring his greyhounds for "disport" in Ashdown Forest.

These counsels to his sister end with the suggestion that whenever she feels "any dullness of mind" she should "use these short prayers following, for every day in the week one. . . . For thus in your heart, you may shortly pray what company soever you be amongst". Here they are:

1. O blessed Jesus, make me love thee entirely.
2. O blessed Jesus I would fain, but without thy help I cannot.
3. O blessed Jesus let me deeply consider the greatness of thy love towards me.
4. O blessed Jesus, give unto me grace heartily to thank thee for thy benefits.

5. O blessed Jesus, give me good will to serve thee, and to suffer.
6. O sweet Jesus, give me a natural remembrance of thy passion.
7. O sweet Jesus, possess my heart, hold and keep it only to thee.

It has already been noted that the English version of the brief *Treatise of Prayer* is possibly from a Latin translation of a lost original. The extracts below are not therefore in the Saint's own words. He deals with the reasons for prayer, the chief fruits of prayer, and the manner of prayer. The final section has an interesting passage on how long we should pray.

Our chiefest labour in prayer must be to inflame and set our hearts on fire, with this fervency of charity, and then as it were, to spin out our prayer, so long until we have attained unto this end. But when through weariness of our frail body we find this heat and fervour in us to grow cold, then must we desist and pray no longer, but presently apply ourselves to some other works of virtue.

He has some remarks on the use of vocal prayer.

I do protest here that it is not my intention to affirm anything in derogation of vocal prayer, such as is either received by custom or ordained by the authorities of the Church, or inflicted by way of penance, or assumed by vow or any other promise whatever by which a man hath bound himself to vocal prayer. But my opinion is, that whosoever is free from these bonds, and in possession of his absolute liberty, and desires to serve God after the best, purest, and most pleasing way unto Him, it is far more profitable for such an one to pray with his heart only than with his tongue and heart together.

Then comes one of his similitudes:

Not unlike with him, who after great labour and long travail hath passed the sea, and is arrived at his desired haven, then he forsaketh the ship that brought him, and applieth himself wholly to the end and purpose for which he came, and is no more solicitous for the poor vessel that brought him thither. So also he that by the help and use of vocal prayer as by a ship hath attained unto the inward consolation of his soul, and to this fervour of charity in God, must then make it his chiefest care and study, that this fervour by no means grow cold, but then leaving of his vocal prayer, he must follow this Holy Spirit who hath brought him to this fervour whithersoever it shall lead him; then he must not use his own words, but whatsoever the Holy Ghost shall suggest unto his heart, that let him desire, not with words, but with burning sighs and joy.

There is one other composition of St John Fisher to which reference should be made as it has become available only within the last few years. Among the papers in the Public Record Office that were taken from Rochester or the Tower (it is not certain which) there are five pages in the Saint's handwriting. These are the draft of a long prayer or meditation written when he knew "the manifold perils" that beset him. The manuscript is in his neat handwriting but is so interlined with alterations that its decipherment proved most difficult. The task, however, was achieved by an Australian priest, and the text was published in *The Month*, and has been reprinted as an appendix to my *Saint John Fisher*.

This survey of the Saint's writings may fittingly end with the concluding sentences of that prayer:

> I beseech Thee to shed upon my heart Thy Holy Spirit by whose gracious presence I may be warmed, heated and kindled with the spiritual fire of charity and with the sweetly burning love of all godly affections, that I may fastly set my heart, soul and mind upon Thee and assuredly trust that Thou art my very loving Father and according to the same trust I may love Thee with all my heart, with all my soul, with all my mind and all my power. Amen.

VII

ST THOMAS MORE

By Bernard Fisher

"Few characters in English history have drawn to themselves such admiration and even love as Sir Thomas More. Men of all classes, non-Catholic as well as Catholic, respect and venerate him as one of the noblest, if not the noblest, Englishman who ever lived. . . . I have come to the conclusion, in reading through his works, that he paid special attention to the study of dogmatic theology. For when he speaks of grace, free will, merit, faith, charity and other virtues, original sin and even predestination, he is so guarded and exact in his statements that a professional theologian could scarcely speak more accurately." These are the words of Stapleton in the *Tres Thomae* of 1588.

More's modern biographers have elaborated on the theme "the noblest of Englishmen" but very little indeed has been written on St Thomas as a theologian or as a saint. As threequarters of More's writings are either ascetical or theological treatises, it is obvious that there is still a great gap in our understanding of the genius of More.

That More was a great saint and great contemplative is easily demonstrable. Mr Richard O'Sullivan has pointed out a certain rhythm in the life of St Thomas. It begins in the cell of the London Charterhouse where he was trying his vocation. He married and was then "forced" to Court. Upon his resignation of the Great Seal he returned home for a time and finished his life in a cell in the Tower. In a letter to Meg, written from the Tower, he says "that among all His great benefits heaped upon me so thick, I reckon upon my faith my prisonment, even the very chief". To the same Meg he remarked : ". . . if it had not been for my wife and ye that be my children . . . I would not have failed long ere this to have closed myself in as strait a room, and straiter too. But since I come hither without mine own desert, I trust that God of His goodness will discharge me of my care, and with His gracious help supply my lack amoung you. . . . Methinketh God maketh me a wanton, and setteth me on his lap and dandleth me." The language here is, surely, the language of a mystic and of a piece with the wonderful phrase in his last letter to Meg, "tomorrow long I to go to God". The passage suggests, too, that this is the happiest period of More's life. The agony in the garden, the period of doubt and fear, comes between 1528 and his confinement to the Tower. His imprisonment was, as he says, a special grace, a period in which he gathered the fruits of a life of great holiness. It is clear also that St Thomas was conscious of the Carthusian roots of his spirituality. It is this aspect that we are concerned with here.

Chambers has shown More's great regard for liberty of conscience. The age in which he lived was a dangerous one for talkers and doubly so as the "king's matter" came to a head. In this crisis St Thomas asserted time after time "that he would meddle with no man's conscience and asked only to be left in peace with his own". The unique circumstance of his case only deepened his extreme and habitual reticence. Thomas More is a silent man. For all his mirth and friendliness, few men have been more careful not to wear their heart upon a sleeve. This inner silence is the key to More's character and it is something he learned from the Carthusians. What is here meant by silence is best illustrated by his conduct on the scaffold. Here he had a great opportunity to deliver himself of a most telling *apologia*. Instead he merely said: "I die the King's good servant but God's first." That is, of course, a superb sentence and it deeply impressed all who were there, but it is essentially meant only for Henry. In 1516, when More entered the royal service, Henry had given him this command "that he look first to God and then to the King". More's words in 1535 are his *Nunc Dimittis*.

Again, until he entered the Tower, More was clean-shaven. The beard was an exact measure of his imprisonment. At his trial he had contended that as he was already serving life imprisonment (for refusal to take the Oath of Succession) before ever the Act of Supremacy was passed, he was, as far as that Act was concerned, dead and therefore untriable. Hence the final jest and the last words he ever spoke as ". . . he bade the executioner stay until he had removed aside his beard, saying: 'That never committed any treason'." His judges of a week before, standing now at the foot of the scaffold, would have understood.

As one would expect, this silence is greatest when it is a question of his relationship with God. None of More's ascetical works were ever intended for publication. The two great works the *History of the Passion* and the *Dialogue of Comfort against Tribulation* were written during his imprisonment in the Tower. They were written out of his experience, no doubt, and partly for his enlightenment and because he was a born writer who enjoyed the discipline and effort of composition. They are not formal and present no system of ascetical theology; they tell us practically nothing of any mystical experiences he may have had. What is obvious, of course, is the spirit and deep faith of the writer, but one could not out of these books alone build up a "way of life".

On the other hand, when dealing with More's spirituality the theological writings cannot be ignored. They are not systematic, they are works of controversy. The matter is never allowed to become a question of pure abstract theological argument. More was acutely conscious that the fight was for souls and it is his constant preoccupation to show the practical effects, morally and spiritually, of the new theological ideas. For this reason, one can find passages in the theological work which reveal his burning faith and charity far more than any passages from the ascetical works.

In the preface to the *Confutation against Tyndale*, St Thomas says that he would that people ceased from reading either his or Tyndale's writings but read "English books as most may nourish and increase devotion, of which be Bonaventure's *Life of Christ*, Gerson on the *Following of Christ* and the devout contemplative book *Scala Perfectionis*". The last is obviously the most important in More's own life. Chambers has shown how rooted in the writings of the early English mystics is the prose of More. So too is his spirituality, and it is with Hilton, "the most theological of these writings", that St Thomas has most affinity. Here, again, the Carthusian influence is at work for three of the surviving MSS. of Hilton are Carthusian copies *c.* 1500-10 and two of these come from the London Charterhouse.

If we had nothing but More's works upon which to base our opinions, we could do little more than guess that Hilton was his mentor. And although he spent long hours in the chapel at

Chelsea, usually behind locked doors, scarcely any prayer written by him would have been found. But the letters he sent to Meg from the Tower, and the two collections of prayers: *A Godly Meditation* (written in 1534) and *A Devout Prayer* (made during the last week of his life) were preserved by the family. The prayers were written and sent to Margaret that father and daughter might pray together for what little time remained to him. They incorporate, here and there, prayers of Margaret, but they are really both a priceless relic of a life of prayer and his last instructions to his most beloved disciple. The whole would cover a mere thirty pages of print and it seems a crime to select from such a source. But it must be done, for the only way to understand More's spirituality is to start from the prayers and to use his ascetical and theological works as a commentary, as it were, upon them.

Give me thy grace, good Lord.
To set the world at nought,
To set my mind fast upon thee.

. . . .

To be content to be solitary,

. . . .

Gladly to be thinking of God,
Piteously to call for his help,
To lean unto the comfort of God,
Busily labour to love him.

. . . .

To bear the cross with Christ,

. . . .

To have continually in mind the passion that Christ suffered for me,
For his benefits uncessantly to give him thanks.

. . . .

Of worldly substance, friends, liberty, life and all, to
set the loss at right nought, for the winning of Christ.

Almighty God, Doce me facere voluntatem tuam. Fac me currere in odore ungentorum tuorum. Apprehende manum dexteram, et deduc me in via recta propter inimicos meos. Trahe me post te. In chamo et freno maxillas meas constringe, quum non approximo ad te.

Good Lord, give me the grace, in all my fear and agony, to have recourse to that great fear and wonderful agony that thou, my sweet Saviour, hadst at the Mount of Olivet before thy most bitter passion, and in the meditation thereof, to conceive ghostly comfort and consolation profitable for my soul.

Give me, good Lord, a full faith, a firm hope, and a fervent charity, a love to thee, good Lord, incomparable above the love to myself; and that I love nothing to thy displeasure, but everything in an order to thee.

Take from me, good Lord, this lukewarm fashion, or rather key-cold manner of meditation, and this dullness in praying unto thee. And give me warmth, delight and quickness in thinking upon thee. And give me thy grace to long for thine holy sacraments, and especially to rejoice in the presence of thy very blessed body, sweet Saviour Christ, in the holy sacrament of the altar, and duly to thank thee for thy gracious visitation therewith, and at that high memorial, with tender compassion, to remember and consider thy most bitter passion.

Make us all, good Lord, virtually participant of that holy sacrament this day, and everyday make us all lively members, sweet Saviour Christ, of thine holy mystical body, thy Catholic Church.

Lord, give me patience in tribulation and grace in everything to conform my will to thine : that I may truly say : Fiat voluntas tua, sicut in coelo et in terra.

The things, good Lord, that I pray for, give me thy grace to labour for. Amen.

One is struck first, by the depth of faith, tenderness of devotion and the beauty of language of these prayers. But they are couched, too, in the careful language of a lawyer and a theologian. Luther had appeared, and these devotions are, therefore, firmly set against a background of faith and works, and the gratuity of faith has been emphasized.

In the fourth book of *Dialogues against Tyndale*, More deals with the question of faith and works. The question has been dealt with, he says, in the time of the Pelagian heresy, and Luther, by his doctrine, is an even worse opponent of grace than Pelagius. All our sufficiency is from God. He does not need either our faith or our works, but He has appointed that these are the conditions of our salvation. One quotation must suffice to show both More's theological exactness and his burning faith.

> Nor that all the laws of Moses, nor all the good works of man, were not able to save one man of themselves, nor without faith and that Christ freely redeemed us. For neither had he or ever shall have any reward of us, for the bitter pains taken in his blessed passion for us. Nor never deserved we unto him that he should so much do for us. Nor the first faith, nor the preaching thereof nor the first justification of man thereby, nor the sacrament and fruit of our baptism, was not given to the world for any good works that ever the world had wrought; but only for God's mere liberal goodness.

The remarkable theological accuracy of the prayers is the first point to be noted. The second is the obvious influence of Hilton. In the space available this latter fact cannot be adequately demonstrated, but here are some indications: "A man shall not come to ghostly light in contemplation of Christ's Godhead, unless he is come in imagination by bitterness, and by compassion and by steadfast thinking on his manhood", says the Ladder. "Imagination by bitterness", "compassion", "steadfast thinking"; all these phrases are apt descriptions of the spirit of More's *History of the Passion* and of his prayers to our Blessed Lord in His agony—"with tender compassion, to remember and consider thy most bitter passion".

Nowhere is Hilton's influence stronger than in the prayer which is the key to More's spirituality.

> Give me, good Lord, a full faith, a firm hope and a fervent charity, a love to thee, good Lord, incomparable above the love to myself; and that I love nothing to thy displeasure, but everything in an order to thee.

"Full faith" is Hilton's "feeling faith". "Feeling faith" had assumed, by 1535, Lutheran overtones and could not now be used with safety. In the early days of conversion, says Hilton, a man who wishes to serve God will need to rely on his "natural wit"; he will need to study and to read and there will be little conscious devotion in his prayers. Soon, if he is faithful in his work and prayer he will be led to some "ghostly contemplation". Under the influence of the Holy Spirit his faith will deepen: he will *realize* more deeply the implications of the dogmas of faith. There are stages in this development; at one time the affections are used more than the understanding, but ultimate perfection in contemplation is both "in cognition and understanding". This "way" to perfection is implicit in More's prayers; it is obvious in the adaptations of St Paul's phrases and in prayer which asks for a "taste of thy holy Spirit". Hilton had been careful to point out, of course, that the higher gifts of contemplation are seldom continuous, for this is not a doctrine of disguised quietism, and there will always be need of formal prayer and meditation. In More's words one must "busily labour to love thee". Hence, too, the hair shirt, returned to Meg only on the last day of his life. This conscious belief in the process by which the soul is gradually "opened" to the influence of grace is evident everywhere in the writings of St Thomas. On persecution, for instance, he can write:

> This manner of ours, in whose breast the great good counsel of God no better settleth nor taketh no better roots may well declare us that the thorns and briers and the brambles of our worldly substance grow so thick, and spring so high in the ground of our hearts, that they strangle, as the Gospel saith, the word of God that was sown therein. And therefore is God a very good Lord unto us, when he causeth like a good husbandman his folk to come afield (for the persecutors be his folk for this purpose) and with their hooks and stocking-irons grub up those wicked weeds and bushes of our earthly substance, and carry them right away from us, that the word of God sown in our hearts may have room therein, *and a glade round about for the warm sun of grace to come and make it grow.*

Such a deep realization of God's providence and the power of grace demands an equally deep appreciation of Man's weakness and the limited nature of his understanding. Luther had gone so far in stressing the effects of original sin, that, as More says, he makes as if "all our works were brought forth out of us without our will . . . out of a brute beast by appetite of sensual motion".

More can put the situation quite simply:

One tribulation is it to good men, to feel in themselves the conflict of the flesh against the soul, the rebellion of sensuality against the rule and government of reason, the relic that remains in mankind of old original sin of which St Paul so sore complaineth in his epistle to the Romans. And yet we may not pray to have this kind of tribulation taken from us. For it is left us by God's ordinance to strive against it and by *reason and grace* to master it, and use it for the matter of our merit.

So much for "full faith" to which "firm hope" is but the natural corollary. Such hope is obvious in these prayers. As an example of humility and hope what better example could there be than the answer he gave to Cromwell? ". . . I have not been a man of such holy living, as I might be bold to offer myself to death, lest God for my presumption might suffer me to fall; and therefore I put not myself forward but draw back. Howbeit, if God draw me to himself, then I trust in his great mercy, that He shall not fail to give me grace and strength."

Now the second half of the important prayer quoted above: "that I love nothing to thy displeasure but everything in an order to thee" is magnificent in its simplicity. Here is a statement of the "way of acceptation"; an affirmation of the goodness of God's creation, the way to perfection of the layman who needs must live in the world. Of this "way" Hilton had written in *The Mixed Life,* but by his example and in his writings St Thomas goes beyond anything Hilton had written. This aspect of More's teaching is so important that it needs special treatment. His adaptation of "Poverty", "Chastity" and "Obedience" to the lay state is especially interesting and here he is well in advance of his age. One example may be given; it is rather complicated and involved, but he is feeling his way to an idea that he is half frightened to suggest.

If there be a man such (as would God there were many) that hath unto riches no love, but having them fall abundantly upon him, taketh to his own part no great pleasure thereof, but, as though he had it not, keepeth himself in like abstinence and penance privily as he would do in case he had it not, and in such things as he doth openly bestow somewhat more liberally upon himself in his house after some manner of the world, lest he should

> give other folk occasion to marvel and muse and talk of his manner, and misreport him for an hypocrite, therein between God and him doth truly protest and testify, as did the good queen Hester, that he doth it not for any desire thereof in the satisfying of his own pleasure, but would with as good a will or better, forbear the possession of riches, saving for the commodity that other men have by its disposing thereof, as percase in keeping a good household in good Christian order and fashion, and in setting other folk a work with such things as they gain their living the better by his means, this man's riches I might (Methinketh) in merit match in a manner with another man's forsaking of all, if there were none other circumstance more pleasant unto God farther added unto the forsaking beside, as percase for the more fervent contemplation by reason of the solicitude of all worldly business left off, which was the thing that made Mary Magdalene's part the better.

The sentence is indeed involved, but the idea is fairly clear. Hilton had said that to neglect business, wife and children in order to contemplate was like dressing the head of Christ with a lovely diadem whilst leaving the body all in rags. More takes the matter further and tries to work the principle out in detail. It is also interesting in that it clearly shows why St Thomas looked upon his imprisonment as the greatest blessing given him by God. At last he had "time and opportunity" for prayer. In earlier years he had had to steal from sleep the time to pray and write his theology. After serving with Martha he now had a few months to contemplate with Mary Magdalene.

Finally, notice the prayers to the Blessed Sacrament given above, ending with the prayer that we may all "be lively members, sweet Saviour Christ, of thine holy mystical body, thy Catholic Church". Again, there is evident here the same theological exactness; for the words "virtually participant" are, surely, a reference to the teaching of Aquinas on the Eucharist as the source of grace. The important feature, however, is that whereas the earlier mystical writers, and even Hilton, had *assumed* the sacramental life, More finds it necessary, because of the advent of Luther, to integrate his great devotion to the person of our Blessed Lord, with the Mass, in a more conscious manner; but beyond that, there is a deep awareness of the mystical Body, an awareness somewhat rare in the sixteenth century. This aspect of More's writings needs an article on its own. Chambers has shown how strong was More's "mediaeval sense of unity". It is more than that. Few men have had a deeper realization of the dogma of the mystical Body, and his passionate defence of European unity is not the oratory of a statesman but the cry of a saint. It is this that makes him such a "saint for today".

There is so much more that could be said. Scarcely anything has been said on penance. No reference has been made to a Kempis or to St Augustine, and both of these exerted great influence on More's spirituality. Since so many societies and groups, of lawyers, civil servants, loyal government officials, politicians, writers, students and many others have taken him as their patron, more attention should be paid to him as a teacher of a "lay spirituality". He is intensely English and directly in the line of the English mystics. Faced with the challenge of Luther, he recast, as it were, the essence of their teaching, in a safe and modern framework of theology. How refreshing, too, to be bidden, as were his children, "to serve God, and be *merry* and *rejoice* in him"!

VIII

FATHER PERSONS, S.J.

By Joseph Crehan, s.j.

If one were to look for a single work of Elizabethan times of which it might be said that this book made martyrs, the most obvious choice would be Fr Persons's *Christian Directory* or the *Book of Resolution,* as it was first entitled. In plan it is little more than an elaboration of the "first week" of the *Spiritual Exercises* of St Ignatius, on creation, sin, judgement, heaven and hell, with some of the exercises of the "second week" added, use being made of the meditation on the kingdom of Christ and—the most original part of the work—a very considerable expansion being made of considerations which could hinder resolution, where something can still be recognized of St Ignatius's meditation on the three classes of men. In origin the work is obviously the result of Persons's own spiritual progress from the time when he made the *Spiritual Exercises* (at Louvain in 1574) after throwing up his post as Dean of Balliol, through his studies in Rome and his brief experience of the mission with Campion. At one point he speaks of having conferred with some priests in England who had impressed upon him the need for meeting the danger of atheism, and thus in the first part of his work he gives a useful exposition of the reasons for accepting the existence of God and a section entitled *Proofs of Christianity.*[1]

It is not the originality of its topics that commends the book but its style, and the power Persons shows of compelling his man to listen and take heed. In a now-famous essay the late Professor Phillimore wrote (*Dublin Review*, July 1913: 1-26) of the tradition of vigorous prose passing from More to the exiles of Elizabethan days, Allen and Persons and Campion, while the native

[1] These sections were inserted by Persons himself in his second edition and were not always printed in subsequent editions. I quote in this article from the edition of 1650, and have modernized the spelling throughout. The problem of counting the manifold editions of Catholic and pirate Protestant presses has recently been handled by Miss J. Derrick in a London University thesis (1954). The *Huntington Library Quarterly*, XXII (1959), 271-300, has a full account of "The Protestant version of Persons's Christian Exercise" by Robert McNulty.

performers in England went floundering after Lyly. R. W. Chambers accepted his claim and made more of it, but in the last twenty years there have been signs of a reaction setting in.

So popular was the work at its first appearance in 1582 that it may be said to have swept over England like a bush-fire. There was a dearth of spiritual writing from the prophets of the new reformation, and the *Book of Resolution* exploded in a void. The Anglicans were so nettled that one of them, Edmund Bunny, pirated the work, removing as far as he could all traces of Catholicism (confession, vows of religion, mortification), and dedicating his theft to Sandys, the Archbishop of York.

Fr Thurston, S.J., did the fundamental research on the use made in Elizabethan times of Fr Persons's book when he was studying "Catholic Writers and Elizabethan Readers" in *The Month* sixty years ago (vol. LXXXII [1894], 457-76). The most impressive piece of evidence he could produce was a letter from the printers of the pirated (Bunny) edition to the Privy Council late in 1585:

> Whereas a book called *The Resolution* was first allowed to be printed by my lord Archbishop of Canterbury his Grace, and after, according to the charter of our company under the great seal of England, entered in our Hall Book to be the copy of John Wighte, bookseller, upon condition that we your poor orators, namely Nynian Newton, Arnold Hatfield, John Jackson and Edmund Bollifant, should be the only workmen thereof—which being the most vendible copy that happened in our Company these many years would have kept us in work for a long time—but to our great hindrance and prejudice, as also to the loss of the owner of the said copy, Joseph Barnes, printer at Oxford, immediately printed one impression of the said book, notwithstanding that the said John Wighte for reverence and good-will to the University then sent his son to Oxford to buy the said impression of the said Barnes, and paid him ready money for it to his contentment, whereupon the said Barnes made faithful promise that he would never reprint the same book; and yet notwithstanding the said Wighte's courteous dealing, the said Barnes, being furnished with money by him, forthwith printed two impressions more, contrary to all honesty and reason and contrary to his faith and promise; which others perceiving to pass without controlment, printed the same book, to our great hindrance, and thereby disfurnished us of work for the most part ever since.

If anyone has read that sentence to the end, he will see that the sanctimonious pirate-printers had been beaten at their own game by a printer at Oxford and by sundry others, and that this book of Persons was "the most vendible copy these many years".

Shakespeare may have read the work, for there can be no doubt it was known to the poets of the time, and there are other links between the two men. Quite apart from the matter of John Shakespeare's will (that was phrased, as Fr Thurston has shown, in the very terms of a Christian testament printed and brought into England by the mission of Campion and Persons in 1580), there is the figure of Falstaff to unite them. In his *Three Conversions of England* Persons gave as part of the work a running commentary on Foxe's *Book of Martyrs*. Upon the name of Sir John Oldcastle, whom Foxe had included as a martyr, Persons had something to say, pointing out that he was really no martyr but a figure of fun, much used by "comediants" upon the stage. This provoked a rejoinder from the Protestant historian and map-maker, John Speed, who bitterly attacked "this Papist and his poet" for their debunking of a Puritan hero. The evidence has been presented by Sir Edmund Chambers twenty years ago (*William Shakespeare*, II, 213-18) but does not seem to have attracted Catholic notice. If a contemporary Protestant regarded the poet-creator of Falstaff as somehow kindred in spirit with the Catholic writer, one cannot think of them as complete strangers to each other. It may some day be the task of a literary researcher to find affinities of phrase between the *Book of Resolution* and the plays of Shakespeare, and it can be no part of the present article to attempt this, but one may offer to such a bookish retriever a morsel to keep him going. In *King Lear* (I, ii) Gloucester is made to say to Edmund:

> I would unstate myself, to be in a due resolution.

Now the word "resolution" had taken on for Elizabethans a special connotation from its use in Persons's title, and there could be a bitter irony in the line, if one took it to mean: "If I were so determined in mind, the result would be to make me lose my nationality." Of course, Gloucester does not, on the surface, mean his words to be taken that way; he is expressing a purpose, not a condition, but at the same time, the wits in the audience could have taken him up that way. In 1608 the result of taking to heart the pleadings of Persons would have been to make a man almost an outlaw, with flight abroad his only safety. One cannot be sure, but in all the bitterness of the play there may be some gall left for this line of Gloucester's.

Persons had no illusions about the kind of writing that was needed to move his audience. Speaking of the style found in the Scriptures, he wrote:

> As great monarchs in their edicts and proclamations are wont to speak to their subjects, not in figures and rhetorical phrases but plainly, briefly and peremptorily, to shew their authority; so the Scriptures, to declare whose edicts they be, do use the like manner of style and phrase to all the world, without alluring or flattering any man, and without respect of monarch, emperor, prince or potentate.... And albeit (as I have said) the Scriptures do use this simplicity of speech, and do not admit that kind of painted and artificial style which human writers do so much covet, yet in persuading, instructing, moving of affections and all other effects which speech or writing can work, there is no comparison (a thing most wonderful) between any other writings in the world and these.

Mr C. S. Lewis in his literary history of the times has censured Allen for "not anticipating the short and easily intelligible sentences of Dryden", and wishes to reject on this account the claim of Phillimore that the true style of English prose was kept by the Recusants, but by some aberration he does not mention Persons at all (though showing awareness in his chronological table of the existence of Persons). Had he done so, it is hard to see why he should have given so much praise to Hooker and spared space for such insignificant writers as William Rankins. When Persons is in full cry there is no stopping him. Here he rails upon vanity:

> We rob and spoil all sorts of creatures upon earth to cover our backs and adorn our bodies. From one we take his wool; from another his skin; from another his hair and fur, and from some other their very excrements, as the silk, which is nothing else but the excrements of worms. Nor yet content with this, we come to fishes, and do beg of them certain pearls to hang about us. We go down into the ground for gold and silver, and turn up the sands

of the sea for precious stones; and having borrowed all this of other creatures far more base than ourselves, we jet up and down, provoking men to look upon us, as if all this now were our own. When the stone shineth upon our finger, we will seem (forsooth) thereby to shine. When silver, gold and silks do glister on our backs, we look big, as if all that beauty came from us. When cat's dung doth smell in our garments, we would have men think that we send forth sweet odour from ourselves.

One shudders to think what Lyly and his disciples would have made of such a topic, how many creatures from the bestiary and how many quaint tropes would have disgraced the paragraph.

Knowing that his book would work where he could not go himself, Persons put into it all that he knew. Foreseeing that his readers would need strength most of all, he enlarges upon the joy of serving Christ:

Two that should pass together towards their country, the one to receive honour for good service done abroad, the other as prisoner to be arraigned of treasons committed in foreign dominions against his Sovereign, could not be alike merry in their inn upon the way. For albeit he that stood in danger should sing, or make show of courage and comfort, and set a good face upon the matter, yet the other might well think that his heart had many a cold pull within him; as no doubt but wicked men have, when they think with themselves of the life to come.

Was he alluding to some episode of his own going into England, when he might have been feeling the cold pull at the heart? On the very next page he puts down what is certainly a piece of his own experience:

I can and do affirm thee upon my conscience before almighty God, that I have had conference with no small number of such persons as myself, and that to my singular comfort, in beholding the strong hand and exceeding bountifulness of God's sweetness towards them in this case. Oh, dear brother, no tongue can express what I have seen therein, and yet saw I not the least part of what they inwardly felt. But yet this may I say, that they that attend in the Catholic Church to deal with souls in the holy sacrament of confession are indeed those of whom the Prophet saith that, "they work in multitudes of waters, and do see the marvels of God in the depths". In the depth (I say) of men's consciences, uttered with infinite multitudes of tears, when God toucheth the same with His holy grace. Believe me, good reader, for I speak in truth before our Lord Jesus, I have seen so great and exceeding consolations in divers great sinners after their conversion, as no heart can almost conceive; and the hearts which received them were hardly able to contain the same, so abundantly distilled down that heavenly dew from the most liberal and bountiful hand of God.

The quality of mercy was indeed not strained in his experience. He shows himself possessed of the true Jesuit spirituality, which was able to make apostolic work an aid to spiritual progress and thus to combine contemplation and action.

Mr C. S. Lewis finds a "racy, fleering manner" in More and Latimer and others which he takes to be truly English and not due to any slavish imitation of the foreigner or of the ancients; one sees it in Persons, though more prominently in his controversial writing than here. Still there are touches of it, as when he exhorts the procrastinator:

It is written among the lives of old Hermits, how that on a time an angel showed to one of them in the wilderness a certain fond fellow that hewed down wood; who, having made to himself a great burden to carry thence, laid it on his back, and, for that it was uneasy and pressed him much, he cast it down again and put a great deal more unto it, and then began to lift it anew. But when he felt it more heavy than before, he fell into a great rage and added twice as much more unto it, thereby to make it lighter. Whereat when the holy man mused much, the angel told him that this was a figure of them in the world, who, finding it somewhat unpleasant to resist one or two vices in the beginning, do defer their conversion, and do add twenty or forty more unto them, thinking to find the matter more easy afterward to be remedied.

Among his character-sketches there is this gem, on the vainglories:

It is a miserable thing for a man to be a wind-mill, which grindeth not, nor maketh meal, but according as the blast en-

> dureth. If the gale be strong, he scourgeth about lustily, but if the wind be slack, he relenteth presently; so, if you praise the vain-glorious man, he will run, but if he feel not the gale blow, he is out of heart. He is like the Babylonians, who with a little sweet music were made to adore anything whatsoever.

He must have been watching a Spanish pack-train the day he wrote out the comparison of the rich man at death to the mule:

> What a misery will death be to many worldlings when he cometh, who now build palaces, purchase lands, heap riches, procure dignities, make marriages, join kindreds, as though there were never any end of all these matters! What a doleful day will this be to them (I say) when they must be turned off, no other wise than Princes' mules are wont to be at the end of a journey; that is, their treasure taken from them and their galled backs only left unto themselves! For as we see these mules of Princes go all the day long, loaden with treasures and covered with fair cloths, but at night shaken off into some sorry stable, much bruised and galled with the carriage of those treasures; so, many rich men that pass through this world, loaden with gold and silver, and do gall greatly their souls in carriage thereof, are despoiled of their burden at the day of death and are turned off with their wounded consciences to the loathsome stable of hell and damnation.

Mr Lewis found in Dryden an "unanswerable ease and gusto, which seems to cost the writer nothing, and kills with nonchalance", and missed such a quality in the Elizabethan prose writers. But he might have found it in Persons.

The Lady of Milan, Isabella Berinzaga, was to set going the new movement in spirituality that so influenced Bérulle and many others some little time after Persons wrote, but it is quite possible that he had seen her on the occasion of his passage through Milan. Later on, he was to play his part in restraining the efforts of those Jesuits who had made themselves her disciples. His own inspiration was mainly scriptural and patristic. He had read widely in the Fathers and some pages of his book are taken up with translations from Augustine, Cyprian, Jerome, Victor Vitensis (whose comments on the Vandal persecutions made him an author most apt for the times) and sometimes Eusebius or Chrysostom. He drew from these sources that clear vision of the Passion of Christ being continued in the life of His Church to the end of time. When he describes the apostles and disciples shut in the Cenacle after the Ascension, he might be speaking of the little bands of Catholics who had assisted at his Mass when he was living secretly in London:

> The whole City was bent against them; themselves were poor and simple people and divers of them women. Lands or revenues they had not to maintain them; nor friends at Court to give them countenance against their enemies. The name of Jesus was most odious; and whosoever did favour Him was accounted a traitor and enemy to the State. There wanted not, perhaps, among them who, considering the great multitude, would imagine with themselves what should become of them, where they should find to maintain and sustain them, what should be the end of that feeble congregation. For abroad they durst not go for fear of persecution; and continue long together they might not, for want of necessaries. Besides that, every hour they expected to be molested and drawn forth by catchpoles and officers. And albeit in these distresses the fresh memory of Jesus and His sweet promises made unto them at His departure, as also the delectable presence of His blessed Mother, and her often exhortations and encouragements unto them, did comfort them greatly, as well may be supposed, yet to them that by human reason should ponder and weigh their present state and condition, it could not choose but seem hard and no ways durable.

It was the custom in the English Province of the Society of Jesus to have some extracts from the *Christian Directory* read publicly at retreat time, a custom which seems to have survived until after the middle of the nineteenth century, but when the work was first read in the refectory of St Omer or Liège, one can well imagine such a passage being received with profound emotion. If one wished to find the influences that went to produce the sober, matter-of-fact, yet deep piety of the English Recusant, it would be right to count this work among the principal. Theologians say that God may sometimes require heroic virtue in those whose whole duty is the keeping of the commandments without any added obligation of the counsels, and one might fairly say that the persecution of Elizabeth and James was such a time for Catholics. The work that Persons compiled had therefore to be, not an appeal to the cloistered and to those under vow, but to the plain men and women of England on whom the weight of persecution fell. The copies of this work that were smuggled in by Barking Creek or Langstone Harbour or at King's Lynn, or ferried to the shore from some merchantman as it passed up the Tyne, in their turn set up another traffic, this time from the shores of England to the seminaries abroad, of men who had seen what Persons saw and were ready to prepare their Pentecost.

As a translator, Persons had qualities which might have helped the work of his friend Gregory Martin (himself no mean stylist), who was wearing himself out with the work of translating and annotating Scripture almost at the very time that Persons was writing the *Christian Directory*. When he cites passages from Scripture, he seems to have made his own versions for the occasion. Thus he has to render a passage of Hebrews when he is speaking of the following of Christ:

> As He by fighting and overcoming was exalted to the throne of His Father, so shall we be to His throne for the like reason. Upon which cause and most comfortable consideration St Paul foundeth himself in his Epistle to the Hebrews, when he exhorteth them so earnestly to the like fight in these words: "Shaking off from us all weight or clog that may hinder us, let us by patience run unto the combat offered unto us, with our eyes fixed upon the author of our faith and fulfiller thereof, Christ Jesus, who setting before His eyes the joys of heaven, and contemning the confusion (or worldly shame) that might thereof ensue, sustained the cross and thereby is come now to sit at the right hand of the seat of God His Father."

Gregory Martin was himself a notable writer of English, though his modesty in not presuming to judge of the meaning of obscure passages made him leave them in their obscurity and so lost him some men's favour. His letters from exile to his sister and to those whom he was hoping to convert show what he could do when not fettered by the text of his author as it lay before him, and it is to be hoped that some day they will be reprinted. St John's and Balliol, Martin and Persons, both must have had reason to read often in the great tome which contained the *Works* of Sir Thomas More, the publication of which in 1557 had been one of the great achievements of the Marian restoration. We know that Persons did, for in his (manuscript) history of the Reformation in England he transcribes long passages from More to illustrate his tale in its earlier stages. The Greek and Latin which Persons had first acquired in Oxford and then polished in Padua and Rome, had taught him to abate somewhat the abundance of More and to thrust sharper with his shorter sentences, but the feeling for the language that was in More passed on to the younger men.

The suggestion is sometimes made that Persons was not very original with his *Directory*, and that he borrowed much of it from the *Christian Exercise* of Fr Gaspar Loarte, S.J. The Protestant publisher of this latter work, W. Leake, who issued the book from the Sign of the Crane in St Paul Churchyard in 1594, claimed on his title-page that it was "the first ground and foundation whence the two treatises appertaining to Resolution were made and framed by R.P.". Describing the book in a Preface, Leake said:

> It was first written in the Italian tongue by a certain Jesuit friar who was named Gaspar Loarte, and afterwards more at large wrought upon and handled in more plentiful discourse by Robert Parsons, Englishman, yet a Jesuit likewise, living beyond the seas.

The fact is that Fr Persons meant his book to lead up to that of Loarte, who was writing to show the practising Catholic how to meditate and how to guard himself against temptation, whereas Persons was certainly not preaching to the converted; he was trying to convince the half-atheist and the wavering "schismatic" that he must resolve to turn away from sin and follow Christ. In his first edition (1582) he says expressly: "No part of this first book of Resolution was handled in that (Loarte's) treatise." The work of Loarte had been put into English (in 1579) by Stephen Brinkley, who was soon to be Persons's printer at the secret press of Green-street House, East Ham. Fr Persons used Brinkley's edition of Loarte to fortify the abandoned Catholics of England, but must have found it inadequate to meet the needs of many of them and so turned to composing his own work, which, being modelled on the plan of the *Spiritual Exercises* of St Ignatius, was bound to have some resemblance here and there to the work of another disciple of Ignatius. But the claim of Leake in 1594 is much rather to be ascribed to a publisher's desire to give his work a good send-off. He knew, without doubt, that the *Book of Resolution* was "a most vendible copy", and, if he could make out that his own product was a key to that work, he would achieve success in his sales. His remarks show no real grasp of the contents of the two works, and one of his phrases, describing Fr Persons as "Englishman yet a Jesuit . . . living beyond the seas", is taken from the preface of the 1590 edition of the *Directory*. Loarte seems to be the original source of the Christian's rule of life which still survives in our catechisms, but he has nothing to compare to Persons's great drive towards the formation of resolution in the sinner.

The atheism of the Elizabethan age is not much featured in the histories of the literature of that time, but it was attacked by Fr Persons most vigorously. The early part of his *Directory* was designed to give the ordinary man some grounds for accepting the existence of God and His Providence, and this was followed by a section entitled *Proofs of Christianity*. How much this was needed can be seen from what he wrote in his *Reply to the Edict of Elizabeth* (1592), where he speaks of "Sir Walter Ralegh's school of atheism . . . and of the diligence used to get young gentlemen to this school, wherein both Moses and our Saviour, the Old and the New Testament, are jested at, and the scholars taught among other things, to spell God backwards". Just as Lord Herbert of Cherbury was to make deism fashionable some twenty years later, so Ralegh does seem towards the end of the century to have led a fashion of bold atheist talking, quite apart from his atheist doing.[1]

[1] Ralegh has been defended against the charge of atheism by a modern American researcher, Ernest A. Strathmann, in two articles: "Ralegh's Skepticism" and. "Ralegh and the Catholic Polemists" in the *Huntington Library Quarterly*, III (1940), pp. 265-87, and VIII (1945), pp. 337-58. He has also produced in the J. Q. Adams Memorial Studies a chapter entitled, Robert Persons' "Essay on Atheism" (1948). He has no new evidence to add to the vital document which was printed in *The Month* for June 1894 by Miss J. M. Stone ("Atheism under Elizabeth and James I"), p. 182. This document was reprinted in full by G. B. Harrison in his edition of *Willobie his Avisa* (1926); it shows that in conversation over the dinner-table Ralegh proclaimed himself quite sceptical about the nature of God and of the human soul. (The distinction between "what is it" and "that it is" was brought up at the time). Mr Strathmann now defends Ralegh on the ground that twenty years later in his *History of the World*, while he has the same reserve about the nature of God, he is ready to accept what the Scriptures say about him. But this does not prove he had cleared away his unbelief, for we do not know how he would have justified to himself or to another the acceptance of Scripture and the very notion of the inspiration of a man by God. He had had time to reflect in the interim, and even to read the *Christian Directory*, but above all to escape from the atheistic counsels of Thomas Harriott, whom Anthony à Wood brands as a complete atheist. One must also remember that men of action are not always quite consistent or logical in their assorted beliefs.

It need cause no surprise to find that when deism was the plague of English society at the end of the seventeenth century the *Christian Directory* was once again appealed to by the Anglican George Stanhope, who in 1700, and again some three or four times in the next decade, issued a bowdlerized version of Persons's work. He claimed that he had put it into modern English, and indeed he has removed most of the verbal power and sharpness of the original and reduced everything to an Augustan smoothness. He was a chaplain to William and Mary and then to Anne, who made him Dean of Canterbury. He brought out an edition of Epictetus, one of Marcus Aurelius and one of the *Imitation of Christ*. His liking for the classics of meditation no doubt led him to undertake the work on the *Christian Directory*, which he must have thought deserved a place with other classics, if only it were put into a modern dress, and this he proceeded to give. The four editions which his work went through in a short space were some reward. The unwary reader who picks up one of them now and thinks that he is reading Persons has been warned.

In his *Elizabethan Recusant Prose* (1950) Dr A. C. Southern has made the claim that Persons shows an indebtedness to the medieval English spiritual writers such as Rolle and Walter Hilton. R. W. Chambers also was in favour of such a dependence, and it is not unlikely. One has to admit that his style is closer to those works than it is to the English versions of Louis of Granada and of Guevara's *Dial of Princes*, the one diffuse, the other euphuistic. Dr Maria Hagedorn, in her *Reformation und Spanische Andachtsliteratur* (1934), gave some passages where Persons may be thought to have borrowed from Granada, but Fr Thurston, commenting upon her work, pointed out that Persons showed no dependence in style and must have been using the Spanish text direct. The debt he owed to the works of St Thomas More is undoubted, as I have already remarked above and have argued more at length in writing of "The Prose of Robert Persons" in *The Month* for May 1940, and whether he felt the influence of the medieval English writers through More and Stapleton or directly it may be impossible to determine until one has definite trace of a copy of their works which he could have used at Rome or at St Omer or in Spain. One other line of transmission of such influence should not be neglected. Fr Thomas Darbyshire was a canon of St Paul's and a man of forty when Queen Mary died, yet he lived on as a Jesuit until 1604 and had much to do with Fr Persons in the meantime. In London he had been the head of a group of priests who called themselves the Table (or Fellowship) of the Name of Jesus. This style implies a devotion to the Holy Name such as was popularly expressed in the *Jesus Psalter*, and Darbyshire, like others, found in the Society of Jesus an organization which seemed to give him new hope of continuing in exile that form of piety which he had known in England. Others had the same idea and in the controversial works of Stapleton there is a notable tribute to the new Society of Jesus written long before any English Jesuit had returned to these shores. It has been noted by an outside observer, Miss Helen White, in her *Tudor Books of Private Devotion* (1951), that there is a link between the old Passion-prayers of English devotion and the Ignatian type of meditation that was being developed in the writings of the latter part of the century. The English exiles who joined the Jesuits in the formative period of the Society under Lainez and Francis Borgia had something to give as well as to receive, and Persons and Campion when in their turn they joined the Society found themselves in a somewhat familiar atmosphere. One should not forget that the novice who in 1568 signed the book of admissions at the Roman noviceship (which had recently begun at St Andrea sul Quirinale) next to Stanislaus Kostka was John Rastell, Fellow of New College, Oxford, and grand-nephew of St Thomas More.

IX

FATHER AUGUSTINE BAKER

By David Knowles

In any list, however short, of English spiritual writers the name of Fr Augustine Baker must find a place. His claim was excellently defined many years ago by Dom Justin McCann, to whom all are indebted for his work upon Baker's life and writings.

> He is [wrote Dom Justin] a striking, if not unique, figure in the history of post-reformation English Catholicism. The fourteenth century in England produced original spiritual writers of the first quality. If we look for any parallel to their work in post-reformation Catholicism, we find one book, and one only, Fr Baker's *Sancta Sophia*, which can be set beside it.

Indeed, we might go further still, and say that it is the only original work in English that gives magisterial guidance over the whole range of the spiritual life. Whatever may be its limitations, or even its errors, it has the stamp of greatness. If Fr Baker is to be judged, it is against the great that he must be measured, against such as St Francis de Sales, St Teresa and St John of the Cross.

The life of David (in religion Dom Augustine) Baker covered almost exactly (1575-1641) the period between the final break with Catholicism in the early years of Elizabeth I and the beginning of the civil disturbances which were to put an end to any hope there might have been of a massive re-establishment of the old religion as a powerful minority among all classes in the country. Seen from another viewpoint, it was the period in which the new Catholicism, that of the Council of Trent, of the Jesuits, and of the Counter-Reformation, made its impact on England; it was a time of anguish and persecution, and yet it was a very real Second Spring, in which the first newcomers from the recently founded seminaries and colleges fired their relatives and converts at home with a zeal that had been lacking in the generation that had lost the faith, and that peopled monasteries and convents in

France and the Low Countries with religious in exile; it was also, unhappily, a time of feuds and quarrels and mistakes, and of a clash of aims and hopes and ideals that ultimately did as much as the spirit of Puritanism to check the spread of the faith in this country. David Baker had experience of all this. Born of well-to-do parents, church-papists, at Abergavenny, he had part of his schooling at Christ's Hospital and part at Broadgates Hall at Oxford where, according to his own account, he lost his virtue and his Christian faith. He then studied law in London and returned to Abergavenny as Recorder. His conversion, begun by a strange escape from imminent death, was completed in 1603 by his reconciliation, and followed immediately by his departure to Italy to become a monk at Padua. At the end of his noviciate his health broke down and he returned to England, where he resumed practice as a lawyer and began his researches into monastic history. In 1607 he took a leading part in the aggregation of a group of English missionary monks to the old English congregation, represented by the last surviving monk of Westminster, Dom Sigebert Buckley, and to him Fr Baker made his monastic profession. He subsequently joined the newly founded monastery of Dieulouard (now Ampleforth Abbey), but never resided there. After ordination abroad, he spent some time in retirement in a Catholic household in Devon, and then worked intensively in London at the command of his superiors on the history of medieval English monasticism for controversial purposes. In 1624 he crossed to Douai to the recently founded monastery of St Gregory (now Downside Abbey), but was sent almost at once as supplementary confessor to the newly founded convent of English Dames at Cambrai (now Stanbrook Abbey). Here he soon found himself as the spiritual director of a young and eager community starting upon their life in religion, and he remained at Cambrai for nine years (1624-33); this was in many ways the happiest and most fruitful period of his life. He was recalled as a result of controversy over his doctrine, and though it was fully approved he was not sent back, but lived a retired life at St Gregory's for five years, till in 1638 he became embroiled in a personal controversy with the prior, Dom Rudesind Barlow, who did not rest till he had secured a presidential order sending Fr Baker, now old and infirm, back to the mission in England. There he lived for some three years, an invalid rather than a missioner, harried about in 1640-41 by the agents of Government in the revived persecution, and escaping their hands only by reason of a rumour of the plague in his house. He died under the care of the mother of one of the nuns of Cambrai in August 1641.

This short narrative will have shown that there was little of monastic observance in the external life of Fr Baker. For only five years, excluding his noviciate, was he the member of a community, and even then, to judge by contemporary accounts, he lived apart from the rest. It may also have shown that Fr Baker was no ordinary man. A gifted lawyer, who consorted on an equality with the lawyers of a great age, a scholar who was admitted to the circle of Selden, Cotton and Ussher, a tireless writer throughout, who produced in the *Apostolatus* a laborious work of great learning, he was also, from the days of his conversion onwards, hoping and striving, with many changes of mind and fortune, to become a man of contemplative prayer.

Fr Baker is often alluded to as a mystic, sometimes even as a great mystic. The justice of the title could be proclaimed—if ever—only after the perusal of the voluminous sources for our knowledge of his life and work; the autobiographical and biographical pieces and his own writings, printed and manuscript. He himself tells us that (like St Teresa) he had twice attempted and abandoned the practice of serious and prolonged mental prayer before a final "conversion", the result of which endured till his death. According to his own account and phraseology he had at one time a "passive union" followed by a time of great desolation during which he returned to an "extroverted" life. After his third conversion he had no specifically mystical experience until the last weeks of his life, when his words are somewhat ambiguous. Three centuries after a life has been lived no one could wish to pose as a competent judge of its character, and the present writer would not have opened the question had it not been for the claims made in Fr Baker's regard, but he confesses that after more than forty years' acquaintance with *Sancta Sophia* he still finds it difficult to assess "that mysterious man" who sits so primly on his chair and gazes so sadly from the traditional portrait. Fr Baker is, indeed, a baffling figure. Powerful of mind and determined of character, sane and central in all his doctrine and able to influence his disciples and contemporaries, not to speak of readers since, to their lasting good, he nevertheless leaves upon us an impression of "queerness", as of a man with whimsies and corners; he was certainly not a "good community man" and fell foul of his confrères more than once. Saints and mystics have before now proved incomprehensible to mediocrity and sanctity always calls forth the resistance of spiritual evil; moreover, ordinary people often fail to understand the motives and ideals of the genius. Nevertheless, Fr Baker seems to lack as a person that indefinable likeness to Christ that is a hallmark of sanctity, and in the same way his writings, luminous and just as they are, fail to carry the ultimate conviction of the mystic that he has seen what he speaks of. That Fr Baker was an admirable and sincere man and a man of prayer, judgement and spiritual insight is certain. More than this, with our limited vision, cannot be said.

Fr Baker, lawyer, scholar and spiritual director, was a voluminous writer. Indeed, "penning", as he called it, was a daily occupation with him on a level with reading and praying. In addition to the *Apostolatus*, four folio volumes of material for monastic history, two autobiographical pieces, a short history of the origins of the English Congregation, lives of Dame Gertrude More and one or two others, and a commentary on the *Cloud of Unknowing*, he left numerous treatises on various ascetical and mystical topics. It was chiefly from these last that a monk of the next generation, himself a distinguished Oxford man and convert, Dom Serenus Cressy, compiled at the request of the Dames of Cambrai and with the warm support of his superiors, the book which he entitled *Sancta Sophia* or *Holy Wisdom*.

Anyone who has glanced at only one of Fr Baker's manuscripts will feel that Fr Cressy achieved a notable feat of editing. He has indeed, to use his own phrase, "methodically digested" Fr Baker's remains and produced an ordered whole, and what appears as a system, out of disconnected and prolix treatises. Nevertheless the method has its disadvantages. Until someone has worked through the existing manuscripts and analysed their contents, we cannot be sure that Fr Cressy has given us the whole of Fr Baker's teaching, and until the revelant passages have been collated with *Sancta Sophia* we cannot be sure that the order and arrangement of the parts fully corresponds to Fr Baker's scheme. Fr Cressy, in short, may have considerably modified the doctrine, for better or for worse. Meanwhile, and in particular for the purpose of this article, we have to take *Sancta Sophia* as we find it, and equate the printed book with Fr Baker's mind.

If Fr Cressy compiled his work out of Fr Baker's treatises, whence did Fr Baker himself derive his doctrine? We may begin with some negative remarks. Fr Baker had not passed through an academic or seminary course of philosophy and theology, and though he had read, as we shall see, some scholastic authors he never writes as a trained theologian, either explicitly, as did, for example, his Carmelite contemporaries at Salamanca or John of St Thomas, or implicitly, as did St John of the Cross. This absence of theological backbone is one weakness of *Sancta Sophia*. Next, Fr Baker, as has been said, never lived the community life of an observant monastery at any time after his noviciate at Santa Giustina. His counsels for religious, therefore, were not the outcome of long experience of the common life, or of the responsibilities of office.

If we now come to the positive influences, we may say that *Sancta Sophia* rests upon Fr Baker's experience, personal and vicarious, and upon his reading. His personal experience, though he never cites it, lies behind many pages, as may readily be seen by comparing one of the personal treatises, such as the printed *Confessions*, with the relevant sections in the book. Yet he may well have learnt most from his own disciples. In his years at Cambrai he found a door open and, though even here he held no official position of superiority, he was able to use his exceptional gifts in forming and directing a young community of zealous and gifted women. In return he unquestionably learnt much of human nature and the ways of God in calling a soul to Himself. When we estimate the extent of his debt to the nuns of Cambrai, however, we must remember that when he arrived at the convent all the nuns were "beginners" in the spiritual life, and though one at least, Dame Gertrude More, advanced towards sanctity in the short span allotted to her, the community of Cambrai in those first years cannot be compared to the galaxy of spiritual talent that St John of the Cross knew at Beas and Granada, or that St Francis de Sales fostered by the lake at Annecy.

Yet when all is said, Fr Baker owed the basis of his teaching to books. He was a scholar rather than an autodidact, and there is abundant evidence, which an editor must some day display, of the breadth of his reading and of his debt to his books. The decades of his maturity coincided with the first great wave of what Bremond has called *L'Invasion mystique*, when the books and first disciples of the great Spanish and Italian saints were arriving in France and the Low Countries to kindle new fires and light new lamps there. Of this invasion Fr Baker was at once a beneficiary and an agent. His sources were many and remarkably well chosen. In the first place, he had the *Conferences* of Cassian and the *Lives of the Fathers*, recently popularized by Rosweyde. From the early Middle Ages he took something from St Anselm, St Bernard and William of St Thierry. He read the *Summa* of St Thomas frequently, and knew the spiritual writings of St Bonaventure. From a later century he took St Catherine of Siena and Blessed Angela of Foligno. Two of the English mystics, the author of *The Cloud* and Walter Hilton, were among his favourite authors; he wrote a commentary on the former and advised his nuns to read the book yearly. Of the Flemish mystics he knew Ruysbroeck and Suso, and of Germans Tauler, Ludolf the Carthusian and above all Herp (Harphius). Of the Spaniards, he cites Osuna and Alvarez de Paz, but these are naturally outweighed by St Teresa (canonized in 1622) and St John of the Cross (not yet beatified); he seems, however, to have been familiar only with the *Ascent* of St John and the *Life* and *Interior Castle* of St Teresa, though both writers had been translated into French in quasi-totality. In consequence, and perhaps unfortunately, he treats them eclectically as supporting authorities without adopting in its entirety the Carmelite mystical theology, perfected by St John, as a regulative norm, and he displays no acquaintance with the Carmelite theologians of Salamanca or the great Dominican theologian John of St Thomas. Among the writers of his own day, his favourites were the two Franciscans, Constantine Barbanson and Benet Canfield, but he knew the *Introduction to the Devout Life* of "the holy bishop of Geneva", the works of Blosius, and several of the Jesuit writers. From all these, but principally from Tauler, Harphius, Suso, the *Cloud*, Barbanson and Canfield he distilled his doctrine, and it is not surprising that the result, which he himself never fused into a system, has a patchwork appearance. He rarely argues from theological principles; the reason given is the opinion of an authority, though it is often critically examined. There are indeed passages of fire and eloquence, which a reader would suppose to be the utterance of experience, but certain of these, at least, can be shown to be precisely those where he is following a printed source.

Sancta Sophia is a carefully arranged series of instructions for one engaged upon the religious life, and especially the "monastical contemplative life", and it aims at reaching from the first entrance of the postulant to the mystical union of perfect souls. It is therefore a treatise of both ascetical and mystical theology, though the strictly mystical teaching occupies only fifty out of 500 pages. No other book is exactly comparable; it stands halfway between a set and formal treatise of ascetical theology and a loosely knit, personal instruction such as is given by St Teresa in her *Way of Perfection*; more comprehensive and orderly than the latter, it is more direct, personal and urgent than the former. It is indeed one of the very few spiritual masterpieces that can be read again and again, and serve as a life's guide. The late Abbot Cuthbert Butler read it at least once a year for more than fifty years on end. It is, however, an unusually difficult book to summarize, for despite the efforts of Fr Cressy's "methodical digestion" it remains a heap rather than a block or a building, and there are many chapters, valuable and indeed indispensable, which cannot be pressed into any logical order and could be excised without leaving a chasm.

Partly of its very nature and partly because of its author's slant of mind, *Sancta Sophia* may also be considered as a guide to prayer. Its sub-title, indeed, is "Directions for the prayer of contemplation". Its scope, however, is really very much wider than this. It is divided by Fr Cressy into three treatises: (1) of a contemplative life in general; (2) of the first instrument of perfection, viz., mortification; (3) of prayer; but these headings give no idea of the richness of the whole. After general instructions on the religious life three particular means of internal enlightenment are discussed; the spiritual director, spiritual reading, and divine inspirations. Then, after sections on the obligations of the religious life, on the noviciate, and on the English mission, the author deals with the mortification of the passions and the practice of solitude and silence; then with the virtues of charity, patience, humility and obedience, after which comes a long chapter on the treatment of scruples. All this takes up some 330 pages. The 220 pages that remain are occupied with prayer; the manner of using sensible devotion and distractions; a full treatment of the three stages of meditation, acts of the will and "aspirations"; instructions for behaviour in distractive offices and in sickness. Finally, an outline is given of the stages of the mystical life.

Fr Baker is diffuse and at times verbose, but he had a trained and masculine intelligence, and the book is dense with the reading and experience of a lifetime. Before discussing it a word of caution may be in place. Like other spiritual classics, such as the *Cloud of Unknowing* and the writings of St Teresa and St John of the Cross, *Sancta Sophia* was composed for a restricted class of readers and will only be read with real profit by those belonging to that class. While it is true that all the books just mentioned may prove of interest, and even incidentally of help, to the casual reader, they were in fact composed for those already committed to a strict religious life and they contain some matter, at least, which can easily be misunderstood by those in other circumstances. In *Sancta Sophia*, indeed, the appeal is wide and the danger of misunderstanding less. It is nevertheless true that the book will prove of real use and value only to a soul committed, or desirous of being committed, to a resolute endeavour to advance in the love of God in an "abstracted" way of life. As Fr Leander of St Martin wrote of Fr Baker's doctrine in 1634, it is "written precisely and only for such souls as by God's holy Grace do effectually and constantly dedicate themselves to as pure an abstraction from creatures . . . and all things which they shall perceive, or be warned of, to be impediments to the divine union of their souls with God" as may be possible, and others will read *Sancta Sophia* at their own hazard.

Having said thus much, it must be added that the doctrine and the manner of presentation throughout the book are sobriety itself. On a multitude of topics Fr Baker gives, with clarity and authority, the central teaching of the masters of the spiritual life throughout the ages. Indeed, if he errs at all in this respect, it is on the side of authority and convention. Nothing in his teaching could be interpreted in an extravagant sense save by a perverse or extremely stupid reader. With this preface, something may be said about three points in Fr Baker's teaching which are of particular value; on mortification, on divine inspiration, and on the first degrees of mental prayer.

As to mortification, or the ascetic life, he is at once simple and bracing, granted always, what he assumes, that the person concerned is living under a firm rule of life. He may be summed up, positively, as finding mortification of the passions in a strict observance of the Rule and religious obedience, and, negatively, in the avoidance of all distraction of the mind; and furthermore in avoiding squandering the will by means of solitude, silence and the renunciation of all activity that results from free, personal choice. More explicitly, perhaps, than any other writer he insists upon the avoidance of all "propriety", that is, the enjoyment of a sense of possession, power, or achievement, whether in regard to things, persons or employments; and upon the value of not-doing rather than doing. Here he is absolutely at one with the Carmelite school as expressed by St John. On the other hand, he discounts the value of purely physical mortifications, and especially of all such as are voluntary and hastily assumed. Nor is he afraid to say that prayer, the kind of prayer he extols, is the best of all mortifications.

As for his teaching on divine inspiration, it is perhaps the most original and valuable part of his work. Many are the souls that have profited and will profit by it, properly understood and practised, and many are those to whom it might bring comfort and strength. It is not, of course, original in the sense of novel, for Christian spirituality has been essentially the same in every age. Not only this, but many writers, from the Fathers of the desert onwards, have given explicit instruction on this very point. It had, however, become obscured in the decay before the Reformation and in the authoritarian climate of the early sixteenth century, and its revival in an heretical and deformed sense had made it something of an unwelcome topic to the spiritual writers of the Counter-Reformation. Yet it may be said that without it there can be no mature and truly strong life of the spirit. The teaching, which is in fact universal Christian teaching applied to a particular point, is that in all cases and on all occasions where a moral or spiritual decision has to be taken, and where no clear law or command makes the will of God here and now apparent, light to see (and strength to act) will be given without fail to one who asks for it with faith and goodwill. The doctrine, it must be repeated, has its fullest relevance only for souls aiming at the highest. Christians who are in and of the world, and even many priests and religious, have not in fact and in the concrete case either the desire or the spiritual capacity to follow the inner light in the "ordinary" decisions of life. But for those who wish to hear and respond to the call to a more perfect following of Christ the doctrine is essential. Those who are honest with themselves will know that the turning points, the crucial decisions for good and bad throughout their lives, have not occurred on a matter of law or expressed command, but in the intimate and unseen region of the soul where the gift or the refusal of the will to God and of love to Christ takes place. How often, if we have any knowledge of ourselves, are we aware that a vital opportunity has been lost precisely because the very existence of a moment of choice has been burked, or, if the opportunity has been taken, that the decision has been made under the guidance of an unseen but intimately experienced illumination. Every sincere Christian knows, on his humble level, what is writ large in the lives of the saints—in St John of the Cross, who wrote:

> Unseeing, on I pressed
> Lit by no earthly rays,
> Nay, only by heart's inmost fire ablaze,

and St Thérèse of Lisieux, of whom the Church sings: "the Lord alone was her guide".

Finally, there is Fr Baker's teaching on the necessity and stages of mental prayer. This is the heart of his book, and its "message" for his generation and for ours. He belonged, as has been said, to the age-group that came to maturity when the writings and exhortations of the saints and leaders of the Catholic Reform were permeating Europe and germinating luxuriantly into flower and fruit, as also into coarse herbage and hybrid growths. Broadly speaking the spiritual reform had taken two directions. There was the efflorescence of intellectual, pastoral and missionary activity —the new education, the Jesuit colleges, the discipline of preaching, retreats and meditation, the renewed frequentation of the sacraments. There was on the other hand a revival of the strict religious and contemplative vocation, accompanied by the appearance of a constellation of saintly men and women who by their example and writings infused new blood into the traditional mystical theology of the Church. The revived English monasticism of men and women, of which Fr Baker had been an active pioneer, was drawn by opposing magnets. On the one hand were the new colleges, the methodical asceticism, the preaching and directing, and the call of souls on the English mission; on the other, the tradition of the monastic past and the vision of the heights of Mount Carmel. Fr Baker had felt the struggle in himself and seen it in the controversies within his own monastic family and in the arguments even within the parlours of the English Dames. He saw it as his vocation to preach and to present the cause of the interior life and of mental and contemplative prayer. For the moment the controversial element in his life can be ignored; for us he is the apostle of the prayer of the spirit. Here, he does but return to the purest sources of monastic and mystical doctrine, the desert fathers, who saw in the prayer of the heart, the prayer of love and adoration, the end of the monastic life and the inseparable companion of all true virtue. But Fr Baker, in emphasis at least, goes even further; for him mental prayer is the centre and the test of all. Neither in his own practice nor in his teaching does he neglect or belittle the sacraments, or the liturgy, as instruments and sources of sanctification, but he is insistent that the monk must be a man of interior prayer, and that only so far as he is a man of prayer, or needs help to make him a man of prayer, are other things of value. As he remarks very truly, the prayer of the heart and will is the only activity incompatible with deliberate sin. The sacraments may be received mechanically or unworthily, vocal prayers may be said with every kind of mental preoccupation, but humble and sincere interior prayer—the explicit or implicit *fiat voluntas tua*—is not compatible with an actual resistance to God's will and love. In his account of the degrees of prayer Fr Baker, who is writing, be it remembered, for those dedicated to a monastic life, passes over formal meditation. This, in his view, should never for the monk or nun be more than a short stage, while for some it should not be a stage at all. For those for whom he is writing, liturgy and meditative reading, both part of their daily life, should take the place of meditation in feeding the mind for as long as it needs to find motive for love. For the monk prayer should soon be immediately and solely an activity of the will, loving, praising God, accepting His will in all things and trusting in His light and help. It is the great merit of Fr Baker that by his description and by the examples he provides he shows the richness, the potentialities and the stages of growing purity in this kind of prayer. Many readers of Fr Baker will of course find, like the would-be literary man of Molière, that they have in fact long been practising something of which they now learn the technical name, but there may be others to whom a chapter of Fr Baker will come as an open door and a new freedom.

Thus far we have laid emphasis upon the excellencies of Fr Baker. A word must now be said of his deficiencies. Such criticisms as follow, it must be remembered, apply to the printed *Sancta Sophia*, and to that alone.

The first criticism is a general and not very serious one. *Sancta Sophia* is a long book, and it would not have lost a great deal if Fr Cressy had been somewhat more ruthless with the pruning-knife. Moreover, it is, at least in its first half, a somewhat sombre book. Fr Baker himself was approachable and sympathetic, especially in his relations with the young, but he lived in a mental climate heavily charged with a dour view of human nature deriving partly from the preoccupation of theologians with the treatises of St Augustine on grace, and partly from the influence of Calvinism and Puritanism on contemporary religious sentiment. There is more than a foretaste in Fr Baker of the sunless outlook of Saint-Cyran and Port-Royal. Three or four passages, indeed, e.g. pp. 200-1, 230, 245, 249-50, 251 in the 1876 edition, seem to exclude the possibility of "natural" moral goodness and to contradict both Catholic teaching and experience in attributing actual sinfulness to all love that is not actually or virtually directed towards God.

More serious, perhaps, is a real confusion in the degrees of the spiritual life and the principles of mystical theology, even if, as is possible, some of the confusion may be due to Fr Cressy's arrangement of the chapters. Put briefly, it would seem that Fr Baker failed to arrive at an adequate definition of contemplation. As has been said, he had read some, though not all, of St John of the Cross, but he had failed altogether to absorb and make use of two of the basic principles of the teaching which the saint drew from earlier tradition and which have since become the common doctrine of theologians. The one is, that no clearly expressible knowledge and no clearly felt emotion in the will can be a proximate means of union with God: the only proximate means are the virtues of faith in the intellect and of hope and charity in the will.

The other is, that normally perfection of the soul cannot be attained without passive purgation of the intellect and will by means of God-sent darkness and aridity which are in fact the impact upon an imperfect being of divine light and love. Hence the need for the twofold purification of sense and spirit in the two "nights" within the soul. Without this clear position, based firmly on the traditional theology of grace and of the functions of the theological virtues and the gifts of the Holy Ghost, Fr Baker had to find his way amid a tangle of schemes based largely on individual experience, his own and that of others. Several serious inconveniences resulted from this.

First, Fr Baker, who was well aware of the elementary part played by the imagination and the reason in prayer, failed to see clearly that in the realm of the will his "forced acts" were equally elementary. Both are activities belonging to the stage of "meditation". Fr Baker, therefore, is at fault when he describes the prayer of the will, *tout court*, as "contemplative", and also when he places his instructions on the season for a change of prayer between the section on meditation and that on acts of the will. Cressy is almost certainly largely to blame for this arrangement. The crucial moment of transition is when both "considerations" and formal "acts" are beginning to give place to the (at first scarcely perceptible) reception of infused love and knowledge. The confusion may have been in part caused by the scheme of St John himself in *The Ascent of Mount Carmel*. There, the saint places the crucial line of division at the moment of abandoning "meditation" because he is treating of the night of the understanding. When he comes to deal with the night of the will he does not, in fact, discuss the point again, but it is clear from many other allusions that he would there have drawn the line at the moment of abandoning express "acts". Common experience corrects Fr Baker. The decision to abandon set meditation can be made very early in a spiritual course by principles of good sense; the other decision is far more serious, demanding true spiritual discretion, and it occurs normally at a real crisis in the soul's growth.

Having once made this initial mistake Fr Baker is drawn into another. Having labelled the prayer of forced acts "contemplative" he is compelled to make the limits of this prayer very extensive, ranging through every degree of increased purity up to what he calls a "passive union"; to clarify matters he makes within it a higher division which he labels (apparently following Barbanson) "aspirations". This arrangement leads him inevitably to a subdivision of contemplation into "active" and "passive" which not only runs counter to the dictum of St John and other great mystical theologians that "contemplation is to receive", but also leaves no place for the division of classical mystical theology between the human and the supernatural "modes" of acting, and between "operant" and "co-operant" grace. Actually, Fr Baker's "aspirations" include two theologically distinct forms of prayer, the one a simplified and elevated form of "acts of the will" and the other an infused prayer. He thus omits entirely (save in a not very satisfactory intercalated chapter) any mention of the true "intermediate" prayer, the so-called "prayer of simple regard", the "acquired contemplation" of many spiritual writers, of which there are several passing hints in St John's treatises and which he is known in practice to have taught to his novices.

Finally, the reader wonders now and then whether Fr Baker, in his flight from the mechanical and artificial "spirituality" of some of the "active livers" with whom he was brought in contact, has not fallen into a Charybdis of his own, by making prayer as an exercise, a pursuit, almost a life, into something with a mechanical efficacy of its own, the one clue and talisman. When all is said, the one single end of the soul's life is to be united in will with God through love of Him and one's neighbour—prayer it is no doubt, in the deepest, simplest sense, but not prayer as an effort or activity distinguished from other virtues or activities of the Christian life.

These flaws in Fr Baker's teaching, if they are really so, may detract from the value of *Sancta Sophia* as a manual of mystical theology and advanced contemplative prayer. They do not, however, seriously affect its value for the "discreet, well-minded soul", the "internal liver" for whom it was so laboriously composed. Such confusion as may exist does not affect at all the practical instruction of the first threequarters of the book, in which its greatest value consists. A soul well established on this basis, and with a sane liberty of spirit, will be directed to other guides, such as the great Carmelite saints, or will be enabled to follow, without book-learning, the guidance of the Holy Spirit. Moreover, Fr Baker is not, so to say, a logical heretic, or even consistent in his definitions. Alongside of the terminology and arrangement to which exception has been taken there are many sections, even in the later chapters of *Sancta Sophia*, which are not open to any criticism; some of them, indeed, would seem from verbal resemblances to be based directly upon St John himself. In consequence, it would be easy to find passages supporting an entirely different theoretical position to that which has been criticized. Perhaps some day a student of all Fr Baker's writings will show that his doctrine developed with his life, and that many of the faults of arrangement are those of his editor.

Whatever the explanation, and whatever the extent of his aberrations, they must not be thought to destroy the excellence of Fr Baker's work. The science of souls and of mystical theology are both extremely difficult fields for the writers of guide-books, partly because both learning and experience are needed, partly because the very simplicity of pure spirituality and the unsearchability of the ways of God elude the theoretician. Even the very greatest—St Teresa, St John of the Cross themselves—are open to criticism on many points of arrangement or expression, whereas the writers of amiable platitudes or arid textbooks can avoid all pitfalls and produce a work that never fired a soul with a single degree of charity. When all is said and done Fr Baker remains among the great, a "summity", as Abbot Cuthbert Butler would have said. When his book was first re-edited in its present form Bishop Hedley, who wrote on that occasion the most weighty appreciation of Fr Baker that has ever appeared (*Dublin Review*, October 1876, reprinted as C.T.S. pamphlet in 1915), remarked that the book was "a noviciate in itself". We may be allowed to end with the words of the editor of the volume, Abbot Norbert Sweeney:

> If it is a duty [he wrote] to apply to holy books the practice which the *Following of Christ* bids us observe towards holy persons, "not to dispute . . . as to who is more holy than another, or greater in the kingdom of heaven", it will not be right to give the preference to this work . . . over the many spiritual books which have helped on souls in the way of perfection. But it will not be right either to give to other books a preference over this.

X

RICHARD CHALLONER

By Joseph Cartmell

Richard Challoner's long life almost spanned the eighteenth century. He was born in 1691 and he died, in his ninetieth year, in 1781. It was the century of Voltaire and the Encyclopaedists. Scepticism was rife in the higher ranks of English society; as for the masses of the people, they were, as Wesley discovered, sunk in paganism. English Catholics could not escape the baneful influence of their environment; and, as an additional evil, they had to endure apparently unending proscription. The tragic result was that a number of prominent families, hitherto loyal, began to defect; and their defection involved in many cases the ruin of the centres of the Faith which they had maintained. One such family was the Gages of Firle in Sussex with whom part of Challoner's boyhood had been spent.

Faced with this critical situation, Challoner's immediate aim, as priest and bishop in London, was to ensure the survival of the remnant. His plan, method and achievement have been well summarized by Mgr Knox:

> Challoner, like his contemporary, John Wesley, saw that if a religious minority was to survive, it must have a culture of its own, a literature of its own. Like Wesley, he settled down with incredible energy to supply the lack himself, and formed, by sheer application, the type of culture which is still, on the whole, that of English Catholics, only leaving Faber to write the hymns. If we have since re-edited (for example) the *Garden of the Soul,* Challoner was the last man who would, or should, have complained. He was himself, like Wesley, an adapter, an abridger, a continuator, rather than an original genius.[1]

But this "culture of their own" which had as its first aim the saving of the Catholics from virtual extinction was not in its essence

[1] "Challoner and the Douay Version", in "Richard Challoner" (*Westminster Cathedral Chronicle*, 1946, p. 33).

something new. It was the traditional Catholicism of England, the faith of the ancient saints and, more recently, of the martyrs. What was in a sense new was the spirit which Challoner desired to infuse into the ancient faith—the spirit of the Counter-Reformation. The means of infusing this spirit, developed by Catholic reformers from the days of Trent, were doctrinal and spiritual instruction and the inculcation of serious, organized personal prayer. Two influences were particularly operative in forming in Challoner's mind and soul the culture he envisaged: Douay and St Francis de Sales. Douay was tenacious of the link through its founding fathers and first professors with pre-Reformation Catholic England. During its 150 years of existence it had been a bulwark of the faith, the intensity of its resistance made manifest by the martyrdom of over 160 of its sons. But Douay had also the distinction of being the first of the Tridentine seminaries, and its life and training were organized accordingly. From Douay, therefore, Challoner brought a love of England's Catholic past, a sense of the greatness and glory of the resistance to the Elizabethan Establishment, a spirit of no-surrender, and also a realization of the need to give Catholics an informed faith and a devotion to prayer.

By its situation Douay naturally came to some extent under the influence of French thought. For Challoner this thought was crystallized in St Francis de Sales. After the Bible St Francis was the chief formative factor in his life. Hence, when he comes to write, it is often the teaching of St Francis that he presents. "The all-pervading subject of the love of God is pure St Francis, even to the turns of expression," writes Canon Burton, and he adds: "so far as Challoner is to be ascribed to a given school, he must without hesitation be classed in the school of St Francis de Sales."[1] St Francis was an innovator. It was he who brought devotion out of the cloister and offered it to people living in the world. In this there is a reason, additional to his own predilection, why Challoner should turn to St Francis; he was writing for Catholics at large and not for priests only or religious. Someone has summed up in a sentence the ethos of Challoner's writing. It is the spirit of Douay successfully united to the method of St Francis de Sales.

Challoner's first major spiritual work was the *Garden of the Soul*, published in 1740. The title was traditional; there had been

[1] *The Life and Times of Bishop Challoner*, I, p. 353.

prayer-books called *Hortulus Animae* and *Paradisus Animae* in use on the Continent from the end of the fifteenth century. They, like all the Continental prayer-books, had been considerably revised and enlarged after the Council of Trent; extravagant prayers and indulgences had been eliminated; and a summary of Christian doctrine on the plan drawn up by St Peter Canisius, various spiritual instructions, and a number of devotions suited to the popular taste had been incorporated. In compiling the *Garden of the Soul* Challoner followed these models, adapting them to English usage. He had two English prayer-books to draw on. One was the *Primer,* a medieval compilation, written originally in Latin. It was put into English at the Reformation in two versions: one, Protestant, and accommodated to the tenets of the new religion; the other, Catholic. The last edition of the Catholic version was issued under James II. The other prayer-book was the *Manual of Devout Prayers*, first published, it seems, in 1583 and based on a Continental model. Challoner himself edited a revised and enlarged version of it in 1757.

The sub-title of the *Garden of the Soul* indicated its wide range of contents; it was "A Manual of Spiritual Exercises and Instructions for Christians who, living in the world, aspire to Devotion". It began with a Summary of Christian Faith, and included Lessons from the Gospels for Meditation; Feasts and Fasts; a Morning Exercise; the Meditations from the *Devout Life* of St Francis de Sales; Instructions and Devotions for Hearing Mass; Devotions for Sundays and Holidays (the *Te Deum*, selected psalms and canticles in English, the Universal Prayer, a paraphrase of the Lord's Prayer, and the Athanasian Creed); Sunday Vespers and Compline (in English); Benediction of the Blessed Sacrament; the Penitential Psalms; Evening Devotions for Families, including the Litany of the Saints (a Douay devotion) and Night Prayers; Instructions on the Spiritual Life; Instructions and Devotions for Confession (with a very detailed examination of conscience); Instructions and Devotions for Communion; Instructions and Devotions for the Sick; Prayers for the Dead; the Litanies of the Holy Name and of our Lady (replacing the Office of our Lady, traditional in the older prayer-books); and the Mysteries of the Rosary. In the seventh edition (1757) Challoner further included: A Manner of Serving Mass; Acts of Faith, Hope and Charity; Instructions and Devotions for Confirmation; the Recommendation of a Departing Soul; Jubilees and Indulgences; and the popular English prayer, the Jesus Psalter. In subsequent editions he made no fresh alterations; but later editors have transformed the book radically.

For a century and more English Catholics perused the *Garden of the Soul* so sedulously that the Oxford converts dubbed them from it. It clearly met a need, which was what Challoner intended; and it created a type of strong, earnest and undemonstrative Catholic of the kind that Challoner himself was. But it did not, as seems sometimes to have been thought, work a transformation in the English religious character. That character in its basic qualities of sobriety, moderation and practical good sense existed long before persecution drove it in upon itself; it can be traced in the English mystics of the fourteenth century, and later in St John Fisher, for example. And, despite the ampler devotional and liturgical life that is ours today and the many changes in our way of life that have come from industrial development and social evolution, the character still endures. "Naturam expelles furca, tamen usque recurret." "After sixty years," wrote the late Abbot Butler (in 1926), "it can be said that English Catholicism has not undergone any radical transformation; the stamp of Manning, Faber, Ward, has not been imprinted on it; no doubt their influence has told; but the old stock of English and Irish Catholicism, fire-tried in the long years of persecution and penal laws, has proved itself the strongest, and has maintained itself in its essential characteristics, and has come out 'dominant'; present-day Catholicism in England is more 'Ullathorne' than 'Manning'."[1]

Along with the *Garden of the Soul* Challoner had been preparing *Memoirs of Missionary Priests* which he published in two volumes (1741-2). Already before entering Douay he knew something of the story of the martyrs. He became a Catholic at Warkworth where his mother was housekeeper to Lady Holman. Lord Stafford, Lady Holman's father, and Philip Howard, her great-grandfather, had been martyred. The material for the *Memoirs* was abundant, and only a fraction of it had been published. The bulk remained in manuscript in the English colleges and religious houses abroad and in the library of Cuthbert Constable in York-

[1] *The Life and Times of Bishop Ullathorne*, II, p. 311.

shire. For the Douay records Challoner had the help of Alban Butler, then professor at the College, who transcribed them for him. His aim was to give a completely objective account. "We do not pretend," he wrote in the preface, "to make Panegyrics of any of these brave men, but merely to deliver short memoirs of what we found most remarkable in their lives and particularly in their deaths." So carefully did he work that later historians, who have had access to official documents which were not available to him and to the archives of the English colleges in Rome and the Iberian peninsula which he did not use, have found very little to correct. Lingard's verdict is well known, that the *Memoirs* were the best State Papers he had ever examined.

The *Memoirs* were designedly incomplete. Challoner confined himself to the missionary epoch, beginning with Cuthbert Mayne, and he dealt only briefly with martyrs, such as Edmund Campion, whose lives had already been written; but he included lay martyrs, perhaps by an afterthought. A point he was determined to make clear was that it was not for the alleged crime of treason that the martyrs suffered.

> As to the odious imputation of Treason [he wrote in the preface] . . . though we pretend not to act the Apologist, but only the Historian; yet we must acquaint our reader that we have inserted no one's name in our list, without being first fully convinced that his religion and conscience were his only Treason; which was certainly the case of all who suffered upon the Penal Statutes of Elizabeth, 27, viz.: either for being made priests by Roman Authority, and exercising their functions in England, or for harbouring and relieving such priests: and it no less certainly was the case of those who suffered for denying the Royal Supremacy, or for being reconciled to the Catholic Church: a thing the more evident, because there was not a man of them all, but might have saved his life, if he would but have conformed in matters of religion.

The one doubtful case that he accepted was that of Mary Queen of Scots.

The bishop's clear, calm objective presentation of facts, so different from the work of Foxe, gave the *Memoirs* genuine controversial value. Trained, as were all the Douay theologians, in the art of controversy, he never let slip an opportunity of upholding the Faith; and he was a formidable controversialist, despite his distaste for this type of writing. He preferred spiritual subjects; and the *Memoirs* had, along with historical truth, the definite spiritual purpose of inspiring his flock with fortitude by the example of the martyrs and with hope in the ultimate triumph of the Faith, since God's power and blessing were manifest in the constancy under torture of so many of their countrymen. However, Challoner's effort did not meet with immediate success. It was not till the next century that the *Memoirs* became standard spiritual reading in Catholic homes.

From the martyrs the bishop turned to the ancient saints and in 1745 published *Britannia Sancta*. Beginning with the dawn of Christianity in these islands, it recorded the lives of the most celebrated British, English, Scottish and Irish saints, 400 in all, with brief references to many others. He compiled it with his usual meticulous care, using the best sources available, St Bede the Venerable, the medieval *Nova Legenda Aurea, Anglia Sacra* (by the non-Catholic Henry Wharton), the Bollandists, and, for the Irish saints, Colgan, O.F.M., of Louvain and the Protestant Archbishop Ussher. It was Challoner's most substantial work; but it did not sell well, owing, in part, to its expensive production.

This work and its much smaller companion, *A Memorial of Ancient British Piety; or a British Martyrology* (1761), were meant to make the saints known not for private devotion only, but as a preparation for the re-establishment of public cult. The Sarum use had gone out with the Reformation; the priests from Douay and the other colleges abroad knew only the Roman rite with a universal calendar and no English Proper. For over twenty years Challoner pressed the Holy See for the restoration of the old English feasts. Benedict XIV conceded a little: in 1749 the feast of St Edmund, King and Martyr, and in 1754 that of St Bede the Venerable; but it was not till 1774 that an English Supplement, containing twenty-two feasts, was granted by Clement XIV. For some of these feasts and for others, which he had hoped for but which were not sanctioned until the next century, Challoner drew up the lessons of the second nocturn.

Between 1748 and 1752 the bishop was engaged in bringing out his revision of the Douay-Rheims Bible. His intention was to provide the Catholic public with a handy edition in a language they could understand, free from the Latinisms, archaic expressions and occasional overliteralness of the original, and with new explanatory notes suited to contemporary need He was assisted, but to what extent is unknown, by Fr Robert Pinkard, a Douay priest, canon of the Old Chapter, and London agent of Douay. Even so, it was a colossal undertaking; and so difficult that the revisers issued three separate revisions of the New Testament between 1749 and 1752, the last being the most drastic of all in its changes. Challoner made considerable use of the Authorized Version, more particularly in the final revision, with the result, in Newman's opinion, that in phraseology and diction Challoner's Bible is nearer to the Protestant than to Douay. In our current Douay Bibles this similarity is not so apparent, since they represent a composite text, based mainly on the earlier Challoner revision of 1749-50.[1]

Challoner's work has been severely criticized. "The version is imperfect," wrote Charles Butler. "A more correct version is perhaps the greatest spiritual want of the English Catholics." Wiseman regretted that no one properly qualified and properly authorized had been found to undertake such corrections and improvements as would finally settle the text;

> to call it any longer the Douay or Rheims version is an abuse of terms. It has been altered and modified till scarce any verse remains as it was originally published : and so far as simplicity and energy of style are concerned, the changes are in general for the worse.[2]

Wiseman's strictures were not directed exclusively at Challoner; for, while the Old Testament remains substantially as he finally revised it, the New Testament has been tampered with time and again since his day. It would have been better if, instead of this patching and darning, as Knox has called it, an entirely new translation had been made; but that would have demanded a leisured scholar, which Challoner was not, and one equipped, as were the original translators, with Hebrew as well as Latin and Greek. However, in spite of its defects, Challoner's version held the field until the appearance of the Knox Bible in the 1940s; nor is it yet superseded. But the bishop's ambition to make English

[1] Cf. *A Catholic Commentary*, 30a and following.

[2] *The Dublin Review*, II, p. 276.

Catholics steady readers of the Bible as a whole was disappointed.

> Whether from inherited distrust or because after all his efforts the Bible remained mostly unintelligible, the result never followed. To this day, so far as English-speaking Catholics are concerned, the Bible consists of a handful of fragments read out in church, two psalms, a remembered phrase here and there in the liturgy, and a few dozen dogmatic texts.[1]

It is clear from the *Meditations* that the bishop himself knew the Bible intimately; quotations, reminiscences and even biblical turns of phrase abound. Such familiarity could be due only to unremitting study and meditation. "To get the full flavour of a herb," wrote St John Chrysostom, "it must be pressed between the fingers. It is the same with the Scriptures." Challoner's Bible must have been the best-thumbed book in his sparse library. Herein lies the ultimate source of his spiritual greatness; in St Gregory's phrase, he found the heart of God in the words of God.

Challoner's first publication, in 1728, shortly before he left Douay for good, was a little book of meditations for each day of the month, with the homely title, *Think Well On't*. It had a wide appeal, and went through many editions. In 1754 he published the much larger work in two volumes, *Meditations for Every Day in the Year*. This work also has been many times republished and, along with the *Garden of the Soul*, it has exerted a profound influence on the lives of many English-speaking Catholics; and of some non-Catholics also. It was always a favourite with John Keble.

The ground-plan of the *Meditations* is doctrinal. Milner considered it "the most valuable and useful body of practical divinity in our language". Into this plan Challoner inserts a second scheme based on the liturgical seasons and feasts. His sources are the Scriptures, dogmatic and moral theology and the chief spiritual writers, notably St Francis de Sales, St Teresa and the *Imitation*. The matter is solid and substantial, with certain key-themes running through it: the love of God and of Christ, the need and value of prayer, faith in the Church's teaching, the seriousness of human life in view of eternity. The style exemplifies the rule set by the Elder Cato: "Rem tene, verba sequentur." It is direct and it drives the points home and at the same time moves with the theme,

[1] Knox: *Challoner and the Douay Version*, p. 36.

reflecting a mind long schooled in thought and prayer. In arranging the meditations Challoner keeps to the mere essentials; three considerations and a conclusion; but in the preface he insists on the necessity of a proximate preparation before meditation and draws up a scheme of concluding affections, arranged in a general way according to the subjects meditated and the degree of a soul's progress in the spiritual life.

Challoner does not accept the view that mental prayer is difficult. It is easy, he writes, to think and love; it is easy to ponder over the great truths of the faith and the mysteries of our Lord's life and Passion; it is easy to talk to God; and in these three things you have the whole sum of meditation. But he knows that many do in fact find it difficult and become discouraged; and so he ends his preface with an exhortation to perseverance:

> What thou art seeking after is a treasure of infinite value; if it costs thee some pains in digging for it, it will abundantly recompense all thy labour. This exercise is the true Christian philosophy, consisting in the search and love of true wisdom; even that wisdom which is so much extolled by the Spirit of God in Holy Writ, and which comes down from God, and carries us up to God; this is the science of the Saints.

How well he himself was versed in that science the *Meditations*—the most self-revealing of his writings—make clear. They confirm Milner's portrait of him in his Funeral Panegyric:

> It was in the exercise of holy prayer, especially of mental prayer, in which he placed his chief delight. This he regularly practised himself for a considerable space each morning, and this he constantly recommended to others, not only to his Ecclesiastics, but to all Christians in general, as the main channel of divine grace, and the only light by which they are enabled to discover the real value of things, temporal and eternal. God alone was witness to the favours he received in this heavenly exercise; but to see him only at his ordinary vocal prayers, and to observe the respect, the recollection, and the fervour with which he performed them, was enough to inspire the most tepid with devotion. To speak the truth, this spirit of recollection was so familiar to him, that he never seemed to lose sight of God amidst the most intricate business, and thus strictly fulfilled the precept of the Apostle, and of Christ Himself, of praying always and without ceasing.

Mystical prayer was somewhat out of favour in Challoner's time owing to the dangers, partly real and partly imaginary, of quietism. Directors encouraged the devout to keep to meditation; it was safe and salutary: it did not encourage illusions, it schooled the soul in virtue, and it was a valuable ascetic discipline. Challoner was therefore at one with his age in stressing the value of meditation to the apparent exclusion of other forms of mental prayer. He was, of course, aware of other, and higher forms; of the prayer of faith or acquired contemplation from his reading of St Francis de Sales, and of infused contemplation in its several degrees from the works of St Teresa. That he had experience of any of these higher forms can only be conjectured. Milner spoke of his remarkable spirit of recollection, and this would seem to indicate that he was, like Hierotheus of the Areopagite, "doctus non solum discens sed patiens divina". "Pati divina" in this sense means to be wise by the gift of wisdom, to be ruled by the Holy Spirit and to have become to a considerable extent a passive instrument in His hands. Prayer and the gift of wisdom are co-ordinated; they grow together, so that, as a man becomes dominated by the gift of wisdom, he reaches a corresponding passivity in prayer, that is, infused contemplation. This does not mean that Challoner attained the mystical flights of a St Teresa. Anything higher than the prayer of quiet, the lowest step on the mystical ladder, would be all but impossible in the workaday, harassed, preoccupied life he had to live. Given the prayer of quiet, he became the saint that everybody said he was (they called him "Venerable") by the full renunciation of his own will in a life of strict asceticism, much trial, and an unremitting apostolate.

We have considered Challoner's chief works only; but there were many others: books of devotion, translations, of which one, *The Following of Christ*, continued to be popular until recent times; a revision, on which our present catechism is based, of the Douay Catechism; a re-edition of the works of his master in the faith and, in part, prototype, John Gother. The writer on English Spirituality in the *Dictionnaire de spiritualité* says that the eighteenth century in England produced no work of note. This is true, if he has in mind original work. But it would be obviously unfair to judge Challoner's achievement by his originality. The age in which he lived did not call for originality; but what it needed he supplied. He was the most widely and permanently influential of the line of writers going back to the Reformation.

At the end of his life Challoner prophesied that a new people would arise. The beginnings of emancipation had in fact already appeared with the passing of the Relief Act of 1778. It is clear that his prophecy was the final expression of his long-cherished and unshaken hope; for his written work and other work also—the founding of the schools at Standon Lordship and Sedgeley Park, for instance—had as their purpose not merely the consolidation of the Catholic position but also, and perhaps especially, the ultimate, though possibly long-delayed, triumph of the Catholic cause.

Hurter has aptly described the greatest of the Vicars Apostolic: "Vir vere admirabilis, Sancto Francisco Salesio et Sancto Alphonso Ligorio comparandus, temporibus difficillimis Ecclesiae Catholicae columen per Angliam."[1]

[1] *Nomenclator Literarius*, V, p. 446 (ed. 1912).

XI

CARDINAL NEWMAN

By H. Francis Davis

Newman's greatest gift was undoubtedly his influence for spiritual good. He knew it, and he always wanted to employ it for God's glory and the salvation of souls. It must have needed all his faith to seem to risk the loss of all this influence when he became a Catholic. Fortunately, his faith in God's providence was great enough to meet this trial calmly. "As to influence," he said, "the whole world is one great vanity, and I trust I am not set on anything in it—I trust not."[1] It caused him much human distress that, during his first years as a Catholic, he seemed to do so little for souls, as contrasted with what he had done as a Protestant. He was, however, consoled before his death with the thought that "it is the rule of God's Providence that we should succeed by failure".[2] When he was made cardinal, the *Whitehall Review* spoke of the unique influence Newman had by then acquired on English-speaking civilization. "There is no man in England more truly honoured and respected." The *Daily News* at his death said that "thousands know that they have lost one in whom their faith rested, one who was a living incarnation of the defensibility of faith, one on whose authority they could quote an argument to sustain them in their acceptance of the unseen". He lived to see his influence as a Catholic more widespread than it ever had been as an Anglican.

Contrary to a superficial view of his talents, Newman was a man of action. It was a need of his nature to help others, and men and women were never wanting who looked to him, and found in him, an inspiration to a new-found faith.

Newman knew of two false kinds of Christianity, a sentimental and a rationalistic, both of them doctrinally agnostic. His lifelong message was that such Christianities were not genuine. To the

[1] A. Mozley, *Letters and Correspondence of J. H. Newman*, 1891, II, p. 471.

[2] W. Ward, *The Life of John Henry Cardinal Newman*, II, p. 285.

agnostic he said, reflecting his own conviction: "It surely cannot be meant that we should be undecided all our days. We were made for action, and for right action—for thought, and for true thought. Let us live while we live; let us be alive and doing . . ."[1] It was in this spirit that Newman by-passed all the committees at the beginning of the Oxford Movement, and undertook, at first almost alone, the unremitting labour of the Tracts, combined with the untiring personal influence of his sermons and friendly correspondence and intercourse.

We are not surprised, then, that his most characteristic message, in season and out of season, was an appeal to a deeper and sincere faith. Faith is what the modern world lacks. Faith is what Christ offers. Faith is that without which Christian prayer and life are impossible. The world has forgotten the very nature of faith; often enough it puts sentiment or opinion in its place. In this way doctrine, God's life-giving word, is lost. Newman himself had begun life, as he always insisted, with a grave temptation against the faith at the early age of fifteen. The grace by which God had saved him from infidelity he always looked upon as the most important grace of his life. In gratitude, he wished only to be able to bring God's word to others.

There were not only unbelievers who were to be brought to the faith, there were believers who were to be taught to live as though they believed, to live as though Christ had come and were their Saviour, to live as though He were the Way and Truth and Life, and as though it really mattered whether we listened to Him. Moreover, when we listen, Newman pointed out, we must not listen to our listening, but to the truths God teaches us. Faith is not feeling, but the acceptance of Christ, who is its Object. It must lead to action with regard to that Object. One without the other would be a mockery.

Faith, for Newman, is self-effacing. It looks out of itself and beyond itself, to the God who reveals Himself.

> Thus the true Christian pierces through the veil of this world and sees the next. He holds intercourse with it; he addresses God, as a child might address his parent, with as clear a view of Him, and with as unmixed a confidence in Him; with deep reverence indeed, and godly fear and awe, but still with certainty and exact-

[1] *Discussions and Arguments*, 1873, p. 214.

ness: as St Paul says, "I know whom I have believed," with the prospect of judgement to come to sober him, and the assurance of present grace to cheer him.[1]

Faith is opposed to that dangerous self-centred type of religion to be found in the world, which is only interested in either our own virtues, or, perhaps still worse, in the power we have of speaking of spiritual things.

> Some persons answer at once and without hesitation, that "to have faith is to feel oneself to be nothing, and God everything; it is to be convinced of sin, to be conscious one cannot save oneself and to wish to be saved by Christ our Lord; and that it is, moreover, to have the love of Him warm in one's heart, and to rejoice in Him, to desire His glory, and to resolve to live to Him and not to the world". But I will answer, with all due seriousness, as speaking on a serious subject, that this is *not* faith. . . . Though a man spoke like an angel, I would not believe him, on the mere ground of his speaking.[2]

It is owing to the fallacy of mistaking feelings for faith that people are led to be disturbed because their attendance at church does not arouse religious emotions. It is owing to the same fallacy when people of the world say that the religion one chooses is a matter of temperament. The fault of too great reliance upon subjective feelings is found even among Catholics, in spite of their objective attitude to the faith. Ultimately it was characteristic of the heresy of modernism, foreseen clearly by Newman, to reduce dogma itself to a codification of religious experience.

> I would say this then [wrote Newman] that a system of doctrine has risen up during the last three centuries, in which faith or spiritual-mindedness is contemplated and rested on as the end of religion instead of Christ. I do not mean to say that Christ is not mentioned as the Author of all good, but that stress is laid rather on the believing than on the Object of belief, on the comfort and persuasiveness of the doctrine rather than on the doctrine itself. And in this way religion is made to consist in contemplating ourselves, instead of Christ; not simply in looking to Christ, but in seeing that we look to Christ, not in His Divinity and Atonement, but in our conversion and faith in them. . . . The fault here spoken

[1] *Parochial and Plain Sermons*, Catholic ed. (hereafter referred to as *P.S.*), viii, p. 211.
[2] *P.S.*, i, pp. 70-171.

> of is the putting the state of a believer as a *more prominent* subject of the Gospel than the nature, attributes, and work of Him who has given it. . . . The true preaching of the Gospel is to preach Christ. But the fashion of the day has been, instead of this, to attempt to convert by insisting on conversion. . . . And thus faith and (what is called) spiritual-mindedness are dwelt on as *ends* and obstruct the view of Christ, just as the Law was perverted by the Jews.[1]

One might say that the centrality of God and Christ in true Faith was not so much one of the root principles as *the* one root principle of Newman's spiritual teaching. He had diagnosed the modern malady, and all his life he sought to apply the only remedy. It is significant of his own firm hold on the faith that there is never the least hint of hesitation as to the Catholic soundness of this position. One has only to look through the titles of his sermons to realize that Newman was ever trying to turn men away from themselves, their own self-righteousness, their self-complacency, their self-seeking, their self-interest, so as to teach them to contemplate God in Christ.

It is important to remember this when we consider what is sometimes referred to as Newman's introspectiveness. Introspective he was by natural temperament. Perhaps this very fact helped to make him the more suspicious of a religion which began and ended in introspectiveness. To him, undoubtedly, as to the two St Teresas and St Augustine, religion did involve a looking inwards. But what he saw when he looked inwards was not his feelings, but two objective beings, the most important beings to each one of us, himself and his Creator. He saw himself as an object in God's presence, the principal object that he had to watch over and perfect with the grace that God would give him. But it was not his own convictions about himself that counted, but Christ's revelation. People too often want "to identify Christian doctrine with their own individual convictions, to sink its supernatural character, and to constitute themselves the prophets, not the recipients, of Divine Truth".[2] It is what I am in the sight of my Maker that counts, not what I seem to my own consciousness. "Sublime, unlooked-for doctrine, yet most true! To every one of us there are

[1] *Lectures on Justification*, ed. 1838, pp. 372-4.

[2] *Oxford University Sermons*, Catholic ed., pp. 172-3.

but two beings in the whole world, himself and God. . . ."[1] This realization that the spiritual life, at the deepest level, is lived out by each individual soul in the immediate presence of God, came to him at his first "conversion" from sin to God at the age of sixteen. It remained with him all his life. ". . . from a boy I had been led to consider that my Maker and I, His creature, were the two beings, luminously such, *in rerum natura*".[2]

An ungrounded fear that this truth was not recognized in the Church of Rome had for a time held him back. He had heard the common accusation made against Rome that dogmas, devotions, rites, sacraments, angels and saints were allowed by her to intervene between God and the soul. It was an immense relief to him to find that this was not so, and that his own childhood conviction had been in harmony with Catholic tradition. He found in the devotions of the Church of Rome that it is again "face to face", "solus cum solo", in the most vital matters between man and his God.

> He alone creates; He alone has redeemed; before His awful eyes we go in death; in the vision of Him is our eternal beatitude. What I can speak of with great confidence is the effect produced on me a little later by studying the Exercises of St Ignatius. For here again, in a matter consisting in the purest and most direct acts of religion; in the intercourse between God and the soul, during a season of recollection, of repentance, of good resolution, of enquiry into vocation, the soul was "sola cum solo"; there was no cloud interposed between the creature and the Object of his faith and love. The command practically enforced was "My son, give me thy heart."[3]

Newman's very conviction of God's existence was in his mind closely connected with this conviction of his life as being lived through in the presence of His Maker and final goal. "I am a Catholic," he wrote in the Apologia, "by virtue of my believing in a God; and if I am asked why I believe in a God, I answer that it is because I believe in myself, for I feel it impossible to believe in my own existence (and of that fact I am quite sure) without believing also in the existence of Him, who lives as a Personal, All-

[1] *P.S.*, i, p. 20.
[2] *Apologia pro Vita Sua,* ed. 1890, p. 195.
[3] Op. cit., pp. 195-6.

seeing, All-judging Being in my conscience."[1] The more Newman was driven back into his own loneliness, the more he found God waiting for him. He consoled his sister on one occasion, when she was worried about him : "I am not more lonely than I have been a long while. God intends me to be lonely; He has so framed my mind that I am in a great measure beyond the sympathies of other people and thrown upon myself. God, I trust, will support me in following whither He leads."

It was a fault of many people, he was convinced, to live by a light other than that of the faith. Too often they forget the presence of God in their souls.

> Common men see God at a distance; in their attempts to be religious they feebly guide themselves as by a distant light, and are obliged to calculate and search about for the path. But the long practised Christian, who, through God's mercy, has brought God's presence near to him, the elect of God, in whom the Blessed Spirit dwells, he does not look out of doors for the traces of God; he is moved by God dwelling in him, and needs not but act on instinct. I do not say there is any man altogether such, for this is an angelic life; but it is the state of mind to which vigorous prayer and watching tend.[2]

It is the same with God's messages. The religious man does not see them, as it were, at a distance. They tell of facts, which affect us here and now. Coming from God, they are accepted as fully as we accept the truth of what we see.

"If it be true (as we hold it to be), it must be of consequence. A religious mind is ever looking out of itself, is ever pondering God's words, is ever 'looking into' them with the Angels, is ever realizing to itself Him on whom it depends, and who is the centre of all truth and good."[3]

The importance of a God-centred view like that of Newman's is evident in deciding the right attitude to sin. A sense of guilt can be something morbid when it is purely a question of subjective feelings. It is the proper attitude of the sinful creature when the sinner puts himself in the presence of the personal God he has disobeyed. "To thee only have I sinned, and have done evil before

[1] Op. cit., p. 198.
[2] *P.S.*, i. p. 75.
[3] *P.S.*, iv, pp. 292, 294.

thee." The non-religious philosopher, Newman tells us, does not mind admitting that sin is an imperfection of our nature, even that it is harmful to our fellow-men, that it destroys our dignity and self-esteem. "But Christianity, in addition to this confession, requires him to acknowledge himself to be a rebel in the sight of God, and a breaker of that fair and goodly order of things which the Creator once established."[1] Some modern writers reflect the subjective attitude to sin when they call it "a growing-pain or a cramp of the evolving powers of our nature" or a species of "mal-adaptation". It is significant that the German Protestant theologian, Schleiermacher, with his very subjective approach to theology, says little in all his works either of the personal God or of sin. ". . . the Christian acknowledges that he has fallen away from that rank in creation which he originally held; that he is guilty in the court of heaven, and is continually doing things odious in the sight of the Divine holiness."[2]

The Christian sense of sin involves a broken harmony between persons, rather than a mere imperfection.

> If, on doing wrong, we feel the same tearful, broken-hearted sorrow which overwhelms us on hurting a mother; if, on doing right we enjoy the same sunny serenity of mind, the same soothing, satisfactory delight which follows on our receiving praise from a father, we certainly have within us the image of some person, to whom our love and veneration look, in whose smile we find our happiness, for whom we yearn, towards whom we direct our pleading, in whose anger we are troubled and waste away.[3]

It is right for us to regard the church as our home, and no one loved more the Catholic practice of visiting the Blessed Sacrament than Newman. Yet the Catholic will never forget the majesty of God whose temple the church is. Regarding the Eucharist, he remarked soon after his conversion: "Catholicism is a different religion from Anglicanism" because of its devotion to the Eucharist, and he spoke of the "blessedness of finding, when you enter a Catholic Church, a Treasure Unutterable, the Presence of the Eternal Word Incarnate, the Wisdom of the Father, who, even when He had done His work, would not leave us, but rejoices still

[1] *Oxford University Sermons*, Catholic ed., pp. 12, 13.
[2] Op. cit., p. 13.
[3] *Grammar of Assent*, 1891, p. 109.

to humble Himself by abiding in places on earth for our sakes while He reigns not the less on the right hand of God." Yet, on the other hand, "we must in all respects act as if we saw God; that is, if we believe that God is here, we shall keep silence; we shall not laugh, or talk, or whisper during the Service, as many young persons do; we shall not gaze about us."[1]

The true Christian attitude is not to demand, "Is religion necessary for man?", "Is prayer necessary to man's self-fulfilment?", "Have I faith?" or "Am I spiritual-minded?"; but rather, "What does Christ tell us?" "How can I please Him?" "How does He wish me to pray?" or "How can I become more like Him?"

Even Catholics frequently fail in not practically submitting their reasons to God's awesome truth, goodness and majesty.

> Men confess that He is infinite, yet they start and object, as soon as His infinitude comes in contact with their imagination and acts upon their reason. They cannot bear the fulness, the superabundance, the inexhaustible flowing forth, and "vehement rushing", and encompassing flood of the Divine attributes. They restrain and limit them by their own standard, they fashion them by their own model: and when they discern ought of the unfathomable depth, the immensity of any single excellence or perfection of the Divine Nature, His love or His justice, or His power, they are at once offended, and turn away, and refuse to believe.[2]

Faith, however, for Newman did not stop short at this living in God's presence. It means, as already touched upon, learning from God. Religion involves revelation, and revelation involves dogma. It is no answer to say that the doctrines of the Creed are not found in Scripture. "If there is a Revelation, there must be a doctrine; both our reason and our hearts tell us so. If it is not in Scripture, it is somewhere else; it is to be sought elsewhere."[3] There were religious theorists in Newman's time, as in our time, who wished to do away with dogmas. He claimed that they would never have much influence with ordinary Christians. People

> want to be assured that what seems to them true, is true; they want something to lean on, holier, diviner, more stable than their

[1] *P.S.*, viii, p. 9.
[2] *Discourses to Mixed Cong.*, 1892, pp. 309, 310.
[3] *Discussions and Arguments*, 1873, p. 132.

own minds. They have an instinctive feeling that there is an external, eternal truth which is their only stay; and it mocks them, after being told of a Revelation, to be assured, next, that that Revelation tells us nothing certain, nothing which we do not know without it, nothing distinct from our own impressions concerning it, whatever they may be—nothing such, as to exist independently of that shape and colour into which our own individual mind happens to throw it.[1]

Religion then offers us an insight into the next world. The spiritual life, from one point of view, consists in making that insight a fruitful one, influencing our lives. Some of Newman's most impressive passages are those where he is describing the fruitfulness of the Christian image of Christ on early Christians. It is not doctrine in the abstract, but the persons and facts to which the doctrine points that form the life of Christianity. "It was the Thought of Christ, not a corporate body or a doctrine, which inspired that zeal which the historian so poorly comprehends; and it was the Thought of Christ which gave a life to the promise of that eternity, which without Him would be, in any soul, nothing short of an intolerable burden."[2] The Christian doctrines are facts, not opinions; they refer to real persons. The doctrine of the Assumption follows from what Mary is, and Christians' contemplation of what she is, rather than a logical deduction from abstract doctrines.

The ancients worshipped; they went out of their own minds into the Infinite Temple which was around them. They saw Christ in the Gospels, in the Creed, in the Sacraments and other Rites; in the visible structure and ornaments of His House, in the Altar, and in the Cross; and, not content with giving the service of their eyes, they gave Him their voices, their bodies, and their time, gave up their rest by night and their leisure by day, all that could evidence the offering of their hearts to Him.[3]

Many people spoke of the realization that Newman succeeded in conveying to them of another world, far greater than the world they see, both in their own souls, and all around them. Like St Leo in his famous Christmas sermon, Newman was at pains to

[1] *Ibid., p.* 133.
[2] *Grammar of Assent,* 1891, p. 465.
[3] *Lectures on Justification,* 1838, pp. 337-8.

give people a deeper and more living faith in the dignity and glory of their own souls in God's sight.

> O fearful follower of Christ, how is it that thou hast never thought of what thou art and what is in thee? Art thou not Christ's purchased possession? Has He not rescued thee from the devil, and put a new nature within thee? Did He not in Baptism cast out the evil spirit and enter into thee Himself, and dwell in thee as if thou hadst been an Archangel, or one of the Seraphim who worship before Him continually? Much and rightly as thou thinkest of thy sins, hast thou no thought, I do not say of gratitude, but of wonder, of admiration, of amazement, of awful and overpowering transport at what thou art through grace?[1]

The way in which Newman spoke of the great invisible world of God around us so impressed people as to make them declare that he seemed himself to be dwelling in that other world, and to visit us to reveal to us its glory. "There are two worlds, 'the visible and the invisible', as the Creed speaks, the world we see, and the world we do not see; and the world which we do not see exists as the world we do see. It really exists, though we see it not. The world that we see we know to exist, *because* we see it. . . . It is an immense world; it reaches to the stars. . . . It is everywhere; and it seems to leave no room for any other world.

"And yet in spite of this universal world which we see, there is another world, quite as far-spreading, quite as close to us, and more wonderful; another world all around us, though we see it not, and more wonderful than the world we see, for this reason if for no other, that we do not see it."[2] He reminds us of the inhabitants of that other world, of those who have lived in this world, whom we think to have died, and yet who live more fully than we do. He speaks of the angels who minister to human beings throughout this world. "We are then in a world of spirits, as well as in a world of sense, and we hold communion with it, and take part in it, though we are not conscious of doing so."[3]

Newman was deeply convinced of the importance for the Christian of choosing whether we shall be dominated by the world we

[1] *P.S.*, iv, p. 140.
[2] *P.S.*, iv, pp. 200-201.
[3] *P.S.*, iv, p. 205.

see or by the unseen world. Since the fall, the world we see is under the control of a spirit which opposes the Gospel. Where the Christian walks by faith, the world walks by sight. Where Christians see through the light of faith, the world walks in the darkness of unbelief. These two comparisons occur; the first, before Newman's conversion, from the pulpit of St Mary's, the second, in his Catholic days, from the pulpit of the Oratory.

The world walks by sight. It seeks for the things it sees. At its best, it strives after good government, the acquisition of wealth, the prevention and relief of want, and all forms of temporal prosperity. It sees nothing beyond this life. It sometimes takes such a hold on shallow religious minds as to persuade them that the millennium has already come, that Christianity is no longer concerned with "obsolete dogmas about another world", but concerns itself with the good of man here below.

The world is impatient of the things that are not seen. They form a challenge to its comfort and sense of security. "Does not the world scoff at all that is glorious, all that is majestic, in our holy religion? Does it not speak against the special creations of God's grace? Does it not disbelieve the possibility of purity and chastity? Does it not slander the profession of celibacy? Does it not deny the virginity of Mary?"[1] The impatience with dogma that Newman witnessed, and the rejection of many distinctively Christian virtues, is common today. Purity, obedience and recognition of authority are not virtues favoured by "the world".

The world that boasts that it has its feet on the earth is sadly blind to the things of heaven. It lacks the light of grace, by which alone it can see. "Not the keenest eyes can see in the dark. Now, though your mind be the eye, the grace of God is the light."[2] Itself not seeing, the world cannot understand those who live by faith. The world thinks the dogmas which are Christianity's life-blood a burden we would gladly reject.

> Yes [comments Newman ironically] that I suppose is the true relief, to believe nothing at all, or, at least, not to be bound to believe anything; to believe first one thing, then another; to believe what we please for as long as we please; that is, not really to believe, but to have an opinion about everything, and let nothing

[1] *Discourses to Mixed Cong.*, 1892, p. 167.
[2] Op. cit., p. 171.

sit close upon us, to commit ourselves to nothing, to keep the unseen world altogether at a distance.[1]

If the world's only defect were blindness to the Faith, its claims would at least be specious to all whose faith is weak. But, mixed with all its specious goodness, there is always sin, even in the world's understanding of the term. In his sermon, "The World our Enemy," Newman shows that the world does nothing without spoiling it. Its great rulers are marred by tyranny and injustice. It substitutes expediency for justice and charity. It has a spirit hostile to meekness and humility.

There is no space in one essay to show how Newman developed this theme of the essential opposition between true Christianity, which lives by faith, and the spirit of this world, which lives by outward appearances. In his own life, Newman always tried to keep free from a love of the world's praise.

> It has been my *lifelong* prayer [he wrote in his private diary in 1860] and Thou hast granted it, that I should be set aside in this world. Now let me make it once again. O Lord, bless what I write and prosper it—let it do much good, let it have much success but let no praise come to me on that account in my lifetime. Let me go on living, let me die, as I have hitherto lived. Long before I knew St Philip, I wished "nesciri". Let me more and more learn from Thy grace "sperni", and "spernere me sperni".[2]

The greatest temptation to the Christian is to try to serve both worlds, with the result that they really live by sight and serve the world, while they appear outwardly even to themselves and show themselves to others as satisfactory Christians. Such counterfeit Christianity is always a kind of insincerity or hypocrisy. The counterfeit Christian has hidden faults that his subconscious carefully prevents him from realizing. He may go into retirement out of laziness and pusillanimity, and persuade himself it is love of contemplation. He practises the outward forms of religion, and thinks he has true Christian holiness. He speaks fluently of religious matters, and thinks he possesses the virtues and the devotion that he

[1] *Ibid.*, p. 185.
[2] John Henry Newman, *Autobiographical Writings*, 1956, p. 252.

praises. He depreciates others and gains a reputation for the virtues he desiderates in his neighbour. And when he finds a deep holiness and otherworldliness he cannot deny, he excuses his worldliness as realism or a keeping of one's feet firmly on the earth. Lastly, he substitutes worldly virtues for true Christian ones, superficial ones for genuine holiness. A deeper commitment than his he regards as fanaticism. His faith is half-hearted.

In one way or another, the spirituality which Newman lived and preached was a call to be faithful to the unseen world of God's revelation, together with a warning of the dangers and speciousness of the unbelieving religion of the world. One of the last of Newman's published sermons, to the seminary students of the Birmingham diocese, in 1873, was on "The Infidelity of the Future." "The special peril of the time before us is the spread of that plague of infidelity, that the Apostles and our Lord Himself have predicted as the worst calamity of the last times of the Church."[1] Could we more fittingly close than with the words of one of Newman's meditations:

> I believe, because Thou hast spoken, O Lord. I joyfully accept Thy word about Thyself. Thou must know what Thou art—and who else? Not surely, dust and ashes, except so far as Thou tellest me.... I wish to lead a life of faith.... O my God, let me never forget this truth—that not only art Thou my Life, but my only Life! Thou art the Way, the Truth, and the Life. Thou art my Life, and the Life of all who live. All men, all I know, all I meet, all I see and hear of, live not unless they live by Thee. They live in Thee, or else they live not at all. No one can be saved out of Thee. Let me never forget this in the business of the day.[2]

[1] *Catholic Sermons of Cardinal Newman*, London, 1957, p. 121; *Faith and Prejudice*, New York, 1956, p. 117.

[2] *Meditations and Devotions*, 1953 ed., pp. 281-2.

XII

NEWMAN'S SPIRITUALITY: ITS VALUE TODAY

By C. Stephen Dessain *of the Oratory*

A French Carmelite, Fr Albert of the Annunciation, remarked recently on the importance of Newman for the General Council which is imminent. The Eastern Patriarchs have already called attention to the Western developments in doctrine which have taken place since 1054, the year of the Schism, as constituting an obstacle to unity. Hence it becomes imperative to show, with Newman's help, that this same development was in progress during the period between the Apostles and 1054. If Newman's teaching on Development has a decisive part to play in promoting unity among Christians, this is perhaps even more the case with his spiritual teaching, which can help to bridge not only the gulf of schism, but that of material heresy, and unite in a common devotion Catholic and non-Catholic Christians in Britain and America.

Newman himself realized that he could be the means of bringing Anglicans and Catholics together, and, with this in view, allowed his friend and former curate William Copeland to publish a large volume of selections from his Anglican sermons. "I think we quite agree," Newman wrote to him on 13 October 1877, "that the object of the selection is to cultivate a unity of ethos among those who otherwise differ," and in his preface Copeland expressed the hope that the volume would be welcomed, because those sermons had been included in it which "from their bearing on the formation of the Christian character may best contribute to the promotion of mutual sympathy between estranged communions and alienated hearts".[1]

This hope of promoting a similarity of outlook between Catholics and non-Catholics was nothing new. Some years earlier Newman wrote to one of the Dominican nuns at Stone about the *Life*

[1] *Selection from the Parochial and Plain Sermons of John Henry Newman*, 1878, p. vi.

they had just published of their saintly foundress and his great friend, Mother Margaret Hallahan, which they seemed to fear had not effected many conversions:

> ... there are two reasons for writing quite distinct from conversion, and, considering all things, I prefer them to any other reason —the one is to edify Catholics. Catholics are so often *raw*. Many do not know their religion—many do not know the reasons for it [i.e. the purpose of it].... The other end which is so important, is what I call levelling up. If we are to convert souls savingly they must have the due preparation of heart, and if England is to be converted there must be a great move of the national mind to a better sort of religious sentiment. Wesleyans, Anglicans, Congregationalists, Unitarians, must be raised to one and the same (what we used to call at Oxford) "ethos". That is the same moral and intellectual state of mind. To bring them to this is "levelling up".

I

Newman's spiritual teaching, leaving aside that done privately, is for the most part confined to his Anglican period and contained in his published sermons. Thus it can still make its appeal to our separated brethren, and speaks a language they understand. Yet it has led many to the Church, in Newman's own day and since, it is fundamentally Catholic, and experience shows that it has the strongest attraction for those who belong to "the most sure sect of our religion" and who are "more abundantly zealous for the traditions". Go to a Cistercian or a Carthusian Monastery and you will find them reading Newman's Anglican sermons, delighting in them, and sometimes even learning English in order to appreciate them better. And we may add, Go as student to St Sulpice and you will be given *Parochial and Plain Sermons* for your spiritual reading. Go to the Gregorian University in Rome, and you will find a course of lectures given there each year, by a distinguished Jesuit, on Newman's spiritual teaching. The French Carmelite already mentioned is writing articles on Newman's spirituality in his Review *Carmel*, and hopes to add to the number of the sermons available in French translations. In Germany the eight volumes of *Parochial and Plain Sermons* have recently been translated and published by the Benedictines of Weingarten, the community that used to be at Erdington. So we have the paradox that these precious sermons are in print abroad but not in England, although it must in fairness be added that sets of the old editions are spread through the libraries.

It is tolerably certain that Newman would not have approved of anyone talking about his spirituality. Spirituality is an abstract word, and he was no lover of abstractions. He held in horror unreal words and professions, especially when they had to do with religion.

> To make professions is to play with edged tools, unless we attend to what we are saying. . . . Be in earnest and you will speak of religion when and how you should; aim at things, and your words will be right without aiming. . . . That a thing is true is no reason that it should be said, but that it should be done; that it should be acted upon; that it should be made our own inwardly.[1]

Newman's spiritual teaching is simply that of the New Testament, made real and driven home. He preaches not a theory or philosophy of his own, but the Christian revelation—not Christian doctrine in the abstract, but the truths of faith in their concrete implications. For piercing, practical, spiritual reading, for the Christian ideal as it is to be lived and realized in this workaday world, we may safely turn to what was preached from the pulpit of St Mary's, Oxford.

How was Newman able to become the preacher of pure Christianity, pure Catholicism, with only faint traces, which grew fainter as each volume of sermons came out, to show that he had been born and brought up a Protestant? How was he prepared for his ecumenical work, acting as link between Catholic and non-Catholic, expounding a doctrine that could win the hearts of both?

Grace builds on nature, and Newman began life with the inestimable benefit of growing up in a lively and united family, where the standards, whether intellectual or moral, were extremely high. For religious teaching he had a mother and grand-

[1] John Henry Newman, *Parochial and Plain Sermons* (henceforth referred to as *P.S.*), V, pp. 33, 45.

mother who were devoted to their Bible. From them he learned to love and study Holy Scripture, and to imbibe its lessons about the duty of man and the loving ever-watchful Providence of God. As he grew older this simple teaching was inadequate against the temptations to unbelief. Looking back later, he accused himself of arrogant self-sufficiency and pride of intellect, and described himself as being at fifteen "an ungodly, unbelieving boy". The turning point of his life was his conversion at the age of sixteen, when he gave himself to God. Helped by a young Evangelical master at his school, he, in his own words, "became a Christian". With his whole heart he accepted the Christian revelation in the purest form available to him. He believed, with the gift of Faith, the chief mysteries which the Catechism tells us every Christian is bound to know, and much more besides. "The conversations and sermons of that excellent man, the Rev. Walter Mayers . . . was the human means of this beginning of divine faith in me. . . . I fell under the influences of a definite Creed, and received into my intellect impressions of dogma, which, through God's mercy, have never been effaced or obscured."[1] We think so generally of Newman as a High Churchman that we tend to overlook his debt to the Evangelicals, the followers of Wesley who remained within the Anglican pale. Newman certainly always looked back with gratitude to the Evangelical teaching, and when over seventy wrote that it

> had been a great blessing for England; it had brought home to the hearts of thousands the cardinal and vital truths of Revelation, and to himself among others. The divine truths about our Lord and His Person and offices, His grace, the regeneration of our nature in Him, the supreme duty of living, not only morally, but in His faith, fear and love, together with the study of Scripture in which these truths lay, had sheltered and protected him in his most dangerous years . . . and had brought him on in habits of devotion till the time came when he was to dedicate himself to the Christian ministry.[2]

Three years before his death he solemnly asserted:

> Did I wish to give a reason for my full and absolute devotion to

[1] *Apologia* (Uniform edition), p. 4.

[2] John Henry Newman, *Autobiographical Writings*, edited by H. Tristram, 1956, p. 79

> the Catholic Roman Church, what should, what can I say but that those great and burning truths which I learned when a boy from Evangelical teaching, I have found impressed upon my heart with fresh and ever increasing force by the Holy Roman Church? That Church has added to the simple Evangelicalism of my first teachers, but it has obscured, diluted, enfeebled nothing of it.[1]

The Evangelical teaching converted Newman to a spiritual life, and with his active temperament this involved a personal striving to put his new faith into practice. "Holiness before peace" and "growth the only evidence of life" were his watchwords. It needs to be emphasized that from the age of sixteen Newman was leading a deep spiritual life. This is clear from his private notes written at the time, and from these written long afterwards:

> When I was growing up and as a young man I had confidence and hope in God, that is I committed myself without anxiety to His Providence, I had the greatest faith in the efficacy of prayer. . . .
>
> When I was young, I thought that with all my heart I gave up the world for Thee. As far as will, purpose, and intention go, I think I did. I mean I deliberately put the world aside.[2]

Immediately after his conversion Newman went up to Oxford, where we find him leading a strict life, trying to attend to the Presence of God, and to purify the motives of his actions. He began to show apostolic zeal in his own family and among his friends, and had plans for becoming a missionary. The next ten years showed him what was lacking or unreal in the Evangelical teaching, his experiences in his very conscientious parish visiting as a curate at St Clement's, Oxford, playing a notable part. Then with the help of his friends at Oriel, especially the High Churchmen, John Keble and Richard Hurrell Froude, he learned properly to understand and appreciate the part played by the sacraments in the spiritual life, and to believe in the Church as a divine institution intended to guide men until the end of time. In particular Hurrell Froude "delighted in thinking of the Saints; he had a vivid appreciation of the idea of sanctity, its possibility and its heights . . . he embraced the principle of penance and mortifica-

[1] Wilfrid Ward, *The Life of Cardinal Newman*, II, 527.
[2] *Autobiographical Writings*, pp. 247, 249.

tion. He had a deep devotion to the Real Presence, in which he had a firm faith". From Froude too, he learned to appreciate virginity for its own sake, and not only as hitherto, for its practical advantage in the apostolic work to which he felt called. Froude "had a high severe idea of the intrinsic excellence of Virginity; and he considered the Blessed Virgin its great pattern. . . . He fixed deep in me the idea of devotion to the Blessed Virgin, and he led me gradually to believe in the Real Presence".[1]

"There is one remaining source of my opinions," Newman adds, "and that far from the least important," the Fathers of the Church. We Catholics of the twentieth century are learning to renovate our religion by going back to the sources, hence the Biblical Movement and the Patristic Movement—*resourcement biblique* and *resourcement patristique*, as the French call them. Newman was already saturated with Holy Scripture: he must now drink deep at the other pure source of authentic Christianity, the Fathers of the Church—and his providential preparation for his life's work would be complete.

> Even when I was a boy [he wrote] my thoughts were turned to the early Church, and especially to the early Fathers, by the perusal of the Calvinist John Milner's Church History, and I have never lost, I have never suffered a suspension of the impression, deep and most pleasurable, which his sketches of St Ambrose and St Augustine left on my mind. From that time the vision of the Fathers was always, to my imagination, I may say, a paradise of delight to the contemplation of which I directed my thoughts.[2]

In the long vacation of 1828 Newman returned to the Fathers with his old devotion and began to read them chronologically, beginning with St Ignatius and St Justin. Studying them in the editions of the Maurists, with the help of Bull and Petavius, he was able to imbibe the full richness of the Catholic Faith. Hence before he was thirty, Newman was, by the Providence of God, in possession of his doctrine. He had learned all that the Evangelicals and the High Churchmen could teach him, he had delved into the sources, he had tried to follow the inspirations of the Holy Spirit. He glimpsed that he was to be an instrument of God. When he

[1] *Apologia*, pp. 24-5.
[2] *Difficulties of Anglicans*, I, 370.

was dying in Sicily in 1833, he said, without understanding what he meant, "I shall not die, for I have not sinned against light". And later, "I have a work to do in England".

II

Newman's spiritual teaching, as we have said, was simply the Christian Faith, but the Christian Faith not merely as something to be believed, but as something to be lived. He appealed to men's consciences in the most direct and plainspoken way. "A passionate and sustained earnestness after a high moral rule, seriously realized in conduct, is the dominant character of these sermons," says Dean Church, who could speak with authority.[1] Yet Newman was no mere moralist. He preached the religious Christian truths as the basis of the life of holiness. His was that doctrinal spirituality which we hanker after, and which has been supplied in this century by such writers as Abbot Marmion and Karl Adam, who satisfy us because they too drank from the authentic sources. For a decade and more Newman put before one of the most intelligent and cultivated of audiences that have ever been, that duty of aiming at perfection which is the conclusion of any practical belief in the Christian faith. The title of the first sermon in his first Volume is "Holiness Necessary for Future Blessedness", and it concludes:

> To obtain the gift of holiness is the work of a *life*. No man will be perfect here, so sinful is our nature. Thus in putting off the day of repentance, these men are reserving for a few chance years, when strength and vigour are gone, that WORK for which a *whole* life would not be enough.... One principal test of our being true servants of God is our wish to serve Him better; and be quite sure that a man who is contented with his own proficiency in Christian holiness, is at best in a dark state, or rather in great peril.... Be ye content with nothing short of perfection ... exert yourselves day by day to grow in knowledge and grace.... Lastly it is our comfort to know ... that we are not left to ourselves, but that the Holy Ghost is graciously present with us and enables us to triumph over, and to change our own minds.[2]

[1] R. W. Church, *The Oxford Movement*, Third Edition, 1892, p. 21.
[2] *P.S.*, I, 12.

The next sermon is on the immortality of the soul and shows what is really meant by leading a spiritual life, "It is face to face, 'solus cum solo', in all matters between man and his God."[1]

> To understand that we have souls, is to feel our separation from things visible, our independence of them, our distinct existence in ourselves, our individuality, our power of acting for ourselves in this way or that way, our accountableness for what we do. These are the great truths which lie wrapped up indeed even in a child's mind, and which God's grace can unfold there in spite of the influence of the external world; but at first this outward world prevails. We look off from self to the things around us, and forget ourselves in them. Such is our state,—a depending for support on the reeds which are no stay, and overlooking our real strength,—at a time when God begins his process of reclaiming us to a truer view of our place in His great system of providence. And when He visits us . . . the unprofitableness and feebleness of the things of this world is forced upon our minds; they promise but cannot perform, they disappoint us. . . . And should it so happen that misfortunes come upon us, then still more are we led to understand the nothingness of this world; then still more are we led to distrust it, and are weaned from the love of it, till at length it floats before our eyes merely as some idle veil, which, notwithstanding its many tints, cannot hide the view of what is beyond it;—and we begin by degrees to perceive that there are but two beings in the whole universe, our own soul, and the God who made it. Sublime unlooked for doctrine, yet most true![2]

This is the doctrine, in almost identical words, of St Teresa and St John of the Cross, but it goes back to the beginning. Rodriguez speaks with admiration of one of the famous Fathers of the Desert, who used to say that a man could not find true repose and satisfaction in this life, unless he reckoned that there is only God and himself in the world. "I want a man," says Newman, "on the one hand to confess his immortality with his lips, and on the other, to live as if he tried to understand his own words." The unseen world must became a reality to us.

Newman, as we know, practised what he preached in this matter, and this holds of another fundamental sermon in the same

[1] *Apologia*, p. 195.
[2] *P.S.*, I, 19-20, 24.

volume, "Self-denial the Test of Religious Earnestness". He was living a detached, ascetical life, not only in a bodily way, but in turning his mind from the glittering prizes which, with his brilliant gifts and wide influence, might so easily have been his. A judge of men remarked of him, "Newman is not looking to get on in life". How clearly he lays it down that we must conquer ourselves, surrender ourselves to God, before His love can take possession of us.

> I must say this ... that the comforts of life are the main cause of our want of love of God; and, much as we may lament and struggle against it, till we learn to dispense with them in good measure, we shall not overcome it. Till we, in a certain sense, detach ourselves from our bodies, our minds will not be in a state to receive divine impressions, and to exert heavenly aspirations. A smooth and easy life, an uninterrupted enjoyment of the goods of Providence, full meals, soft raiment, well-furnished homes, the pleasures of sense, the feeling of security, the consciousness of wealth,—these and the like, if we are not careful, choke up all the avenues of the soul, through which the light and breath of heaven might come to us.... If we attempt to force our minds into a loving and devotional temper, without this preparation, it is too plain what will follow,—the grossness ... the affectation ... the unreality, the presumption, the hollowness (suffer me, my brethren, while I say plainly but seriously what I mean), in a word, what Scripture calls the Hypocrisy, which we see around us....

Again and again Newman tries to bring home the fundamental Gospel law of self-denial. "What then is it that we who profess religion lack? I repeat it, this: a willingness to be changed, a willingness to suffer (if I may use such a word), to suffer Almighty God to change us. We do not like to let go our old selves." And elsewhere:

> We cannot have our eyes at once on this world and on the other. Those who live in the sun's glare can see nothing in twilight; but those whose eyes are used to the shade, see many things which others will not believe they can see. So it is with our souls; the minding of the flesh, aiming at this world's goods, seeking to rise or succeed in life, gazing on greatness, rank, distinction, abundance, pomp and show, coveting wealth, measuring things by wealth, eating and drinking without restraint, placing no curb

upon the passions, exercising no self command, living without rule . . . all this makes the heart irreligious.[1]

If Newman could bring home the law of self-denial, he was far too much of a realist to other-worldly in the bad sense. A famous sermon is entitled "Doing Glory to God in Pursuits of the World", and begins:

When persons are convinced that life is short . . . when they feel that the next life is all in all, and that eternity is the only subject that really can claim or can fill our thoughts, then they are apt to undervalue this life altogether, and to forget its real importance. They are apt to wish to spend the time of their sojourning here in a positive separation from active and social duties : yet it should be recollected that the employments of this world, though not themselves heavenly, are after all the way to heaven . . . but it is difficult to realize this. It is difficult to realize both truths at once, and to connect both truths together; steadily to contemplate the life to come, yet to act in this. . . . In various ways does the thought of the next world lead men to neglect their duty in this; and whenever it does so we may be sure that there is something wrong and unchristian, not in their thinking of the next world, but in their manner of thinking of it.

Newman suggests various remedies: among them is this:

The Christian will feel that the true contemplation of his Saviour lies *in* his worldly business; that as Christ is seen in the poor, and in the persecuted, and in children, so is He seen in the employments He puts upon His chosen, whatever they be; that in attending to his own calling he will be meeting Christ; that if he neglect it, he will not on that account enjoy His presence at all the more, but that while performing it, he will see Christ revealed to his soul amid the ordinary actions of the day, as by a sort of sacrament.[2]

This leads on to another fundamental and of course biblical theme, the all-pervading Providence of God, which is continually being touched on by Newman and underlies his whole spiritual

[1] *P.S.*, V, 337-8, 241; VI, 116.
[2] *P.S.*, VIII, 154, 165.

attitude. Here is just one quotation from the sermon "A Particular Providence as Revealed in the Gospel" :

> It is very difficult, in spite of the revelation made to us in the Gospel, to master the idea of this particular providence of God. If we allow ourselves to float down the current of the world, living as other men, gathering up our notions of religion here and there, as it may be, we have little or no true comprehension of a particular Providence. We conceive that Almighty God works on a large plan; but we cannot realize the wonderful truth that He sees and thinks of individuals. We cannot believe that He is really present everywhere, that He is wherever we are, though unseen. . . . We do not in any sufficient sense believe that he is . . . "about *our* path, and about *our* bed, and spieth out all *our* ways". We cannot bring ourselves to get hold of this solemn fact, that He sees what is going on among ourselves at this moment; that this man falls and that man is exalted, at His silent, invisible appointment.[1]

III

Having laid the foundations deep and sure, Newman is ready to go on to speak of the grandeur of the Christian life and the privileges of the sons of God. He is no mere preacher of morality or of unconnected and heterogeneous Christian practices. As Christians a wonderful loving union with God is offered to us, we are to strive to live in His presence, we enter into relations too sacred to speak of, with the three Persons of the Most Holy Trinity. Newman has much to say about the Sacrament of Baptism, and the grace and privileges it brings with it. His teaching is centred on our Lord : it is bound to be in view of the sources from which it is drawn :

> When men are to be exhorted to newness of life, the true Object to be put before them, as I conceive, is "Jesus Christ, the same yesterday, today and for ever"; the true Gospel preaching is to enlarge, as they can bear it, on the Person, natures, attributes, offices, and work of Him who once regenerated them and is now ready to pardon; to dwell on His recorded words and deeds on earth; to declare reverently and adoringly His mysterious greatness

[1] *P.S.*, III, 115-16.

as the Only-begotten Son, One with the Father, yet distinct from Him . . . and to combine and contrast His attributes and relations to us as God and man, as our Mediator, Saviour, Sanctifier and Judge. The true preaching of the Gospel is to preach Christ.[1]

The Movement of which Newman was the life and soul made a great change.

> The great Name [says Dean Church], no longer stood for an abstract symbol of doctrine, but for a living Master, who could teach as well as save. And not forgetting whither He had gone and what He was, the readers of Scripture now sought Him eagerly in those sacred records, where we can almost see and hear His going in and out among men. It was a change in the look and use of Scripture, which some can still look back to as an epoch in their religious history.[2]

There also followed a new appreciation of the sacraments as the means by which our Lord acts through the centuries upon His disciples, and conforms them to Himself. This is how Newman describes the connection of the Sacraments with Christ:

> ... instruments of the application of His merits to individual believers. Though He now sits on the right hand of God, He has, in one sense, never left this world since He first entered it; for, by the ministration of the Holy Ghost, He is really present with us in an unknown way, and ever imparts Himself to those who seek Him. Even when visibly on earth He, the Son of Man, was still in heaven; and now, though He is ascended on high, He is still on earth. And as He is still with us, for all that He is in heaven, so, again, is the hour of His cross and passion ever mystically present, though it be past these eighteen hundred years. Time and space have no portion in the spiritual Kingdom which He has founded; and the rites of His Church are as mysterious spells by which He annuls them both.... Thus Christ shines through them, as through transparent bodies, without impediment. He is the Light and Life of the Church, acting through it, dispensing of His fulness, knitting and compacting together every part of it.[3]

No one has described the Mystical Body of Christ, in English, like Newman:

[1] *Lectures on Justification*, p. 325.
[2] R. W. Church, op. cit., p. 191.
[3] *P.S.*, III, 277.

Christ formed His Apostles into a visible society; but when He came again in the Person of His Spirit, He made them all in a real sense one, not in name only. For they were no longer arranged merely in the form of unity, as the limbs of the dead may be, but they were parts and organs of one unseen power; they really depended upon, and were offshoots of that which was One; their separate persons were taken into a mysterious union with things unseen, were grafted upon and assimilated to the spiritual body of Christ, which is One, even by the Holy Ghost, in whom Christ has come again to us. Thus Christ came, not to make us one but to die for us : the Spirit came to make us one in Him who had died and was alive, that is, to form the Church. This then is the special glory of the Christian Church, that its members do not depend merely on that which is visible, they are not mere stones of a building, piled one upon another, and bound together from without, but they are one and all the births and manifestations of one and the same unseen spiritual principle or power, "*living* stones", internally connected, as branches from a tree, not as the parts of a heap. They are members of the Body of Christ. That divine and adorable Form, which the Apostles saw and handled, after ascending into heaven became a principle of life, a secret origin of existence to all who believe, through the gracious ministration of the Holy Ghost. . . . So that in a true sense it may be said, that from the day of Pentecost to this hour there has been in the Church but One Holy One, the King of kings, and Lord of lords Himself, who is in all believers, and through whom they are what they are; their separate persons being but as separate developments, vessels, instruments, and works of Him who is invisible. Such is the difference between the Church before the Spirit of Christ came, and after. Before, God's servants were as the dry bones in the Prophet's vision, connected by profession, not by an inward principle; but since, they are all the organs as if of one invisible, governing Soul, the hands, or the tongues, or the feet, or the eyes of one and the same directing Mind, the types, tokens, beginning, and glimpses of the Eternal Son of God.[1]

Few of the recognized Catholic spiritual writers give as much attention to the Holy Eucharist as Newman. He had a firm belief in the Real Presence which is so plainly taught in Scripture, and although he did not believe in Transubstantiation until he was a

[1] *P.S.*, IV, 169-71.

Catholic, that doctrine was in a true sense implicated in his teaching. He even used it as an argument *a fortiori*:

> Nothing can show more clearly how high the blessing of Holy Communion is, than to observe that the Church's tendency has been, not to detract from its marvellousness, but to increase it. The Church has never thought little of the gift; so far from it, we know that one very large portion of Christendom holds more than we hold. That belief, which goes beyond ours, shows how great the gift is really. I allude to the doctrine of what is called Transubstantiation. . . .[1]

That comes in a sermon on The Eucharistic Presence. Let us see one or two more passages where Newman explains the Blessed Sacrament to us:

> We must not suppose that in leaving us [at the Ascension] He closed the gracious economy of His Incarnation, and withdrew the ministration of His incorruptible Manhood from His work of loving mercy towards us. . . . Blessed for ever be His Holy Name! before He went away, He remembered our necessity, and completed His work, bequeathing to us a special mode of approaching Him, a Holy Mystery, in which we receive (we know not how) the virtue of that Heavenly Body, which is the life of all that believe. This is the Blessed Sacrament of the Eucharist, in which "Christ is evidently set forth crucified among us"; that we, feasting upon the Sacrifice, may be "partakers of the Divine Nature". Let us give heed lest we be in the number of those who "discern not the Lord's Body", and the "exceeding great and precious promises" which are made to those who partake it.
>
> In the Church He dispenses blessings, such as the world knows not of. Blessed are they if they knew their blessedness, who are allowed, as we are, week after week, and Festival after Festival, to seek and find in that Holy Church the Saviour of their souls! Blessed are they beyond language or thought, to whom it is vouchsafed to receive those tokens of His love, which cannot otherwise be gained by man, the pledges and means of His special presence, in the Sacrament of His Supper; who are allowed to eat and drink the food of immortality, and receive life from the bleeding side of the Son of God! Alas! by what strange coldness of heart, or perverse superstition is it, that any one called Christian keeps away

[1] *P.S.*, VI, 141.

from that heavenly ordinance? Is it not very grievous that there should be any one who fears to share in the greatest conceivable blessing which could come upon sinful men?[1]

Then, as usual practical:

He has shown us *how* to come to Him, and I see that men do *not* come to him in that way which He has pointed out. He has shown us that to come to Him for life is a literal bodily action; not a mere figure, not a mere movement of the heart towards Him, but an action of the visible limbs; not a mere secret faith, but a coming to church, a passing on along the aisle to His holy table. . . . If then a man does not seek Him where He is, there is no profit in seeking Him where He is not. What is the good of sitting at home seeking Him, when His Presence is in the Holy Eucharist? . . . The true reason why people will not come to this Holy Communion is this,—they do not wish to lead religious lives . . . and they think that that Blessed Sacrament does bind them to . . . live very much more strictly and thoughtfully than they do at present.[2]

This is the conclusion of a sermon on "The Gospel Feast":

May we not regard the Blessed Sacrament in a cold, heartless way, and keep at a distance from fear, when we should rejoice! May the spirit of the unprofitable servant never be ours, who looked at his lord as a hard master instead of a gracious benefactor! . . . Nor let us be of those, who come in a formal, mechanical way, as a mere matter of obligation, without reverence, without awe, without wonder, without love. . . . But let us come in faith and hope, and let us say to ourselves, May this be the beginning to us of everlasting bliss![3]

IV

We must pass over so much else of Newman's teaching on our Lord, on the Passion, on how we pray with Christ, on the Liturgy, and hasten on to the supreme Christian privilege, the Indwelling of the Blessed Trinity in the soul, which comes to us, as we have seen, through Christ's Body, His Church. Indeed the sermon on that subject which has already been quoted, begins as follows:

[1] *P.S.*, II, 144-9.
[2] *P.S.*, VII, 149-50.
[3] *P.S.*, VII, 177-8.

It was the great promise of the Gospel, that the Lord of all, who had hitherto manifested Himself externally to His servants, should take up His abode in their hearts. This ... is frequently the language of the Prophets; and it was the language of our Saviour when He came on earth : "I will love him," He says, speaking of those who love and obey Him, "and will manifest myself to him.... We will come unto him, and make our abode with him". Though He had come in our flesh, so as to be seen and handled, even this was not enough. Still He was external and separate; but after His ascension He descended again by His Spirit, and then at length the promise was fulfilled. There must indeed be a union between all creatures and their Almighty Creator even for their very existence.... But far higher, more intimate, and more sacred is the indwelling of God in the hearts of His elect people;—so intimate, that compared with it, He may well be said not to inhabit other men at all.[1]

Again and again Newman returns to this truth, which is the culminating point of the Christian Revelation. Whole sermons are devoted to "The Indwelling Spirit", and to "The Gift of the Spirit".[2] The Holy Spirit has come to finish the work of Christ, in regard to us.

To Him it is committed to apply to us severally all that Christ has done for us.... For if all gifts of grace are with the Spirit, and the presence of the Spirit is within us, it follows that these gifts are to be manifested and wrought in us.... As a light placed in a room pours out its rays on all sides, so the presence of the Holy Ghost imbues us with life, strength, holiness, love, acceptableness, righteousness.

We shall still have a natural fear of entering the presence of Christ our Judge, but "if we have lived, however imperfectly, yet habitually in His fear, if we trust that His Spirit is in us, then we need not be ashamed before Him. We shall then come before Him as we now come to pray—with profound abasement, with awe, with self-renunciation, still as relying on the Spirit which He has given us."[3] And how practical Newman makes this doctrine!

[1] *P.S.*, IV, 168.
[2] *P.S.*, II, 217; III, 254.
[3] *P.S.*, V, 138, 55.

When are we the more likely to dread sinning, when we know merely we ought to dread it, or when we see the exceeding peril of it? When are we more likely to keep awake and be sober, when we have a present treasure now to lose, or a distant reward to gain? Is it not more dreadful, when evil thoughts afflict us, more encouraging and ennobling in affliction, more kindling in danger and hardship, to reflect (if the words may be said) that we bear God within us, as the Martyr Ignatius expresses it, that He is grieved by us or suffers with us, according as we carry or renounce His Cross.

And Newman adds:

Has not this thought more of persuasiveness in it to do and suffer for Him than the views of doctrine that have spread among us? Is it not . . . deeper and more sacred than [that] which makes . . . heavenly grace a matter of purchase and trade; more glowing than [that] which depresses it almost to the chill temperature of natural religion.[1]

As he develops this doctrine, so fundamental for the spiritual life, Newman is led on to explain

that the thought of God, and nothing short of it, is the happiness of man; for though there is much besides to serve as subject for knowledge, or motive for action, or means of excitement, yet the affections require a something more vast and more enduring than anything created. . . . He alone is sufficient for the heart who made it. . . . But there is another reason why God alone is the happiness of our souls, to which I wish rather to direct attention:—the contemplation of Him, and nothing but it, is able fully to open and relieve the mind, to unlock, occupy, and fix our affections. We may indeed love things created with great intenseness, but such affection, when disjoined from the love of the Creator, is like a stream running in a narrow channel . . . it is not an expanding of the whole man. Created natures cannot open us, or elicit the ten thousand mental senses which belong to us, and through which we really live. None but the presence of our Maker can enter us; for to none besides can the whole heart in all its thoughts and feelings be unlocked and subjected. "Behold," He says, "I stand at the door and knock; if any man hear my voice and open

[1] *Lectures on Justification*, p. 191.

the door, I will come in to him, and sup with him, and he with me...." "God hath sent forth the Spirit of His Son into your hearts." It is this feeling of simple and absolute confidence and communion which soothes and satisfies those to whom it is vouchsafed.[1]

V

Here we must pause, and consider for a moment what Newman has to say about Mysticism, that is about the experimental knowledge and love of God. Up till now he has been describing what is known as ontological mysticism, the wonderful objective presence of God in the souls of true believers and the loving union that flows from it. This is something known by faith, and not in itself a matter of experience, or something that falls under the senses, even though the humblest Christian may from time to time be allowed a certain awareness of it, if only from its effects. In confining himself chiefly to the teaching of Faith in this matter, Newman was, of course, conforming to the pattern of the New Testament, which puts before us the Christian privileges in their fullness, but is comparatively reticent about the experience to which they may lead. It illustrates once again how authentic and solid was the teaching that went out from the pulpit of St Mary's, the doctrine of St John and St Paul made real once more.

A great deal of what the great Christian spiritual writers have to say is concerned with psychological mysticism. They describe, St Teresa and St John of the Cross for instance, the experiences of the soul under the influence of grace, and what the reactions of the soul should be. This was a sphere into which Newman did not often feel called to venture, partly out of a humble distrust of himself, partly because he was dealing with ordinary Christians and not with a specialized audience, but chiefly because his mysticism is that of the New Testament and Christian antiquity. (Indeed once, in 1860, when asked about the works of St John of the Cross, he replied, perhaps after the humble manner of his patron St Philip Neri, that he knew nothing of them, but as an ordinary Catholic was content, after the New Testament, with the *Imitation*.) He helped to direct many people along the road to sanctity, but he

[1] *P.S.*, V, 316-18.

would certainly have agreed with the violent strictures St John of the Cross passes on the unskilful directors who interfere between the soul and its God, and who forget that the Holy Spirit is the paramount Director. Newman urged men on to the heights, as they felt the call, but was little inclined to set up as a master where there was so much scope for unreality and unreal words. Yet he too, in spite of what some people have maintained, had that experimental knowledge of God's presence in the soul, which is the essential part of mysticism. This we may deduce from his effect on his contemporaries and the way they spoke of him, and from various references in the sermons, all the more convincing for their reticence.

> A thick black veil is spread between this world and the next.... In the Gospel this veil is not removed; it remains, but every now and then marvellous disclosures are made to us of what is behind it. At times we seem to catch a glimpse of a Form which we shall hereafter see face to face. We approach, and in spite of the darkness, our hands, or our head, or our brow, or our lips become, as it were, sensible of the contact of something more than earthly. We know not where we are, but we have been bathing in water, and a voice tells us that it is blood. Or we have a mark signed upon our foreheads, and it spake of Calvary. Or we recollect a hand laid upon our heads, and surely it had the print of nails in it, and resembled His who with a touch gave sight to the blind and raised the dead. Or we have been eating and drinking; and it was not a dream surely, that One fed us from His wounded side, and renewed our nature by the heavenly meat He gave.[1]

Then there is this passage, less passionate :

> A true Christian may almost be defined as one who has a ruling sense of God's presence within him. As none but justified persons have that privilege, so none but the justified have that practical perception of it.... "I have set God always before me," says the Psalmist.... Let us in all circumstances thus regard Him.. In all circumstances, of joy or sorrow, hope or fear, let us aim at having Him in our inmost heart; let us have no secret apart from Him. Let us acknowledge Him as enthroned within us at the very springs of thought and affection. Let us submit ourselves to His guidance and sovereign direction.... This is the true life of saints.

[1] *P.S.*, V, 10-11.

And finally:

> Christians, on looking back on years past, will feel, at least in a degree, that Christ has been with them, though they knew it not, only believed it, at the time. They will even recollect then the burning of their hearts . . . they will experience a sort of heavenly fragrance and savour of immortality, when they least expect it, rising upon their minds, as if in token that God has been with them, and investing all that has taken place, which before seemed to them but earthly, with beams of glory.[1]

About the active and contemplative life, Newman speaks in a very balanced practical way. There are two ways of serving God, by active business and quiet adoration,

> those who are like Martha, those like Mary; and both of them glorify Him in their own line, whether of labour or quiet, in either case proving themselves to be not their own, but bought with a price, set on obeying, and constant in obeying His will. If they labour it is for His sake; and if they adore, it is still from love of Him. And further these two classes of His disciples do not choose for themselves their course of service, but it is allotted by Him.[2]

For most people it is the part of Martha, but Newman suggests a few classes that perhaps are called to the more favoured portion of Mary. First, the old "whose season of business is past, and who seem to be thereby reminded to serve God by prayer and contemplation. . . . Next those who minister at the Altar. . . . And next I may mention Children as in some respects partakers of Mary's portion". Their school time ought to be in some way a contemplation of their Lord and Saviour. Then, of course, the unmarried, and finally many people during their times of leisure. Newman clearly sees the prayerful life as open to most men, and at the same time no one is more emphatic that love is proved by deeds. He denounces those who "sit at home speculating, and separate moral perfection from action", and also literature which leads "men to cultivate the religious affections separate from religious practice".[3] His was an active temperament, and he insists that we are justified by the deliberate and heroic works of righteousness and

[1] *P.S.*, V, 225, 236; VI, 134.
[2] *P.S.*, III, 321ff.
[3] *P.S.*, II, 288, 373. *Lectures on Justification*, p. 296.

not by feelings, yet he sums up his teaching at the end of the sermon on Faith and Love:

> We are Christ's, not by faith merely, nor by works merely, but by love; . . . we are saved by that heavenly flame within us, which, while it consumes what is seen, aspires to what is unseen. Love is the gentle, tranquil, satisfied acquiescence and adherence of the soul in the contemplation of God; not only a preference of God before all things, but a delight in Him because He is God, and because His commandments are good. . . .[1]

After that quotation it is perhaps hardly necessary to notice an objection sometimes made that Newman's spiritual teaching is too gloomy, and that he has not shaken off the pessimism and rigorism of Evangelicalism. It is true that, until his later Anglican sermons, Newman thought all deliberate and wilful sin was grave, and that if committed after baptism it could only be forgiven by non-sacramental means. But for Catholics too, it remains a mystery how fully deliberate sin can be venial, and it is the first enemy to be attacked by anyone who is beginning a spiritual life. Newman's teaching is austere certainly, as all true religion must be: he is serious and full of reverence, dealing with the most important of all questions. He protests against "an exclusively cheerful religion" but he is emphatic that "gloom is no Christian temper". He himself was a humanist; he was attracted by the joyful optimism which underlies the spiritual teaching of St Ambrose and St Athanasius and the Greek Fathers. He wrote to Pusey in 1835 that "Gloom as connected with the Monastic rule came in with the Gothic ethos." His preference was for the cheerful architecture of humanism, while his humour has been described by Fr Lockhart, who lived with him at Littlemore:

> There was at times in him a great vein of humour, and at times a certain playful way which he had of saying things which were full of meaning, and called to mind some passages in St Paul's writings, suggesting, too, that perhaps there was in him, as in this, so also in other things, a certain likeness to the Great Apostle who made "himself all to all that he might gain all to God".[2]

Joy and peace were for Newman the keynotes of the Christian

[1] *P.S.*, IV, 317-18.
[2] William Lockhart, *Cardinal Newman*, 1891, p. 4.

character, and by way of proof and also of conclusion, his description of this must be given :

> The Christian has a deep, silent, hidden peace, which the world sees not. . . . He is the greater part of his time by himself, and when he is in solitude, that is his real state. What he is when left to himself and to his God, that is his true life. He can bear himself; he can (as it were) joy in himself, for it is the grace of God within him, it is the presence of the Eternal Comforter in which he joys. . . . He can lay his head on his pillow at night, and own in God's sight, with overflowing heart, that he wants nothing,—that he "is full and abounds",—that God has been all things to him, and that nothing is not his which God could give him. More thankfulness, more holiness, more of heaven he needs indeed, but the thought that he can have more is not a thought of trouble, but of joy. It does not interfere with his peace to know that he may grow nearer to God. . . . The Christian is cheerful, easy, kind, gentle, courteous, candid, unassuming; has no pretence, no affectation, no ambition, so singularity; because he has neither hope nor fear about this world. He is serious, sober, discreet, grave, moderate, mild, with so little that is unusual or striking in his bearing, that he may easily be taken at first sight for an ordinary man. There are persons who think religion consists in ecstasies, or in set speeches;—he is not one of those.[1]

The historians of that outpouring of divine grace which we name the Oxford Movement have often described the effect of Newman's teaching, and that calls our attention to another of its characteristics. It was what is now so sought after, a spirituality adapted to those in the world, to the laity, and to ordinary life. Newman set before men the ideal that should be theirs from the fact of their being baptized. He was not preaching to sheltered monks and nuns, although it is noticeable that they are among his greatest admirers, he was appealing for Gospel holiness and perfection to the young men of the English educated classes of his time. When they came up to Oxford their Christianity had, for the most part, no very profound hold on them, whether as to faith or morals.

> On such as these [writes Fr Lockhart again] Newman's sermons came down like a new revelation. He had the wondrous,

[1] *P.S.*; V, 69-71.

> the supernatural power of raising the mind to God, and of rooting deeply in us a personal conviction of God, and a sense of His Presence. He compelled us to an intuitive perception of moral obligation—of that Natural Law of right, which is written in the mind by the Word and Wisdom of God.[1]

In a speech in the House of Commons, many years later, Sir John Duke Coleridge bore witness to the way Newman prepared men to live the Christian life in the world:

> There was a man in my time, of admirable genius, of saintly life, of singular humility and self denial, who taught us not any peculiar theological dogma, but simple religious truth; whose example kept a lofty standard before our eyes; who led us by his life and by his teaching to all things "lovely and of good report"; to whom many in Church and State owe it that their sense of responsibility was awakened, and that they are now in their degree, doing, in some poor and imperfect way, their duty both to God and man.[2]

The testimonies of those who owed their spiritual life to Newman could be multiplied indefinitely.

Newman's own spiritual and recollected life had begun when he gave himself to God at the age of sixteen. His entry into the Catholic Church made little change in this respect. "I was not conscious to myself, on my conversion, of any change, intellectual or moral, wrought in my mind. I was not conscious of firmer faith in the fundamental truths of Revelation, or of more self-command; I had not more fervour; but it was like coming into port after a rough sea."[3] Even his devotion to what he called "the bright and beautiful character" of St Philip Neri dated from long before his entry into the Church. He saw a likeness in him to John Keble, who shares with Hurrell Froude the honour of being the "saint" of the Oxford Movement:

> This great saint reminds me in so many ways of Keble, that I can fancy what Keble would have been, if God's will had been that he should have been born in another place or age; he was formed in the same time of extreme hatred of humbug, playful-

[1] William Lockhart, op. cit., pp. 25-6.
[2] E. H. Coleridge, *Life of Lord Coleridge*, 1908, II, 49.
[3] *Apologia*, p. 238.

ness, nay oddity, tender love for others, and serenity, which are the lineaments of Keble.[1]

No convert was more docile than Newman. He was struck with the simplicity and the objective sense of spiritual realities that he found among Catholics, but he knew that things were at a low ebb. He wrote to Keble in December 1844, less than a year before he was received: "No one can have a more unfavourable view than I of the present state of the Roman Catholics—so much so, that any who join them would be like the Cistercians of Fountains, living under the trees till their house was built. If I must account for it, I should say that the want of unity has injured both them and us."[2] Newman had done much to recatholicize the Church of England, but he did not find among Catholics enough of his own appreciation of the Christian privileges, of the mystic beauty of the Church as the Body of Christ, of the Indwelling Presence of the most holy Trinity in the soul. Père Boyer, the Jesuit professor of dogmatic theology at the Gregorian University in Rome, has pointed out, as one of the blessings of the entry of our separated brethren into the Church, that it would call our attention to spiritual treasures which we do not sufficiently utilize.[3] This recalls Newman's remark that the Church must be prepared for converts as well as converts for the Church. May we not say that something of this has been happening of recent years? The Bible is once more being studied and made the basis of their spiritual life by ordinary Catholics, the Fathers are becoming known and translations of their works spread in collections like that *Library of the Fathers* which Newman initiated. They are read for their spiritual teaching, and no longer merely for the arguments they can furnish in apologetics. This is all part of the levelling up of which Newman spoke, and which will bring together the Christians of different communions. His own synthesis of the biblical and patristic teaching on the spiritual life we are now better able to appreciate and to use for our spiritual nourishment. To Anglicans for whom it was originally drawn up, it has always had an appeal, since it is derived from the twin sources they hold in honour, and goes back

[1] Anne Mozley, *Letters and Correspondence of J. H. Newman*, 1891, II, 474.
[2] *Correspondence of J. H. Newman with J. Keble and others, 1839-1845*, 1917, p. 364.
[3] *Unitas*, 1948, I, pp. 14-15, quoted in R. Aubert, *Problèmes de l'Unité Chrétienne*, 1953, pp. 14-15.

behind the more philosophical and juridical expositions of medieval and modern times. St Bernard is called the last of the Fathers because in him dogma and piety and literature are still one, and his mysticism is simply the experience of the data of the New Testament. Newman, who leaves later developments on one side, took over where St Bernard left off, and perhaps should be allowed to succeed to his title.

XIII

CARDINAL MANNING

By George Andrew Beck, A.A.

I

To most Catholics, particularly to the clergy, Manning's fame as a spiritual writer rests on his classic, *The Eternal Priesthood*. Some would say that, apart from this one book, Manning should be regarded as an apologist, a controversialist, a great preacher but not strictly as a spiritual writer. Neither Purcell nor Shane Leslie gives more than a passing reference to this side of his pastoral and priestly activity. Hutton devotes a chapter to the Cardinal as a writer and a preacher and is, on the whole, unsympathetic to this aspect of his work. Only in some parts of Mr Reynolds' *Three Cardinals* and in the essay by Mgr Davis, in the symposium, *Manning: Anglican and Catholic*, is his work as a spiritual writer considered and assessed.

It is true that most of Manning's writings were apologetic. He felt himself called upon to defend the Church and to explain her teaching on a wide range of social and political topics, from parental rights in education to the unity of the Church, from rights of labour to Catholic teaching on civil obedience.

Hutton notes that most of Manning's Catholic sermons were unwritten when delivered, and were only afterwards written out for publication. This gives them, he suggests, a certain thinness and he states that they lose much of their power through dissociation from the presence and calm of the preacher.

> The conscious air of authority with which he spoke, his recollectedness, the ease with which an appropriate word or phrase came to his lips, the slight and not ungraceful action, the forefinger being at times slightly raised and then, in emphasis, pointed downwards,—all this being absent when the sermons are at a later time read, there is nothing to distract attention from the fact that, though the words are well chosen, and many of the phrases

happy and well to the purpose, the argument, if flawless, is slight and unconvincing; it is to assertion and not to reasoning that you are expected to bow, and the conviction grows upon you that the preacher has never really touched the "bottom facts" of the case. Nevertheless, taking the standard of pulpit utterances at what it is, every fair critic must admit that Cardinal Manning's sermons were always far above the average, were always interesting and always worth hearing, though one cannot add that they are always worth reading [pp. 222 and 223].

Surveying a number of Manning's writings, including *The Grounds of Faith* (1852), *The Temporal Mission of the Holy Ghost* (1865), *The Fourfold Sovereignty of God* (1871), and *The Internal Mission of the Holy Ghost* (1875), the author suggests that "these somewhat conventionally able and learned treatises" are to the modern reader more wearying than convincing:

> They deserve no doubt respect and praise; many striking passages might be culled from them; there are apt references and quotations, and there are vigorously-drawn conclusions from premisses not equally well established; but a reader cannot for ever sit patiently and be lectured as a catechumen; and it is the prevalence of assertion over every other kind of proposition that must always render these volumes unreadable to the great mass of men. Cardinal Manning was apparently aware of this defect, and in his latest apologetic work, the *Religio Viatoris*, he begins at any rate with an effort to gain his reader's confidence by treating him as if, to some extent, on equal terms. He is almost playful in his repudiation of assumptions; and the thing goes on smoothly for a while; but soon the didactic temper finds its way in; and before the book is half finished, the author is again laying down the law, and is speaking, as he could not fail to speak, considering the force that he believed he had behind him, as one having authority, not to argue but to teach [pp. 223 and 224].

II

It may well be true that Manning's style is wearisome to the modern reader. We may agree that he asserts rather than argues. His writings, however, take on an added interest when one begins to appreciate the overriding purpose which inspired so much of what he wrote. We owe it to Mgr Davis to have offered us a synthetic view of Manning's work which gives a unity to so much of what would otherwise seem occasional sermons and addresses. Mgr Davis draws a comparison between Newman and Manning and speaks of them both as being prophets to their age.

> Each had a prophetic intuition of some of the grave problems of his time, and each as an apostle of truth offered his solution. The problems they dealt with and therefore the solutions they offered were in different spheres. There were more ways than one in which Victorians were drifting from the truth. Newman thought that the challenge of rationalism, atheism and indifferentism was the most dangerous. Manning was more anxious about the Catholics who were not Catholics; Catholics who no longer knew the Spirit and His work within them, or had forgotten that the Church is God dwelling among men : Catholics who were so ready to appear friendly to their fellow-countrymen that they were in danger of compromising the divine truths of the faith. . . . In the case of Manning fortunately all his spiritual writing is fired by one inspiration, to bring home to clergy and laity a vivid sense of the supernatural reality of the Church and what this involves in her individual members. Failure to realize God's presence in the Church, sacraments and inner spiritual life of the Christian was seen by Manning to be the dominant fault of non-Catholics of his century. Catholics themselves had been only too often affected by this naturalistic outlook of the world around them [pp. 150 and 151].

With this principle of unity as a guide, it is possible to take up Manning's works not only with a new interest but even with some spiritual excitement. In the Preface to *The Glories of the Sacred Heart* (1876), for instance, we find the important principle concerning the doctrinal or dogmatic foundation for devotion and the spiritual life.

> I believe firmly that when divine truth is fully and duly apprehended it generates devotion; that one cause of shallowness in the spiritual life is a superficial apprehension of the dogma of the Incarnation; and that one divine purpose in the institution and diffusion of the devotion of the Sacred Heart, in these last times, is to reawaken in the minds of men the consciousness of their personal relation to a Divine Master [p. ix].

Manning returns to this theme in the third chapter of the book which is entitled "Dogma and Devotion", and he sums up this principle of his teaching in two paragraphs:

> The Sacred Heart is the key of the Incarnation; the Incarnation is the treasure-house in which are all the truths of the Father, Son, and Holy Ghost. The Incarnation casts off two rays of light; on the one side, the mystery of the Holy Sacrifice of the Altar; on the other, the devotion due to the Blessed Mother of God. Anyone who knows the Sacred Heart aright will know, as I said in the beginning, the whole science of God and the whole science of man, and the relations between God and man and between man and man. These truths are the dogma of dogmas, the treasures hid in the Sacred Heart, the tabernacle of God.
>
> Make yourselves, then, disciples of the Sacred Heart; learn to know it, and that knowledge will never pass away. Faith will pass into vision, but dogma is eternal; dogma is the truth impressed upon the intelligence by faith. The obscurity of faith will pass into the light of vision; but that impression of the truth upon the glorified intelligence will abide for ever when Truth Himself shall be seen face to face [p. 97].

Similarly in the first chapter of *The Temporal Mission of the Holy Ghost*, supported by a wealth of quotations from the New Testament and the Fathers, he develops one of the earliest modern statements on the Church as the mystical body of Christ, the "incorporation of those who are sanctified" and the union of the Holy Spirit with the mystical body and its members. In this, as in other matters of doctrine and practice, he was in advance of his age. Many of his addresses are remarkable summaries of Christian doctrine, interspersed with practical and pastoral advice of considerable acumen and force. He was concerned to show the richness and majesty of Catholic teaching and to urge his hearers to a more vivid appreciation of their inheritance.

III

It might be argued that Manning's works hitherto mentioned are not strictly spiritual writings. They are sermons, public addresses, statements of teaching intended only indirectly for personal meditation and the spiritual guidance of individuals. There are, however, aspects of Manning's work here and elsewhere which go deeper, and are concerned with personal conduct and personal ideals in the spiritual life. He noted on several occasions how happy he had been during the eight years (1857-65) when he had been superior of the Oblates of St Charles at St Mary's, Bayswater. In dedicating *The Temporal Mission of the Holy Ghost* to the Fathers of the Congregation, he spoke of them as "you with whom I have spent eight of the happiest years of my life". For the Oblates he had drawn up a rule of life, based on that of St Charles Borromeo, and before leaving them he set out for his successor a rule of life for superiors which may be taken to express both his own ideal and the standard he would expect in this congregation of missionary priests. The rule as Manning left it to Fr Dillon is as follows:

1. Try to be gentle, calm, silent as possible.

2. Never contradict anybody.

3. If you are forced to differ say: "I should hardly have thought so", or "I thought it was so and so", or "Can you be sure that it is so?"
Contradictions seldom convince and almost always irritate.

4. Never reprove anyone in the presence of others.

5. Find all the excuses you can for them, that they may be ashamed of excusing themselves.

6. Never refuse permission unless compelled and then with gentleness, kindness and regret. Let them know that you are going against yourself.

7. Try to cheer and amuse everybody especially if they are ill, or in trouble or out of sorts, that they may turn to you as the refugium and requies peccatorum.

8. Watch over your manner and tones of voice and look.
Be very courteous, considerate and delicate in dealing with others, especially those you are a little impatient with.

9. Pray very much against prejudice and dislike of persons.

10. Look through the largest window in the house, not through the keyhole.

11. In giving obedience don't order but ask. "Be as good as to do so and so." "Would you do so and so," and offer to do it sometimes yourself.

Here are ten commandments for you and one over [p. 55].

It is perhaps too much to expect a clearly defined spiritual doctrine to emerge from Manning's writings. He was, above all, concerned with practical things. Wilfrid Ward thought that, while having nothing of Newman's depth, precision or consistency, he had in a remarkable way the practical man's flair for going to the crux of any problem. In matters of philosophy, Ward thought that he was "sensitive as to generalities, but densely ignorant of all particulars", and that he tended, when faced with a difficult question, to oversimplify the issue, finding some particular phrase or maxim which supplied the one solution to the problem. Ward noted that this key to the problem "might be a maxim of the schoolmen or it might be some idea of his own".[1]

There is such a phrase which occurs in Manning's writings, and from which he develops a maxim of the spiritual life—somewhat vaguely expressed but apparently firmly held. Manning calls it the "Law of Liberty". At times he seems to carry it to the dignity of a principle closely akin to St Augustine's *libertas*, a fruit of the gift of Wisdom; while at other times it seems to be no more than a peg on which to hang notions of obligation and perfection in the spiritual life, perhaps little higher than a sense of loyalty and honour—what might be termed Christian or priestly *noblesse oblige*.

Manning first refers to the Law of Liberty in the Lenten sermons published in 1874 under the title *Sin and its Consequences*. He refers vaguely to the Law of Liberty in two of the earlier conferences, speaking of it as "the law of love, of gratitude, and of generous freedom, which is written by the Holy Ghost on the heart of all those who, being born again in Baptism, are united to our Lord and Saviour Jesus Christ by the bonds of charity". In dealing with temptation he says:

There is a law of liberty by which we are to be judged at the

[1] See the penetrating and sympathetic study of the Cardinal in chapter XIII of Maisie Ward's *The Wilfrid Wards and the Transition*.

Last Day. St James says : "So speak ye and do as being to be judged by the law of liberty." Now I am appealing to you in the liberty of Christians, in the generosity and gratitude of those who have been redeemed by the Precious Blood of Jesus Christ. I say, deny yourselves in these trivial but dangerous things.

It is, however, in the sixth conference, dealing with "The Joys of the Resurrection," that he sketches more fully the doctrine of the "Law of Liberty". At this stage it seems to be an effect of the virtue of detachment. We are free to love the creatures of God provided they do not bring us into bondage. In these conferences it is the negative side of liberty which is emphasized. Manning's teaching has some affinity with the Ignatian doctrine on the right use of creatures.

Manning returns to the theme and develops it more fully in *The Internal Mission of the Holy Ghost* in the conference on the "Gift of Counsel". He introduces the law of liberty as follows :

Saint James writes : "So speak ye and so do as being to be judged by the law of liberty." What is this law of liberty? If it be liberty, how are we bound? If it be a law, how are we free? It is precisely the law of counsels. If we love God and our Divine Redeemer; if we hunger and thirst after justice; if we would make sure of eternal life; if we know the will of God, and "This is the will of God, your sanctification"; if we desire to be sanctified, if we desire to be conformed to the likeness of our Divine Lord and His Immaculate Mother,—then the gift of counsel and the prompting of generous love will make us press onward and rise higher in the spiritual life.

He refers to the Sermon on the Mount and says it is the law of perfection given to the Christian people of the world.

Our Divine Master calls us to use our liberty as Christians, to rise above the low level of that which is absolutely necessary by the law of commandments, and to ascend up by the law of liberty towards Him, upon the mountain where He, our Light and our Life, dwells eternally [p. 339].

He says Christian perfection is an invitation "revealed to us in the Face of Jesus Christ" to use our liberty in love and generosity to go beyond the minimum set out in the commandments.

Christians are the first-fruits of the Holy Ghost. Look at the heathen nations, out of which we were taken. Compare the Christian people with the nations of the ancient world. I may say, compare the one Holy Catholic Church with the nations which, once of its unity, have now fallen away from it. Tell me where is to be found the Sermon on the Mount; where is to be found voluntary poverty; where is to be found obedience even unto death; where the spirit of martyrs; where the self-denial of confessors; where the meekness of the forgiving, and the mercy of those who die for their brethren? These things are to be found wheresoever the law of liberty and the gift of counsel are the light and the guidance of men [p. 340].

In the following year he developed this theme a little more fully. In the sixth conference in *The Glories of the Sacred Heart*, he speaks of the effect in the temporal order of the Incarnation and of its fruit both in individual souls and in Christian civilization.

If any man be in Christ Jesus—and all who are baptized and are born again are in Christ Jesus—"old things are passed away; and all things are become new". Wherever the hearts of men have been thus changed, first one by one, then by households, then by villages and towns and cities and peoples and nations, the world has changed its face. It has put off its own likeness, and has put on the image of Jesus Christ. The outward life and the inward Heart of our Divine Redeemer have become the pattern and law to men. And as the world was changed in individuals, households, and kingdoms, the Church of God became the mother and the queen of the nations. They were thereby redeemed from the bondage and corruption of sin into the glorious liberty of the sons of God. In them have been verified the words of Jesus Christ, "If the Son shall make you free, you shall be free indeed." "You shall know the truth, and the truth shall make you free."

He notes that Satan tempts men to a false liberty which would rob them of the freedom of the sons of God, and he explains more fully the Christian idea of liberty.

Liberty is not license; liberty is not the freedom of madmen; liberty is not the power to do wrong, nor to believe falsehood, nor to err out of the way of justice. Liberty means redemption from sin, from falsehood, from human teachers who may err and therefore can mislead. It is redemption from all spiritual tyranny of man over man, and the liberation of the whole man, with all his

> faculties, his intellect, his heart, his will, his affections; it is a redemption of the soul in all its actions towards God, in its obedience, in its faith, in its adoration, by the divine authority of Jesus Christ, who has purchased us with His Precious Blood, and has folded us within a unity where falsehood cannot enter, and under the divine guidance of a Teacher who can never err. Such is true liberty, and there is no other.

Above all, in the fifteenth chapter of *The Eternal Priesthood,* the chapter entitled "The Priest's Liberty", Manning gives more completely his conception of the law of liberty and the type of obligation it engenders.

He speaks of it as a law binding every member of the mystical body of Christ, and above all the chief members of the body, the bishops and priests of the Church.

"This law is anterior to all other laws, bonds, or vows; it is universal, and constrains every regenerate soul. It is supreme, and has no limit in its requirements except the power we have to fulfil it." This liberty of the sons of God is far more than freedom from the restraints of the Mosaic law. It is more than freedom from the guilt of original sin. It supposes the power and desire to fulfil the commandments of God. "There is no duty of a son of God that the regenerate cannot fulfil if they have the will. They have both the power and the freedom. This, then, is the first step in the liberty of the children of God."

In Manning's mind, however, the law of liberty carries the Christian soul to greater heights. It is the law of love, the desire of total giving and all that goes with the gift of self. In a remarkable passage manifestly influenced by St Augustine he sets out the ideals of Christian liberty, the true liberty of the priest.

> To serve God is to reign. To love God is perfect liberty. *Ubi spiritus, Domini ibi libertas. Charitas Dei diffusa est in cordibus nostris per Spiritum Sanctum, qui datus est nobis.* Where the Spirit is, there is liberty; for the Spirit of God is love, and where love is, there is liberty. There can be no liberty where love is not. Where the love of God is not, the love of creatures, and of the lowest of all creatures, the love of self, reigns. There can be no greater bondage than this. The love of creatures brings with it jealousies, disappointments, resentments, and manifold temptations. A priest who has lost his liberty by any unbalanced attach-

ment is in bondage. He is dependent for his happiness and for his peace upon something below God, which is changeful, uncertain, and transient. St Augustine describes his own state, before the supreme love of God set him free, as a bondage of iron chains, not forged by the hands of other men, but by his own iron will [pp. 194 and 195].

IV

We begin to see that Manning's law of liberty is less a theological doctrine than the exposition of a sound psychological and educational principle—the principle of personal responsibility and personal response to the Divine generosity. The spiritual life of the Catholic laymen and the Catholic priest depends not on outward conformity but on inward awareness and conviction. There are no limits to generosity and self-sacrifice except the limits of love. The practical consequences are manifold and ultimately depend on the generosity of each individual. Manning's teaching may be no more than an elaboration of the *Ama et fac quod vis* of St Augustine. It is, however, for those not bound by formal rule and observance, a teaching of great importance inspired by acute psychological insight. Ultimately in the spiritual life as elsewhere, each of us establishes personal standards and personal ideals. Examinations of conscience, days of recollection, annual retreats, are occasions to judge how far we come up to those standards and to renew the ideals. Such was Manning's purpose in enunciating the "law of liberty" for layfolk and for priests. It is above all in *The Eternal Priesthood* that this quality in Manning's teaching emerges. The assertions are there as are the quotations from earlier writers. But the style is more sober, the zeal more controlled, the insight into human frailties no less keen; while throughout the book are so many sound practical counsels of priestly wisdom.[1]

Manning has been criticized for the somewhat narrow and rigorist attitude which he adopted with regard to some aspects of the social duties of an Archbishop and a Cardinal. He exagger-

[1] This aspect of Manning's spiritual writing was treated very fully in an anonymous article entitled "Cardinal Manning and The Priesthood" published in *The Clergy Review* in November, 1940. It seems unnecessary to go over the ground covered by that article of which use has already been made in these pages.

ated the division (if indeed there was division) between the religious Orders and what he preferred to call the pastoral clergy. He was perhaps unduly preoccupied with the need for what Gioberti had called *un clero colto e civile*, yet nobody who reads his notes in Purcell's twenty-eighth chapter, especially his notes entitled "Law of Liberty; Expiation" can fail to be moved by his earnest preoccupation with the things of God and the service of his Master.

> Under the old Law of commandments the people are bound to pay tithes. Under the new Law of liberty people are free to give as they will, and the measure of their gift is the measure of their will. The will is regenerated in Baptism, and the law of God is written on the heart, and the heart is united by love to the love of God, and the will is conformed by love to the Will of God, *pondus voluntatis amor*; and the will in all its liberty becomes a law to itself. What limit ought a bishop to put upon the use of his liberty in the services of his Divine Master? No limit short of the use that our Lord made of His liberty for us. He gave Himself for us, and we ought to give ourselves to Him. And if a priest is called to this use of His liberty : how much more a bishop as the head and leader of his priests?
>
> Therefore "*summa dicere*" means "*summa semper velle, et summa facere.*"
>
> I should not have written what is in this Journal if I had not been bid to do so. What I have written will perhaps seem to some to be extreme, but it seems to me that someone ought to be extreme, that is, to pursue Truth to the utmost, and to hold up in everything the highest standard. There will always be many, too many, and those good men, who will refine and palliate and enlarge the ways of liberty. Let one then, at least, bear witness for the higher and the best, the happiest and the safest way.

Perhaps the most fruitful of his spiritual writings are in the journals and notes which he left after his death. As we read them we can well endorse the words of Wilfrid Ward's tribute—a tribute to a priest whose teaching and example did much to bring the fullness of Catholic teaching and ideals of Catholic holiness before the clergy and the people of this country. "Seldom has one felt better suited to a man's life-work and personal appearance alike, the great antiphon, so often sung as he entered his cathedral, and recited by those who prayed over his grave : *Ecce sacerdos magnus, qui in diebus suis placuit Deo, et inventus est justus.*"

XIV

FATHER FABER

By Ronald Chapman

Faber's reputation is not a happy one. His name is not actually forgotten but it exists at the edge of people's minds. Only a few vague impressions cling to it. He is, of course, remembered as a hymn-writer—not, strangely enough, as first Superior of the London Oratory. The pejorative remarks of Pusey may be recalled, and Newman's "As to Faber I never read his books" is not easily forgotten. Then Faber's low opinion of the Old Catholics is remembered against him. His spiritual writings are often dismissed by those who have not read them as extravagant, Italianate, Victorian.

It is true that if you pick up one of his books and glance through it Faber's faults as a writer are quickly apparent. He can be prosy, repetitive and sentimental. He has a *penchant* for private revelations and is at times simply silly. He openly delights in purple patches. There are great slabs of passages, sometimes chapters at a time, which glow with ethereal light but have little content. There are lapses of taste.... For the modern reader it is a formidable undertaking to sift the gold from the rubbish. For gold there is, pure gold. It is the purpose of this article to show that it exists.

Frederick William Faber was born in his grandfather's vicarage at Calverley, Yorkshire, in 1814. Educated at Harrow he gained a scholarship to University College, Oxford. Good-looking, eloquent, a born leader, ardently religious at a time when Oxford was never more religious, he quickly made his mark. Faber had been brought up with strong Calvinist leanings but on Septuagesima Sunday, 1836, he heard Pusey preach on baptism. This caused a sudden change of opinion and he fell under Newman's spell. A single-minded Yorkshireman, it was not long before he found himself on the Romeward fringe of the Oxford Movement. He won the Newdigate prize in 1836 and was elected to a fellowship at his college in 1837. But he was never at home in Oxford. He was happier at Ambleside talking Tractarianism with Wordsworth, writing long nature poems, or travelling abroad scrutinizing Continental religion.

At this time of his life Faber almost decided to make a career as a poet. He would not have succeeded in becoming anything but a dilettante. Nevertheless it needed a great effort of the will to tear himself away from the enjoyable, if purposeless, life he was leading. In 1842 he accepted the college living of Elton, Hunts., but after reading himself in immediately set out on a Continental tour. He was within an ace of becoming a Catholic in Rome and returned to Elton in October 1843 much shaken in his loyalty to the Church of England. For the next two years he lived and acted as nearly as possible as if he were a Catholic priest living in a Catholic country. He wished to work the parish "in the spirit of St Philip and St Alphonso". It was a strange experiment and perhaps no one but Faber would have succeeded as well as he did in the attempt.

A few weeks after Newman's conversion in 1845 he was received into the Church. He quickly formed a small community from his former parishioners and other converts called "Brothers of the Will of God". In 1846 Lord Shrewsbury handed over Cotton Hall near Cheadle to the new community and Faber was ordained in April 1847. But on 1 December of the same year, to the consternation of the other Brothers, Faber suddenly felt called to join Newman as an Oratorian. Such was the man's personality that the whole community followed suit and offered themselves as Oratorians.

In 1849 he was sent by Newman from Birmingham to London to establish a new Oratory. This was at first in King William Street, Strand, and was then moved in 1854 to its present site in Brompton. Faber was not a strong man and had always overtaxed his strength. From this time till his death he was more or less an invalid, burnt out by his immense labours. He died after a long and painful illness in 1863, aged only forty-nine.

Faber's spiritual works were written within seven years, at the end of his life, and they form an unusually coherent whole. They were the fruit of long thought and experience gathered when at long last he had the leisure to write. He often wrote when he was ill and regarded his writing almost as a means of relaxation. This explains many of his faults as a writer. By 1853, the date of *All for Jesus*, his theological opinions and style were fully formed. There is no sign of development in the eight books written in the seven years. They might all be volumes of one large work. It was apparently in this way that Faber thought of them. They can therefore be conveniently treated as a whole with only a few words on individual books.

Faber's work is in a *genre* of its own. It is not pure theology, nor mere devotion (even when it most appears to be so), nor explanatory apologetic, but a very individual mixture of the three. It undoubtedly owes a lot to the popularization of science which had already begun in his lifetime. He hoped to make intelligible to English readers the truths of dogma in the same way as the truths of science were being made intelligible. "We seek," he wrote in *Bethlehem*, "for men, or if so be a man, who shall wed all the sciences with theology, who shall reconcile faith and reason in one large lucid philosophy." Strange as it may seem to those who only think of Faber as a devotional author this was his ideal of himself as a writer. Whether he is discussing the possibility of other beings peopling other worlds or describing the beauty of an Italian landscape or the habits of animals, his vision is single. There is one simple explanation to all things, "one large lucid philosophy"—God.

In a passage at the beginning of *The Creator and the Creature,* too long to quote, he describes the view of London on the day that the conclusion of the Crimean war was celebrated. He notes the canopy of smoke above the city, the booming canons, the ringing church bells, the songs of birds, the insects on the foliage close beside him. In the garden a fleet of young perch are sailing round in the pond. "What a mingled scene," he concludes, "of God and man!" In all his books Faber delights to return to this mingled scene of God, man and creation. "All created life must in its measure imitate the uncreated life out of which it sprang. The very habits of animals and the blind evolution of matter are in some sense imitations of God. The fern that is for ever trembling in the breath of the waterfall, in its growing follows some pattern in the mind of God." "All the inferior animals, with their families, shapes, colours, manners, and peculiarities, represent ideas in the divine mind and are partial disclosures of the beauty of God, like the foliage of trees, the gleaming of metals, the play of light in the clouds, the multifarious odours of wood and field and the manifold sound of waters." Describing the birth of our Lord he writes, "When the first cry of the Infant Jesus sounded in the cave, the melancholy splashing of those far western waters was mingled with the imitated howls of beasts in that strange typical festival of heathenism."

It all comes back to God but God revealed by Jesus Christ—the God of love. Love is the beginning, the midde, the end of Faber's work. It is the key to morality, to creation, to theology. It is not merely a system—it is a deeply felt personal vision, experienced and pondered over. "We cannot look at Him as simply external to ourselves. Things have passed between us; secret relationships are established, fond ties are knitted; thrilling endearments have been exchanged, there are memories of forgiveness full of tenderness . . ." "O how often in the fluent course of prayer does not this simple fact that God is loving us, turn round and face us." "Pain or ease, sorrow or joy, failure or success, the wrongs of my fellow creatures or their praise—what should they all be to me but matters of indifference? God loves me." "He chose us when as yet we lay in the bosom of the great void. . . . He had a special love for something we by grace might be, and which others could not or would not be." "St John states it; no one can explain it; earth would be hell without it; purgatory is Paradise because of it; we shall live upon it in Heaven yet never learn all that is in it—God is love." "I cannot tell how men endure life who do not profess this faith in the Creator's special love." "Surely God cannot have been to others as He has been to us; they cannot have had such boyhoods, such minute secret buildings up of mind and soul; we have a feeling that about our own lives there has all along been a marked purpose, a divine speciality. Yet in truth how many millions of such tender and equally special biographies is the most dear and blessed God living in men's souls throughout all years and all generations! We are not singular among men; it is God's love which is singular in each of us."

Love is at work everywhere at the root of everything. "Creation is simply an act of divine love." "Creation is His love of Himself strongly and sweetly attaining its end through His love of His creatures and their love of Him. Perhaps all the works of God have this mark of His triune Majesty upon them, this perpetual forthshadowing of the Generation of the Son and the procession of the spirit, which have been and are the life of God from all eternity." "Why then does God love us? We must answer because He created us. This then would make mercy the reason of His love. But why did God create us? Because He loved us. We are entangled in this circle and do not see how to escape from it." "Because God is God creation must needs swim in joy. . . . From the joy therefore of the highest seraphim to the blythe play of the Christian child on the village green all joy is from Him. . . . The joy in the bright eyes and inarticulate thanksgivings of animals are from Him."

Faber was a clear thinker and he realized the implications of this philosophical vision on his approach to the spiritual life. "If this account of creative love be true, if God redeemed us because He persisted in desiring, even after our fall, to have us with Him as participators in His own eternal beatitude, salvation ought to be easy, even to fallen nature. If it is easy, then it might appear to follow that at least the majority of believers would be saved." Faber addressed himself to this "majority of believers". He called them "invalid souls" or the middle class of the spiritual world, or more explicitly his "poor Belgravians". He hoped to clarify their faith and thus raise them up to God. He did not expect to make saints of them, he did not write of the higher paths of sanctity, he hardly mentions dark nights of the soul. He believed it was this sort of person St Philip Neri set himself to sanctify in Rome and to whom his sons were called by God.

At bottom a severely practical man, Faber set out in his books to remedy a lack which was painfully obvious to him. His "poor Belgravians" wished to lead spiritual lives, their vocation was in the world—and what spiritual food were they given? Books written for enclosed religious—"dry books" as he called them, very well for those to whom they were addressed but hopeless for the poor Belgravian. What was meat to the one might be poison to the other. The spiritual books designed for those called to a high vocation when read by those living in the world could be the cause of deception, pride and more often than not of despair. Faber's books attempt to beguile his readers from the world, to attract them to God, almost, one might say, tempt them to religion.

Of course Faber's approach has its disadvantages. His enemies said he had, as it were, debased the coinage. Salvation can appear too easy and religion unreal. This never happened in Faber's mind. If his books are read carefully a structure of hard common sense and well-mastered theology is seen below even his most saccharine effusions. He also had a masterly understanding of the human heart. But it is true that out of their context or read by a hostile eye there are passages which seem to dissolve away the realities of the spiritual life. Religion seems to have gone to be replaced by emotion. Similarly, his critics complained, what if the candles at Benediction cease to be merely an attraction to religion and become a substitute for it?

That was the crux of the argument of those who rejected Faber's way of attraction. But in doing so it is hard to see (except on aesthetic ground) how St Francis de Sales and St Philip Neri would not have to be rejected also. Faber has his own answer.

> We hear people condemning unlucky devotees because they are fond of functions and Benedictions, of warm devotions and of pictures of the Madonna, of feasts and foreign devotion.... Now does it follow that because persons are fond of these things they have nothing else in their piety? Because they have one characteristic of good Catholics are they therefore destitute of the others? Because they like flowers do they reject fruit? Oh, but mortification is the thing.... Souls are gravely warned, without regard to time, or place or person or condition to be detached from the gifts of God and to eschew sweet feelings and gushing fervours, when the danger is rather in their attachment to their carriages and horses, their carpets and their old china, the parks and the opera and the dear bright world.... Better far to flutter like a moth round the candles of a gay Benediction, than to live without love in the proprieties of sensual ease and worldly comfort, which seem, but perhaps are not, without actual sin.

Yes, it is easy to be saved because we are loved by God. He only demands love in return. And what is easier, one might say more natural, than to love God? "Is it hard to find our joy in God? Rather is it not hard to find our joy in anything else?" "Our hearts bound upwards because God is above. We cannot help ourselves. The very purling of our blood in our veins is joyous because life is a gift direct from God." "To serve God because you love Him is so easy." "You must love. You must love. You must love. There is no other way. There is no help for it. Love will teach you everything." The argument comes round again. If we can love God, even a very little, then we shall be saved. And does it really matter that we have loved Him, even the small amount we do, because of a row of candles, an altar of flowers or even because of a purple patch in a spiritual book?

All for Jesus (1853) is the best known of Faber's works and in many ways the most characteristic. Its sub-title "Easy ways of divine love" shows its purpose. As an introduction to the spiritual life and to the practice of Catholic devotions it was extremely popular. Unfortunately it is aggressively Italianate and openly emotional. The parochial, the trivial and the sentimental are cheek by jowl with fine passages on the love of God. It is like a Catholic chapel in the worst taste—the real thing but not a little repellent. Even so when all is said and done the book is still a success. As likely as not the old magic after a hundred years will work on the modern reader. *Growth in Holiness* (1854) is a very different book—a manual on the spiritual life, sane, shrewd and erudite. It almost entirely lacks the rhetoric of Faber's usual style.

The Blessed Sacrament (1855) is full of high-flown language which can distract the reader from the originality of Book III. This turns out to be a bold, almost daring, piece of apologetic. It is remarkable that Faber never passed through a period of scepticism except in his schooldays. Yet this book reads like the apology of a converted sceptic. Faber argues with a shadow and the argument goes like this: either this amazing thing is true or else there is—nothing. It is the wrestling of Blanco White with a different outcome.

The Creator and the Creature or *The Wonders of Divine Love* (1858) is *All for Jesus* with a theological bias. Faber himself wrote that "it stands to the author's other work in the relation of source and origin". It contains the essential Faber and Faber at his least parochial. It breathes the confidence of a man to whose faith nothing is alien. It is in this book that he formulates most fully his conception of creation as an act of divine love. Faber, a poet by instinct if not in fact, here delights to stress over and over again the goodness and beauty of creation.

The Foot of the Cross (1858) is a highly wrought, often moving, but extremely long meditation on the seven dolours of our Lady. *Spiritual Conferences* (1859) contains little that is not elsewhere but is often shrewd. *The Precious Blood* (1860) on the Redemption is the work of a tired man. *Bethlehem* (1860), on the other hand, recaptures his early spirit and contains passages as good as any he ever wrote.

Faber was a startling phenomenon in mid-nineteenth-century London. His contemporaries and fellow Catholics were uneasy about him. What was this man, preaching his embarrassing message of love, couched in a Baroque idiom, doing in the world of Dickens, of steam engines and progress? He did not seem to belong.

Yet Faber did belong. The intellectual history of the nineteenth century is a series of reactions against Utilitarianism or what Chesterton called "atheist industrialism". Cobbett, Dickens, Carlyle, Ruskin, Arnold were as much in reaction against their age as was Faber. Yet we regard these men as of the very bone of Victorian England. Faber's reaction, if it can be called such, was a very different thing to theirs. But then the Oxford Movement differed from the Pre-Raphaelite Brotherhood. Looked at in this way Faber is most nearly akin to Dickens. The reaction of Dickens was the emotional reaction of the natural man, Faber's was the emotional reaction of the spiritual man. Is it fantastic to say that what Christmas was to Dickens, Marian devotions were to Faber? It was the attempt in both cases to redress the balance, to bring back into life what had been driven out by Bentham, in the one case human brotherhood, in the other the religion of love. The one was no less of his age than the other. Faber shows himself to be a Victorian in a hundred different ways. He is betrayed by his style, by his optimism, by his sugary taste, by his sentimentality. We don't like his referring to our Lady as Mamma. ("Won't Mamma be pleased!" he exclaimed after a crowded procession with the Neapolitan Madonna.) But then, we also don't like Little Nell.

Faber knew well enough the gulf which existed between his message and his readers. Could he have failed to do so? A less promising age for preaching the gospel of love could hardly be imagined.

We live [he wrote] as if we would petulantly say: ". . . you devout people in reality stand in the way of religion. It is hard for us to define religion; but you surely are enthusiasts. What we mean is, You are all heart and no head. . . . All this incarnation of a God, this romance of a gospel, these unnecessary sufferings, this prodigal blood-shedding, this exuberance of humiliations, this service of love, this condolence of amorous sorrow;—to say the truth it is irksome to us: we are not at home in it at all; the thing might have been otherwise. . . . Might we not put this tremendous mythology of Christian love, with all possible respect, a little on one side, and go to heaven by a plain, beaten, sober, moderate path, more accordant to our character as men, and to our dignity as British subjects? If the Anglo-Saxon race really fell in Adam why obviously we must take the consequences. Still, let the mistake be repaired in that quiet, orderly way, and with that proper exhibition of sound sense which are so dear to Englishmen."

Well! If it must be so, I can only think of those bold words of St Mary Magdalene of Pazzi: "O Jesus! Thou hast made a fool of Thyself—through love!"

That was Faber's apology to his age—and to us.

But does this really meet the case? Is it fair that Faber should shield his extravagances in this way? It is no good making preposterous statements and then calling them Christianity. That in effect was Pusey's charge—which Newman tacitly endorsed. But *was* Faber's theology extravagant? It is true there are exuberant phrases and occasional verbal exaggerations. It is also true that some of his sermons and many of his earlier writings are exaggerated. But no unbiased reader can fail to see that his theology was carefully thought out. As to his Mariology I doubt whether many modern Anglo-Catholics would object to it. He expressly does not teach the presence of our Lady in the Blessed Sacrament. Nor does he teach the presence of the Blessed Sacrament in heaven at the end of time. He mentions the belief only "to leave it in the uncertainty of a devout opinion".

Faber's future as a spiritual writer remains in doubt. He will certainly never again be read at length except by the few. He is, however, a very difficult author to anthologize. Several anthologies have been made without success. The difficulty is that it is not simply a question of choosing extracts. He not only says telling things on the subject of God's love but to get the feel of the man's mind it is also necessary to follow his argument. His books need to be epitomized and then illustrated by the telling passages. It would be a vast undertaking, but if well done would be worth the trouble. Perhaps Faber needs, like Augustine Baker, a Fr Cressy to compile a readable redaction of all his works into one work.

XV

JOHN CHAPMAN

By B. C. Butler, O.S.B.

Only one "spiritual" book stands to the credit of Dom John Chapman: the posthumously published *Spiritual Letters*.[1] I hope to show that, despite the paucity of published material, he deserves his place in this series of English masters of spiritual doctrine.[2]

Born in April 1865, the youngest child of the Archdeacon of Sudbury, he might be described as a product of Barchester—Victorian, well-to-do, Conservative, English of the English despite his unusual familiarity with the French tongue. Health precluded him from a public school education (he would otherwise have gone to Eton); but not from Oxford (Christ Church, of course), or a First in Greats, or the moderately High Church theological college of Cuddesdon. What could have checked this brilliant and profound young ordinand in a meteoric career to the heights of Bishopthorpe or Lambeth? *Dieu dispose*. After an intellectual and spiritual struggle of great acuteness ("My difficulties are a real terror and agony. I am in a great strait. People talk lightly about 'secession' as the 'easy path'. If only they knew what it feels like! And I have known it for six months almost unbearably") he was received into the Church in December 1890. He tried his vocation with the Society of Jesus but failed, and was ordained priest and solemnly professed at the Beuronese Benedictine Priory of Erdington in 1895. In 1913 he became temporary superior of the newly

[1] The editor of this volume, Dom Roger Hudleston, tells us that no idea that these letters would be published ever entered their author's mind. It is to be regretted that they were not accompanied, on publication, with a theological commentary. A number of passages have been pointed out where it needs to be shown that the thought and/or expressions do not contradict authoritative decisions especially various condemnations of sentences of the Quietist Molinos. In general, it may be said that these sentences, as condemned, appear to lack the qualification "in the intermittent act of contemplative prayer", a qualification supposed by Chapman, though not always stated.

[2] In what follows, unassigned quotations are from the above-mentioned volume. I have used the following abbreviation: BC=M. Bremond and Père Cavallera, *Downside Review*.

converted community of Caldey Island (now Prinknash Abbey), and in 1915 an army chaplain. The Erdington foundation was a casualty of the 1914 war, and Dom Chapman was allowed to transfer his stability to Downside, whither he was recalled from his work on the Vulgate Commission at Rome to become Prior under Abbot Ramsay in 1922. On Ramsay's death in 1929 Prior Chapman was elected to succeed him, and himself died in office in November 1933.

I

One of the most obvious things to say about Chapman is that he was a very great New Testament and Patristic scholar. Here, as in the ascetico-mystical field, his published books represent him quite inadequately; though *John the Presbyter*, now largely forgotten, is a striking example of poised, acute, original scholarship, taking its own line in serene independence of the greatest names of the pre-1914 learned world, and never refuted. He was, I think, the first to pioneer the road to a true solution of the vexed question of the "Primacy Text" in St Cyprian's *De Unitate*, chapter iv; but for his work on this subject, as for so much else (e.g. his explanation of the "brethren of the Lord"), you have to search the pages of the learned reviews of the years 1895-1930. *Saint Benedict and the Sixth Century* was not only a work of Benedictine *pietas* (by which I do not mean "piety"), but an audaciously brilliant attempt to "see" the work and place of St Benedict in sixth-century Church and Empire, as no one before Chapman (and perhaps no one since) has seen it. The posthumous *Matthew, Mark and Luke* is a sort of tragedy. Chapman, like all the best critics of his generation, had come to regard *Mark* as the earliest of the four Gospels, and as a source used independently by the authors of *Matthew* and *Luke*. The Biblical Commission appeared to favour a different view, and on Salisbury Plain, during the war, Chapman began to re-examine the question for himself. The result was revolutionary. He thought he saw clear evidence that *Mark* was dependent on a source indistinguishable from *Matthew*. Material for a book began to accumulate, and had reached impressive proportions by about 1931 (when he showed thc manuscript to me). But the cares of an uncongenial office, and then the onset of a fatal disease, prevented the completion of the work; and the devoted editing of Mgr Barton could not turn the torso into anything that could hope to win the sympathetic attention of non-Catholic critics. The book was published just before the 1939 war, and has hardly been heard of during the past fifteen years. Yet anyone who, with competence and an open mind, will read and re-read it, and then read it again, will find—whether or not it proves to him that *Mark* depends on *Matthew*—that it has shattered his belief in the dominant solution of the Synoptic Problem.

But such scholarship was only a part of Chapman's multifarious intellectual activity. A connoisseur of painting and music, he was an accomplished pianist, and once (disastrously) undertook to teach the resident community at Downside how Plainchant ought to be rendered. More importantly, he had enjoyed his philosophical studies at Oxford, and as a Catholic he could not keep his mind or his pen off dogmatic theology. I am not sufficiently in sympathy with him on this speculative side of his interests to be a fair judge of his philosophical and theological insights. I always thought that to have read the *Summa Theologica* at the rate of seventeen columns an hour did not necessarily qualify him as a master of Thomism. But he was not lacking in natural self-confidence, and there is a Downside story that he once undertook to teach to some young monks the treatise *De Trinitate*, with the remark that he was the only man who "understood the Trinity".

That story should be taken along with the warning, specially necessary for readers of the *Spiritual Letters*, that Chapman's humour was chronically irrepressible, fantastic, Carrollian, verging on the realm of pure nonsense, and often tumbling over into wild, straight-faced absurdity. A non-Catholic visitor, after a fascinating half-hour with the Abbot, was alleged to have reported that, charming as those monks were, they really did live in an odd world of their own; why, their Abbot had spent half an hour proving to him that the world was flat! He once excused the awkward gait of a young aspirant from the Antipodes, with the kind comment that of course he could hardly be expected to have learnt, so soon, to walk the right way up. Years before, he had got into trouble with his Jesuit preceptors because it was discovered that he had spent the time, during a noviciate walk, in proving to a companion that Napoleon never existed; this was thought to tend to undermine a proper faith in historical evidence.

A second warning may also be not out of place. Few spiritual writers have been so lacking in "unction" as Chapman was. He had a thoroughly masculine intellect, was a great realist, and by nature and habit was extremely reserved about his innermost feelings, which in any case he regarded as profoundly unimportant. There is a letter of 1912, to a nun whom, I suspect, Chapman did not yet know well, in which a paragraph of not very convincing "unction" is followed without warning by a sudden outbreak of the real, scandalizing, but intensely serious, Chapman:

> I must enclose a line to you, to wish you and all the Community all Christmas blessings and graces. May we learn to become very little with our Lord, if He is to do great things in us, as we wish. If His love has drawn Him down from heaven so low, that He may make Himself like us, how much He must long to lift us up, and make us like Him. It is a cruel road that He has chosen, taking our miseries and our sufferings, in order to be able to give us His joy and His glory. He makes our road very easy by comparison, though we complain, and think He is very cruel to us. I always feel the Crib so sad, as well as so sweet. It is not like Easter, which is nothing but rejoicing.
>
> I have come to the conclusion that one can remain united to God even when one goes to sleep in time of prayer. Don't laugh! (pp. 116 ff).[1]

Yet occasionally the veil is lifted, as in a letter to a young Jesuit

[1] It has been pointed out that the following proposition has been condemned: *Etiamsi superveniat somnus et dormiatur, nihilominus fit oratio et contemplatio actualis: quia oratio et resignatio, resignatio et oratio, idem sunt, et dum resignatio perdurat et oratio* (Denzinger-Bannwart, 1245). Two comments seem called for: (1) the condemned proposition should be taken as a whole; and it gives as the explanation of its thesis that *dum resignatio perdurat, perdurat et oratio*—as though prayer were identical with a *habit* of resignation. This Chapman would emphatically deny: "Prayer (even 'habitual prayer') is an *act* not a *habit*. The habit which produces the prayer is not the essence of the prayer. The essence of electric light is not electricity, but light" (pp. 55f, 1930). (2) Later in the letter quoted in the text above, Chapman writes: "I mean, quite seriously, that it is best to remain simply united to God's Will (making any acts to fill up the time, that come of themselves, or none at all if none come), and not to mind if one's internal attitude is very much that of *trying* to go to sleep. But of course one can do one's best to keep off actual sleep by fidgeting, or changing one's position, and so forth."

He is giving advice to a contemplative religious who is obviously past the stage of "meditative" prayer; see above.

whose spiritual experience and intellectual difficulties had plainly stirred Chapman to his depths:

> The ordinary person—and you yourself when not in a state of prayer—finds God far off—unimaginable, cold—a bare desert of perfection.
>
> He prefers—with Omar Khayyám—a glass of wine, which is here and now, and warming; and love means something nearer, and lower, and hotter to him.
>
> And God has answered.
>
> He has translated Himself into human language—He has come —*in propria venit.*
>
> Ηλυθες ὦ φίλε κοῦρε, τρίτῃ σὺν νυκτὶ καὶ ἠοῖ
> Ἤλυθες οἱ δὲ ποθοῦντες ἐν ἤματι γηράσκουσιν!
>
> (Don't be shocked—for the Saints use human language. Why shouldn't I use Theocritus?). (p. 229).[1]

Who but Chapman would have found two lines from a love-poem of Theocritus to express the yearning of his whole nature (below the "apex" of the soul) for the Word made flesh and the rising "on the third day"?

It is possible to spend a lifetime on the study of Christian origins and in theological speculation without constructing a theology of the spiritual life or becoming a master of the theory and practice of prayer. But Chapman was something more than a scholar and a thinker. His published writings give us little that is autobiographical, but there is a passage in the letter to a Jesuit quoted above which may be important:

> At 12 (or 13) years old I felt that religion ought to be transcendent, infinite, necessary—I suppose the vague, unexpressed notion that was in my head was "The One" of Parmenides, and the idea that the ultimate explanation of everything must be "The One". Of course I knew nothing of philosophy, and very little of Christianity (p. 206).

It is probable enough that the thirteen-year-old son of the Archdeacon of Sudbury had not read much philosophy, though it is also probable that he knew more of Christianity than most non-

[1] Thou'rt come, dear heart; this third night—nay, this dawn—
Thou'rt come—but in one day starv'd love grows old.

Catholic children of that age. But however much or little he knew by human tradition, I think the passage suggests that, like de Condren and Newman, Chapman had from boyhood a recognition of what I can only call the godhead of God; and the quest of this divine reality became the ruling passion of his life. It was, we are told (p. 4, from the Memoir by G. R. Hudleston), at Cuddesdon that he "began that inner life, with its habits of prayer and regularity, which, humanly speaking, led him to the cloister, and made him essentially a contemplative". That he became a fervent religious goes without saying. But it is also clear that after twenty years as a Benedictine he was still groping for light in his spiritual path.

It was inevitable that one so enamoured of God, and at the same time so intellectually alive and curious, should feel the need of a spiritual theory that would "work". This was at last achieved, when he was already in his forty-eighth year. He writes in April 1913:

> I really had no theory worked out until last November; and the reason I am writing now is because I believe I can be much more useful to others now I have thought things out more definitely, with the help of two or three "contemplatives" who, of course, know much more experimentally than I do, though they are younger, and have not directed people, or very little (p. 118).

This passage comes from a letter written to a canoness regular of the Lateran. Chapman gave retreats to a number of communities of religious; and it is probably not far from the truth to say that it was personal contact with those who, like the English canonesses of Bruges, were leading the contemplative life and carrying on the practical tradition of prayer which came down ultimately from the great days of the Flemish mystics, that drove him with renewed concern to his questionings, and perhaps suggested the basic answer. And it was in 1913 that he was sent to take temporary charge of the newly converted, formerly Anglican, community of men on Caldey Island (now Prinknash Abbey, Caldey Abbey itself having since been taken over by the Cistercians). Here he closely questioned members of the community who seemed to him to be experienced in prayer, and so was able to check his theory against their practice.

II

The "theory" (it is really an *ars* rather than a *scientia*) supposes that the devout Christian will "meditate" on the truths of revelation. To meditate is to occupy one's mind with a subject, meaning by the mind the reasoning reason and/or the imagination. Chapman had no doubt that meditation was indispensable:

> We must not forget that meditation is *necessary for all.* We must all *taste* the truths of the faith, assimilate them. For priests there is the study of theology, *theologia mentis et cordis,* and the preparation of sermons; for the laity there is devout reading and the hearing of sermons; monks and nuns have the Divine Office, and so in a way have priests. But more than this—for all of us it may be necessary and possible, even if we are Saints, upon occasion to use the lower faculties, to picture hell and heaven, to make present by fancy the sacred Humanity of our Saviour : sometimes a glance will be enough; but there is surely no rule, for dispositions and facility vary so greatly (BC, p. 15 n.).

In the modern centuries, however, two developments had taken place. It had become part of the rule of constitutions of most religious Orders and Congregations, and a devout practice for some of the laity, to devote a regular period of time daily (often half an hour) to personal prayer, apart from the Divine Office, the rosary, the Stations of the Cross, and other prescribed forms. And it had further become common to take advantage of this period of personal (or "mental") prayer for the practice of meditation. Indeed, it was quite normal to refer to the period of mental prayer as one's "meditation", and so recently as about the beginning of this century it was customary in my own monastery to read out in choir, the evening before, suggested "points" for the morning half-hour of "meditation".

Two reasons can be given for this use of meditation in time of prayer. The first is that, by it, the memory, imagination and reason are diverted from the pull of creaturely interests. We come to our daily prayer trailing clouds not of glory but of worldliness, or at any rate business. But if we can occupy our attention for a time with the mysteries of the faith or with sayings or incidents from the Gospels, there is a chance that this clamour of creatures will be temporarily suspended, and the claim of God on our faculties may be heard more clearly and persuasively. Hence Chapman would argue that, while for an enclosed religious half an hour of prayer might be enough, for people living in the "world" a much longer period would probably be needed—he did not, so far as I am aware, suggest how so long a time might be made available for the busy housewife or the rising barrister. In general, his doctrine about prayer was that the longer one spends on it the better it goes:

> The only way to pray is to pray; and the way to pray well is to pray much. If one has no time for this, then one must at least pray regularly. But the less one prays, the worse it goes. And if circumstances do not permit even regularity, then one must put up with the fact that when one does try to pray, one can't pray—and our prayer will probably consist of telling this to God (p. 53).[1]

The other reason for meditation in time of prayer is, that it provokes pious emotions, feelings, "realizations", which the will can then utilize in "acts" or "aspirations". Recall to the memory and the imagination the Child in the manger at Bethlehem; picture Him shivering slightly in the cold of the winter night, under the vague flickering of a Roman lamp; hear Him (in your imagination) whimpering for food. Then reflect that this "helpless" suffering Child is He who, even now while He shivers and hungers, is giving food and warmth to all living things—*per quem nec ales esurit*; and that these sufferings, a prelude to Calvary, are an effect and an expression of a love for yourself that is literally infinite. And now, reverting to the actual present, and knowing that He is here now, by His sacramental presence, by sanctifying grace, or because He is always omnipresent, present and "waiting" for your recognition of Him—will you not automatically turn to Him with acts of adoration, repentance, gratitude, trust and love? Thus your meditation has passed over naturally into "prayer", the "lifting up of the mind and heart to God". And as repentance is

[1] From a letter to a layman. The problem here raised obviously deserves further investigation. (1) Has one only prayed well when one *thinks* one has prayed well? (2) Is one's "prayer" to be identified with what happens when one is engaged on a set period of "mental prayer"?

not real unless it includes a firm purpose of amendment, it seems equally natural that you should pass on to an appropriate "resolution", which should be definite and relevant to your known circumstances. If, finally, you choose, out of the devout thoughts of your meditation, some one that may serve as a motto or "spiritual bouquet", to be recalled to your mind from time to time in the ensuing twenty-four hours, and so to bring your heart back to the pious sentiments aroused in the period of prayer, you will have completed the outline of a type of meditation which must be familiar to many of my readers.

"Meditation", thus understood and practised during set times of "mental prayer", "is an excellent devotional practice for those who can do it" (BC, p. 6). At least at a certain stage of the spiritual way it is "useful, fruitful and possible" (ibid.).

> The method of St Ignatius in particular seems an admirable instrument for converting from a worldly life to a devout life. The Saint intended his exercises for young men of good education and good abilities, who had not yet given much attention to spiritual things, but could be persuaded to try this month's retreat as an attractive novelty.... The same exercises ... will have a great effect upon those to whom meditation is an untried effort: for the first time the truths which they had learnt in the catechism and the creed are made real instead of notional.... It can be the means of leading to a new life and to any degree of sanctity (ibid., pp. 6 ff.).

But, argued Chapman, there are limits to the usefulness of this device; and I suppose that in a general way everyone would agree. To begin with, there are the "mystics"; their experiences are often held to be extraordinary and could therefore be left on one side by framers of systems of normal spirituality.[1] Secondly, one comes across people who, from the first, appear to have no "facility" for meditation, at least for formal systematic meditation. Thirdly, there is, in the practice of meditation (or so Chapman argued) a law of "diminishing returns":

[1] Chapman had his own explanation of mysticism, and those who are interested may be referred especially to the article "What is Mysticism?" printed as an appendix to the *Spiritual Letters*. This is *scientia* rather than *ars*; so far as I can see, it can be rejected without affecting the practical teaching with which I am here primarily concerned.

> The meditations lose their vivacity and their effort by custom. The imagination works less freely on matter which is too familiar, and emotions refuse to arise (BC, p. 8).

The vital point here is the last: *emotions refuse to arise*. It seems sometimes to be assumed that, as progress is made in mental prayer, the strictly "meditative" element will occupy a smaller portion of the "half-hour", but that the extra time thus available will naturally be used for a greater quantity of "affective"[1] prayer, those warm holy sentiments and fervent "coloquies" which are held to be the really prayerful element in the whole exercise. "That would be nice. But it is the opposite of what happens" (ibid., p. 10). The reader should note this appeal to experience. Chapman was not trying to wean from meditation and emotional prayer those who are intended for that kind of prayer and can find profit in it. He is dealing, like St John of the Cross, with those who are faced with a breakdown in the kind of prayer which they have been taught or have taught themselves—a breakdown which, it is presupposed, is not due to tepidity or ill-health. And his first comment is, as we have seen, that such a breakdown was to be expected for psychological reasons. We cannot expect that our five-hundredth meditation on the Child in the manger will let loose the same flood of emotion as overcame us when we first seriously applied our imagination and reason to this subject. The novelty has worn off; and it was as a novelty that the subject first enraptured us.

But Chapman offered a deeper, theological, reason for this breakdown, when it occurs in the prayer of those who are really seeking God and trying to lead a good life. He regards it as a symptom of what, with St John of the Cross, he calls the Night of the Senses. Meditation and "affective" (i.e. emotional) prayer, co-operating with the good will of one who is making serious efforts to reform his life, have "consolidated" the *pure will's* love for God, which has now become a "power in the soul". This pure-will love of the soul for God is one in act with "imperceptible contem-

[1] The word "affective" is equivocal. As used above, it means "emotional"; but in the classical tradition of spirituality it means rather prayer of the *will*, as distinct from both discursive and emotional prayer. It may be suspected that confusion of the two meanings has worked havoc in modern theory.

plation"[1]; it is, in fact, an "infused" love (for we are incapable by ourselves of loving God-revealed as we ought); and its operation, which the activities of the reasoning reason, the imagination, and the emotions, can only (in their direct effect) lessen or interrupt, tends by its very nature to inhibit the (prayerful) activities of these lower faculties. This inhibiting is called by Chapman "the ligature", and he has a favourite example of it:

> Reasoning about spiritual things produces conviction once for all: it can and must be recalled, but cannot be drawn out again for the same time it took to think out on the first occasion. And it is often dry, difficult and tiresome. Even if it were otherwise, the ligature stops it in prayer time, when the simplest words seem to have no meaning, and it proves impossible to understand the Our Father (BC, p. 12).[2]

Chapman ardently denied that what he was talking about was "high mysticism":

> I shall be told that this is mysticism, unproved and improbable. By no means. It is just ordinary religion. . . . What is a Christian to do when he wants to keep a good resolution? Is he to meditate, by using his imagination to rouse his emotions, which in their turn will move his will? No, for emotion is treacherous and short-lived. Is he then to think over all the reasons, and to work out syllogisms to convince him of his duty? Evidently not, for he is already convinced . . . every Christian knows the solution of this apparent difficulty: He is to PRAY. We all know that Divine Faith has to rule our human intellect, and that only the prayer of faith will save us, and not our own considerations. Not our reasoning powers, not "delectatio" is to draw our will and rule it, but *what we receive from God, infused faith and strength* (BC, pp. 12 ff.; my italics).

[1] The word "contemplation" derives from the Platonic vocabulary of the early Greek Christian Fathers. It emphasizes an aspect of prayer to which, in his practical theory, Chapman did not find it necessary to pay much attention, being more concerned with the volitional ("affective" in the classical sense) aspect. But every act of prayer is simultaneously cognitional (or contemplative) and volitional (or affective). The cognitional element can be almost "imperceptible", because the object of prayerful attention is God, and He is beyond our imagining and conceiving; we may be more conscious of the act of will by which we seek to attend.

[2] It should hardly be necessary to point out that Chapman does not allege that it is impossible to *recite* the Our Father, but to *understand* it.

And again:

> It is a dry land, where no water is; and *consequently "sicut desiderat cervus, etc."*. Only the desire is a *will*, not an emotion.
>
> All depends on whether you have the courage for so dry a prayer. And yet it has a supra-sensible consolation. It is one long act of love—not of my love to God, but of His to me. It is always going on—but in prayer you put yourself into it by an act of faith.
>
> What I am writing about is a prayer of "beginners", I know nothing about any other. There is nothing high about it. It is for those who have got beyond the stage where they want to *think about* our Lord as absent (pp. 46 ff.).

In fact, these people do not want to "think about" God at all—in time of prayer; they "want God, and not thoughts about God" (cf. p. 118). Their prayer is not spent in "thinking":

> The time of prayer is passed by beginners in the act of *wanting God*. It is an idiotic state, and feels like complete waste of time, until, gradually, it becomes more vivid. The strangest part is when we begin to wonder whether we mean anything at all, and if we are addressing anybody, or merely using a formula without sense. The word "God" seems to mean nothing. If we feel this, we are on the right road, and we must beware of trying to think what God is, and what he has done for us, etc., because this takes us out of prayer at once, and "spoils God's work"; as St John of the Cross says (pp. 119 ff.).

A word may be required about the phrase "using a formula". The *Spiritual Letters* includes, as an appendix, "A Few Short Rules" for contemplative prayer. These date from 1913, shortly after Chapman had arrived at his "theory", and they tell us that:

> All those who find it impossible to meditate, not from laziness or lukewarmness, and find they cannot fix their thoughts on a subject unless they cease to feel that they are praying, are meant to cease *all thinking*, and only make acts of the will. . . . *Let the acts come*. Do not force them. They ought *not* to be *fervent*, excited, anxious, but calm, simple, unmeaning, unfelt. . . .
>
> The acts will tend to be *always the same*. . . . The *principal* stage consists in this: "O God, I want Thee, and I do not want

anything else."—This is *the essence of pure contemplative prayer,* until the presence of God becomes vivid. (Then it *may* change, and praise or exultation may be the chief or sole act. But I imagine there is no rule.)

I think it is fairly clear that the "formula" of the letter is the verbal content (so to say) of the "act" or "act of the will" of the *Few Rules*. But I also think that in these (not to speak of other) passages Chapman has expressed himself in ways that may be misleading. The unwary reader might infer that his doctrine is that "pure contemplative prayer" *consists in* such formulated "acts of the will"; and, although Chapman says clearly that these acts are "not to be forced" but "allowed to come", the inexperienced practitioner may well find that either he forces an act, or else he is left without any such "act" at all. In fact, I suggest, there are "acts" which "suggest themselves" (what some writers seem to mean by "aspirations"), and there are acts which are deliberately induced ("forced acts"); and whether an individual uses the former or the latter or a combination of the two sorts may be a matter of temperament, circumstance, or grace. But the important thing to realize is that these "acts", whether forced or quasi-automatic, are *not* the essence of pure contemplative prayer; and that Chapman himself, at least in his mature view, did not think that they were.

We get nearer to his real opinion in a letter to an Ursuline nun, dated 1925:

> ... Hence the *distaste for meditation* which we are conscious of in the time of prayer. We want to use our Will to "want God", and not to keep our thought in order. We want to be "wanting God", and detached from everything else.... While our will is making its intense (but almost imperceptible) act of love, our imagination is running about.... The distractions, which are so vivid to us, are not *voluntary* actions, and have no importance; whereas the *voluntary* action we are performing is the *wanting* God, or giving ourselves to God.... The best and usual way to keep it (sc. the imagination) quiet is to repeat certain words, texts, ejaculations.... But the *real prayer* is the *act of the will* (wanting, loving, etc.) behind all this. You cannot *feel* this act of the will; but you can know it.... We have to learn to live by this higher part of our soul, and to pay no attention to anything else (pp. 180 ff.).

This repetition of "certain words, texts, ejaculations" is, I think, the same as the "acts" of the passage from the *Few Rules*. If so, it is significant that these acts are here distinguished from the "real prayer". The latter is indeed (rightly) described as an "act"; it is even called an action. But it is an "unfelt" act; it is a "wanting to want" God. We seem "to be idle, mooning, wasting time" (ibid., p. 179). The "real prayer", then, is neither a "forced act" nor an "aspiration", but something that is more continuous than these, something that goes on during their intermittent recurrence and after they have ceased and during involuntary distractions; something that actuates a "higher part of the soul".

We want a word to denote this "act" of the apex of the soul, this act which is "unfelt" and "almost imperceptible", so that while it is actually going on "we seem to be idle, mooning, wasting our time". St John of the Cross speaks of a "loving attention" to God; but, true though this description of the "act" of prayer in its contemplative aspect no doubt is, it may not at first be of great help to the person who seems to himself to be "full of distractions, and not praying at all" (ibid., p. 180). How, such a person will ask, can I be "attending" to God and at the same time "full of distractions"? Let us turn to another passage of the *Spiritual Letters*:

> What *does* matter is the upper part of the soul; but that is something which we can't *feel*, but only *know*. But we have to make sure that the highest part of our soul ... is united to God, and *nothing else matters* at all in this world. The right intention is the only way I can describe it. *The essential interior act of religion* is the giving ourselves to God, turning to Him, and remaining turned, uniting ourselves to His Will and renewing this union as often as we think of it, or simply remaining united (p. 175).

It is not clear that in this passage Chapman is speaking specifically about set times of mental prayer. But we shall see later that he came in the end to attach little importance to the distinction between "times of prayer" and the rest of the waking life of a devout person (our letter is addressed to a Canoness Regular of the Lateran).

The word that we seem to need, and we find it in this passage, is *intention*. Our intention is precisely the basic determination or orientation of the pure will in act, and it is what settles the moral worth of our life. The saying that hell is paved with good intentions is precisely not true. What hell is paved with is velleities which stopped short of becoming intentions—poor little potential intentions that aborted and never came to birth. Every priest knows that, granted the right form and matter, the sufficient condition for a valid Eucharistic consecration is ministerial intention. And every priest knows that this is compatible with extreme "distraction". Intention is the one thing that is completely under our own control. No pious thoughts, imaginations or emotions would amount to "prayer" if the intention to pray were absent; and on the other hand, granted the intention of praying, no amount or quality of distraction (*ex hypothesi* involuntary) can destroy the reality of the prayer. And an intention persists until it is retracted or *de facto* terminated by an act of the will, substituting some other intention.

We are not realistic enough in our discussions of prayer. Viewed from the human side, prayer is like any other deliberate self-determination. Intention is what unifies every moral entity. What makes the difference between a number of venial sins of theft and an accumulation of small thievings which amount to a grave sin is that, in the latter case, the materially distinct small acts are unified by a single intention. The writing of this essay has been done at various times, and has been subject to many major or minor interruptions. But it has been a single moral act, because it has been controlled throughout by a single intention; and the intention has been informed by a single intellectual grasp of an end to be attained. Of course, when our intention is directed to a finite external object, circumstances may occur to frustrate its realization, and this means that such an intention may fail to be completely "born". When our intention is directed to spiritual union with God, no created circumstance can frustrate it; and God will not frustrate it, because he is *Deus auxiliator*, the Redeemer of Israel.

It remains to mention the other big distinction between prayer and some other intentions. It is a truth of philosophy and faith that only by grace can the creature refer himself, or be referred, to God as self-revealed. Hence the intention of anyone who prays in a state of grace is an effect at once of habitual and of an actual grace. All such prayer is "infused" : and if "contemplative" means the same as "infused", all real prayer (in a state of grace) is contemplative.

Those who have studied and understood St John of the Cross

will recognize that Chapman's doctrine of prayer is identical with that of the great Spanish "mystical doctor", and the *Spiritual Letters* show that Chapman was conscious of this fact, and of his debt to his great predecessor.[1] But such teaching was not common, at least in England, in the first quarter of this century. Some idea of what we owe to Chapman may be gained by reading the chapter on Benedictine mysticism in Cuthbert Butler's invaluable *Benedictine Monachism* (1919), if we remember that Butler was the representative of a very sound practical tradition of contemplative prayer. Chapman's achievement was to discover for himself, at the cost of how much spiritual struggle, scientific observation, and hard ratiocination, that St John of the Cross had been right after all:

> For fifteen years or so, I hated St John of the Cross, and called him a Buddhist. I loved St Teresa, and read her over and over again. She is first a Christian; and only secondarily a mystic!
>
> Then I found I had wasted fifteen years, so far as prayer was concerned! Naturally I had a gradual revulsion against St Teresa (p. 246, written in 1920).[2]

A further incidental, but by no means unimportant, service was to extract the essence of the doctrine of prayer from the Carmelite, Spanish, sixteenth-century, personal trappings that clothe it in the writings of St John of the Cross himself, and to present it afresh in twentieth-century English dress. Thirdly, I suggest that by giving more emphasis to intention than to attention, Chapman has made the doctrine as a whole less Hellenic and more Christian.

III

The year 1912, when he formulated to himself his theory of

[1] There is, however, a difference of emphasis, as suggested above. Chapman underlines the volitional, affective, aspect of prayer, while St John of the Cross uses the traditional language of "contemplation", thus emphasizing the cognitional side—but it is a "general", "obscure", non-conceptual, sort of knowledge As such knowledge tends to elude our processes of reflexion, the person praying is often hardly if at all aware that he is "attending" to God. He should be told that he has nothing to worry about, provided he *intends to attend*.

[2] Anyone who suspects that there is a fundamental contradiction between the spiritual doctrines of the two great Spanish Carmelites is recommended to read "Contemplative Prayer in St. Teresa", by Dom David Knowles, *Downside Review*, April 1933 and following numbers.

prayer, was an important date in Chapman's life. Another was about 1920:

> I have been reading (for the first time) some of *Père de Caussade's l'Abandon à la Providence divine.* It is extraordinarily good. But, like St John of the Cross, it makes one realize that a simple *remise à Dieu* is not so simple. It is as easy as jumping into a fire, which you had not seen, and has the same effect. It burns your clothes first, then your flesh, and then your bones. It is a fearful thing to fall into the hands of the Living God. But He is Infinite Wisdom and Infinite Love all the same. It is quite a question whether the broad way is any more comfortable than the narrow one (p. 62, 1920).

This discovery of de Caussade meant a lot to Chapman, and as he was a principal influence in England in spreading the knowledge of the eighteenth-century Jesuit, it has meant a lot to many others.[1]

What did Chapman get from de Caussade? In one sense, very little that he had not already worked out for himself, or found elsewhere, as the following quotations, all from dates earlier than 1920, will show:

> Be sure that if you give yourself up blindly to God's Will, all will come right, though it may seem all wrong. Do not worry, but be confident (p. 35).
>
> A contemplative is always doing the same thing all day and all night. He is praying, or having breakfast, or talking, or working, or amusing himself; but he is principally conscious that he is *doing God's Will*; the different external activities seem to him a sort of varied outcome of one continuous internal intention (p. 38).
>
> How is it possible to be anxious, worried, self-conscious, bewildered, "with simplicity"? The answer is *abandon*—which is a French word (*une âme abandonnée* always sounds to me like "an abandoned character").

[1] Friedrich von Hügel was reading de Caussade away back in the nineteenth century. Chapman's discovery was made in 1920, and he owed it to a *Lady Living in the World* (p. 98). But already in 1914 the Anglican Bishop Chandler, in a remarkable book with the significant title *The Cult of the Passing Moment,* was quoting *L'Abandon,* and taking as his theme the view that the spiritual life is "a communion with God, or a waiting upon God, from one moment to another, with the corollary that fresh and progressive indications of His will may be thus received" (Preface). A copy of Chandler's book came into my possession in 1925, when I knew little of Chapman except as a scholar and a controversialist. When, some years later, I met the influence of de Caussade again in Chapman's own monastery, it was like the joy of meeting an old friend.

The point is that all anxiety, worry, etc., has its seat in the lower (not the lowest) part of the soul—in the imagination and emotion, or even in the intellect, but above this (or below it if you like) is the "apex" or "ground" of the soul, wherein prayer takes place, and union with God (p. 42).

God's Will towards us is:

(1) *Voluntas beneplaciti*—(permission).

(2) *Voluntas signi*—(precepts and counsels).

Hence two general virtues—including all others:

(1) Conformity (Rodriguez's name) or Indifference (St F. de Sales and St Ignatius's name) or *Abandon* (Mgr Gay's name).[1]

(2) Obedience (*a*) to commandments of God and the Church,
(*b*) to counsels, according to our state,
(*c*) to inspirations, according to supernatural prudence.

Also . . . our duty is summed up in giving ourselves to God, as He gives Himself to us (p. 233, written in 1911).

Thus, well before 1920, Chapman knew what one may call the bare bones of de Caussade's doctrine. He knew that, more important than the method of your prayer, your one all-governing task in the spiritual life was "to give yourself up blindly" to God's will; not to worry but to be confident; that times of "mental prayer" derived their total value from the same source as times of legitimate amusement—from the acceptance of God's will; that all virtues are included in "conformity" and "obedience"; and he even knew the name for the doctrine: *l'abandon*.

Yet he tells us, in his Introduction to Thorold's translation of de Caussade's *On Prayer*, that there was something in de Caussade which he thought was a "novel contribution to ascetical literature":

[1] Charles Gay, Vicar General of Poitiers, was the author of *De la Vie et des Vertus Chrétiennes considérées dans l'Etat Religieux* (three volumes, 1877). The fourteenth chapter (vol. 3) is entitled "De l'Abandon à Dieu", being preceded by chapters on Charity and Christian Sorrow, and followed by a chapter on Fraternal Charity. Gay's treatment of *abandon* is very beautiful, and depends (like de Caussade's) on Bossuet. But, whereas Gay devotes one chapter, and that neither the first nor the last, of his book to *abandon*, de Caussade makes it the whole substance of the spiritual teaching contained in his treatise.

We can be perfect here and now by being exactly as God wishes us to be here and now; perfection is not an aim to be realized in a dim and doubtful future, but it is for this minute, this very minute, and not the next minute or two : *hodie si vocem eius audieritis* : this moment is the most precious of all moments, for it is the moment in which we have the power of abandoning ourselves wholly to God's Will. No other moment is in our power. We need not worry about what is to come; by hope we abandon to God the care of the morrow, of our perseverance, of our death, of our eternity; but by charity we abandon ourselves to His Will now. . . . We all know that it is only in the present moment that we merit, only in the present that we act, only in the present that we love. But (de Caussade) connects this necessary fact with our duty of confidence as to the past and the future : he insists on it as the safeguard against worry and despondency, the great dangers of all dangers, and he expresses it in a startling phrase : "the Sacrament of the Present Moment".

God is everywhere, and in past and future : He is above all space and time; but to me, it is not the distant but the near, not the past and future but the present moment, which is the veil of God, or rather the unveiling of God. I cannot always tell His Will for the future, but I can never doubt it now; and I can always be sure of being united to His Will now. If we seek Him, we have found Him.

In de Caussade, Chapman found, then, a synthesis of spiritual truths which he had been discovering piecemeal for himself over a period of thirty years. It was a synthesis developed and presented by an eloquent writer who was also a religious genius of a high order. And it was worked out and applied by de Caussade with astonishing vigour and completeness in the four interdependent spheres of creation, history, redemption and psychology. It was utterly mystical and at the same time utterly Christian and evangelical. And it finally enabled Chapman to overcome the dichotomy which had bothered him for so many years : the painful contrast between the transcendence, infinity, necessity of God and the complexus of this unnecessary, contingent, arbitrary universe of finite realities, within which Christianity is situated, and to which it makes its own contribution of "unnecessary, contingent, arbitrary facts and doctrines" (pp. 205 ff.). Of course he had known all along that there was only one rational "solution" of the contrast :

God made the Cosmos.

Why? It was a *very* odd thing to do!

And what an extraordinary universe to invent! Just fancy inventing *matter*! and thinking of such a thing as time—or space! Very clever of Him, no doubt—most ingenious, to imagine such curious facts as co-existence and succession. But very arbitrary and absurd—one might say, insane. . . .

Of course there are many odd and (*a priori*) most improbable things besides space and time and matter—such as colour and light, music, right and wrong (conscience), pain, wonder and so forth—not to speak of the moon; and there are many questions one might ask, which philosophy would find it hard to answer, such as why England is not an island, why things don't fall upwards, why I cannot describe heat and cold, why things don't look larger in the distance (pp. 205-8).

A rational solution is one thing. A realized, practical, lived solution is another. And all along there was that discomfort with the arbitrary, driving him to wild humorous outbursts of jeering at its absurdity—the other side of the mastering desire for God:

You remember that I sent you a huge series of papers of theology—a theodicy—a theory of the world on the Christian hypothesis. Now, oddly, I can't say that *any* of that is my real spiritual life. I did not know this till lately.[1] It is my Faith—it leads me to God—it is most useful out of prayer. But in prayer always—and out of prayer also—the mainspring of everything is wholly *irrational,* meaningless, inexpressible. "I want God"—and the word "God" has absolutely no meaning. I find so many in this positively absurd and obviously mystical condition; I suppose one "contemplates" without knowing it. Of course it simplifies people's spiritual life into nothing but the desire of God's will. The whole object of life becomes to want nothing but God. *Only there is no reason for it.* The word "God" means *nothing*—which is, of course, theologically correct, since God is nothing that we can think or conceive. St John of the Cross describes the state at length in three places. Hardly anyone seems to understand it. I could have been in it—with immense profit—twenty-two years ago, or more. But no one told me it was possible (p. 248).

What de Caussade brought to this tormented, hungering, spirit

[1] He is writing a few months after the invention of the "theory".

was the lived and life-giving unification of the two contrasted orders of reality, summed up in the triumphant phrase: the sacrament of the present moment. No longer only *over against* but utterly *within*, the complexus of created, historical, contingent finites, as this complexus becomes actual for us in the passing moment in which alone we are so arbitrarily actually alive, de Caussade points us to the eternal and the necessary, "made flesh" for our salvation which is identical with His glory.

The significance of this discovery for Chapman in his personal life may be dimly conjectured by those who know something of the disappointments, frustrations, and sorrows of his last years, in an office which was distasteful to him from the first, and which prevented so much that he would have wished to do,[1] and of the last months of a weary illness that brought premature death. But this is not a biography of Chapman, and it is more to the point to indicate the effect that it had on his direction of others, of which a sample may be given from a letter to a Benedictine nun, written in 1925:

> We have to learn in practice what we always knew in theory: everything that happens is God's Will. God's Will always intends our good. God's Will is carving us into the likeness of His Son.
>
> Every moment is the message of God's Will; every external event, everything outside us, and *even every involuntary thought and feeling within us* is God's own touch. We are in living touch with God. Everything we come in contact with, the whole of our daily circumstances, and all our interior responses, whether pleasures or pains, are God's working. We are living in God—in God's action, as a fish in the water. There is no question of trying to *feel* that God is here, or to complain of God being far, once He has taught us that we are bathed in Him, in His action, in His Will.

[1] "It is really a great blow to become Abbot. There are so many things I wanted to do. I shall value your prayers . . . that I may not do much harm." (p. 187).

XVI

MONSIGNOR RONALD KNOX

By Thomas Corbishley, s.j.

It is rarely safe to prophesy about the taste of posterity, but it seems difficult for us not to suppose that the name of Ronald Knox will be chiefly remembered for his translation of the Bible. Whatever opinion men may come to hold of the merits of the translation as a translation, the achievement itself will surely always remain to impress the imagination. In the context of this article it is tempting to suggest that the ten years or so which went to that achievement had a profoundly modifying effect on his spiritual outlook. It is possible to point to a *Retreat for Priests,* published in 1946, and show how much it makes use of biblical figures as pegs on which to hang spiritual teaching. But if this argument is meant to suggest that the spiritual teaching was somehow a by-product of the work of translating the Bible, we shall be hopelessly wrong. One of the features of Ronald Knox's earliest religious writing, even in the days before he was a Catholic, is the intimate knowledge of the Bible which it displays.

Take for example that trenchant piece of polemic, *Some Loose Stones*, published in 1913. Already we see his concern for the inspired Word of God, his uneasiness about the critics' attempts to undermine the Christian's faith in its inerrancy, his refusal to accept the latest fashionable hypothesis, on the ground that it sprang from a wrong approach to the Bible.

> The argument has been, not that we should distrust hypotheses because of their uncertainty, but that we should distrust them because of the certainty with which inconsiderate people hold them. Everybody knows that all hypotheses are in the last resort partial and insecure as a representation of the truth; at the best, they cannot be positively proved, they can only escape refutation. This alone would give strong ground for doubting that the first principles of our faith were ever meant to rest on foundations so precarious. But it is not merely that they are insecure avenues

to truth: my complaint is that they contain definite provocation to error. And on the ground of this constant temptation, of which I am myself fully conscious, if I could not preach the Christian faith in its fullness on a basis of absolute *a priori* certainty, I would give up preaching it altogether.

He does not, indeed, concern himself there primarily with the content of the Bible; but throughout the book his knowledge of and love for it are patent and emphatic. It seems fair to claim that it was not the translating of the Bible which moulded and refined Ronald Knox's spiritual teaching, but rather that, because he had from the beginning felt this devotion to it as a primary source of religious truth, in his later years he was happy to spend so much of his precious time in the task of making it more accessible to the ordinary Christian.

The passage just quoted may serve to illustrate what was perhaps the least expected characteristic of Ronald Knox's whole religious and spiritual outlook, its complete and absolute normality. I say "perhaps the least expected" because of his early history. After a record at Eton which was outstanding (Christopher Hollis has described him as "perhaps the greatest schoolboy of all time"), he went up to Oxford where a career of equal brilliance awaited him. Not merely was he accepted as an unusually gifted scholar, collecting with a certain inevitability the highest classical awards, but he was equally successful as a member of a society of young men who shed lustre on Balliol in its heyday. At the Union he was, and remained almost to the end of his life, a speaker of recognized genius.

Yet none of this turned his head, or, as far as we can judge, ever impaired that natural modesty which was the basis of a profoundly Christian humility. When Modernism was particularly vigorous in the Church of England, he employed his talents, not in developing new theories, but in defending the traditional views. Had he felt so inclined the Higher Criticism would have found in him one of its most gifted adherents. His linguistic ability, his skill in textual criticism, his insight into what may be called the psychology of authorship might have seemed to lead naturally to alliance with the Streeters of the day. Although, as we know, he numbered several of the more radical critics amongst his friends, he held Scriptural truth too sacred to be a theme for mere cleverness. All his cleverness was turned to the defence of orthodoxy.

He was saved from the perils to which his unusual qualities might have exposed him by an absolute faithfulness to the practices of piety. Mgr Vernon Johnson has given us a precious picture of him, after some spectacular success at the Union or in some other company, slipping quietly into Pusey House for the early service there. The habit grew on him, when it was no longer allegiance to what Pusey House stood for that claimed him. To the end of his days, at the height of his fame and amidst the press of work, he never faltered in the simple regularity of the devout priest. Just as he always had time for correspondents, guests, casual callers, so he always had time for the detail of regular observance.

The most remarkable feature of his life at every level was that he matured surprisingly early, and that, having matured, he neither ran to seed, as so often happens, nor was he content to rest on his early laurels. His mind was richly stored from his early days; yet he was ever adding to its riches. His flashing wit was a sign of the quickness of his thought; yet he never relied on this quickness. All his public utterances, sermons, conferences, lectures, speeches, were prepared with meticulous care. Even after they had been written out, as they invariably were, he would work over them in preparation for the actual delivery, marking the pauses, underlining the emphatic word. It was this thoroughness which made his spiritual teaching so effective.

If we ask what is the content of that spiritual teaching, we must surely reply by saying that it is simply the orthodox, "classical" teaching of the recognized masters of the spiritual way. It is, indeed, so conventional, in a sense, that it is not easy to single out any special features for comment. Yet it is the experience of most of us that we have never read or listened to a conference, a broadcast talk or a sermon by Ronald Knox which has not illuminated for us some aspect of our faith, enabled us to appreciate more precisely the importance and the desirability of an interior life. What was his secret?

It was quite simply that he was himself a man at once wholly dedicated to the living of a full Christian life and possessed at the same time of a remarkable gift for communicating to every type of listener the significance of that life. "To every type of listener"

—that is the point. Until comparatively modern times, we feel, "spiritual reading" was an activity indulged in by priests and religious, and as a work of supererogation by a handful of the laity. During the past forty years, a great change has come over the scene. More and more publishers of spiritual literature are consciously aiming at a growing public of lay readers. And though it would be false to claim that Ronald Knox was a pioneer in this movement, there can be little doubt that he has enormously accelerated its growth.

In some ways, he could be seen at his most characteristic in the short sermons which he wrote for a number of years for publication in the *Sunday Times*. Without in any way seeking to water down the full truth of Catholic doctrine, he was yet able to present it in a way that would make it, if not acceptable, at least intellectually respectable and entirely compatible with wit and urbanity. Typical of the author were the refusal to compromise, the insight into human nature, the gift of compressed, at times epigrammatic, statement of profound truth. Here are a few specimens of what he so justly called *Stimuli*:

> Any organised Church gives you not gold waiting to be minted, but ore waiting to be smelted; there will always be dross.
>
> We moderns are contemptuous of outward appearance; it does not follow that we are humble.
>
> Much easier to find a man who has corrected a tendency to pull his drives than a man who has conquered the habit of uncharitable talk.
>
> The difference between the Old and the New Testaments is the difference between a man who said: "There is nothing new under the sun" and God who says: "Behold, I make all things new."

A wholly different audience, and yet, as we know, one no less important in his eyes, was the school which found shelter, with him, in the Actons' home at Aldenham Park. Had it not been for the accident of war and evacuation, we should never have had the precious *Slow Motion* books—precious, again, not so much for what they say as for the inimitable way in which they say it. For example, we are all familiar with the distinctions between "notional" and "real" assent, as made by Newman. We have, in fact, become so used to it that our very acceptance of it has itself become almost a "notional" affair. How fresh it becomes when we read the following passage:

> To *believe* a thing, in any sense worthy of the name, means something much more than merely not denying it. It means focusing your mind on it, letting it haunt your imagination, caring, and caring desperately, whether it is true or not. Put it in this way. If somebody says to you, "Of course, your own country's rule in the Colonies is every bit as brutal as German rule in Poland," you don't reply, "Oh, really? I dare say it is." You care furiously about a statement like that. You may not have the facts at your fingers' ends, but you are not going to let a statement like that pass without examination. It would alter your whole idea of what the world is like if you thought a statement like that could be true. And it has, or ought to have, the same sort of effect if somebody tells you that some article of the Christian creed isn't true. . . . If you really *believe* a thing it becomes part of the make-up of your mind; it lends coherence to your thought, colour to your imagination, leverage to your will. It *matters* enormously.

I have quoted this passage, not merely because it illustrates the Knox technique; it also illuminates the man himself, in a profoundly important way. He was a man for whom the basic reality of this world was the faith of Christ as taught by His Church. There is a passage in *The Belief of Catholics* which brings out the same point even more emphatically.

> Where you see men, in the old world or in the new, full of the conviction that there is one visible Church, and that separation from it is spiritual death; where you see men, in the old world or in the new, determined to preserve intact those traditions of truth which they have received from the forefathers, and suspicious of any theological statement which has even the appearance of whittling them away; where you see men distrustful of the age they live in, knowing that change has a siren voice, and the latest song is ever the most readily sung; where you see men ready to hail God's Power in miracle, to bow before mysteries which they cannot explain, and to view this world as a very little thing in comparison of eternity; where you see men living by the very high standards of Christian ambition, yet infinitely patient with the shortcomings of those who fall below it—there you have the Catholic type.

We do well to ponder this passage, with its surely deliberate echoes of the style of the great Newman, for it expresses the soul of Ronald Knox. He was first and foremost a Catholic.

He spoke for the Catholic Church, and when he spoke to the members of that Church, whether they were schoolgirls, undergraduates, pious laity in retreat, the members of an ordinary congregation or priests of God, he spoke to them always in a way that might help them to appreciate more fully their Catholic heritage. Versed as he was in the lore of Enthusiasm, appreciative as he was of the contribution to Christian holiness of men like Wesley or Bunyan, closely as he had studied the French mystical writers, he yet knew that the greatest assistance he could give to his fellow-Catholics in their struggle to achieve sanctity, was to enable them to understand the basic truths of the Church's teaching.

That is why he was prepared to bend his mind to the task of instructing those schoolgirls at Aldenham, translating the language of theology into words of one syllable which they could follow, not scorning to use their own familiar slang where it might help. So he can explain the effects of the Fall.

> Sometimes we get indigestion, and you will find that with older people, sometimes even with schoolmasters and schoolmistresses, indigestion puts them in a bad temper. Indigestion puts them in a bad temper—do you see what has happened? Indigestion, which is a matter concerned with the body, has given rise to bad temper which is a matter concerned with the soul. The body, which ought to be taking its orders from the soul, is giving its orders to the soul instead! That is the kind of thing the Fall has let us in for.

Or this, on the Communion of Saints:

> The floor of heaven is like a window with a muslin curtain across it; we can't see in, but the Saints can see out. They see what we are doing and are interested in what we are doing.

So, in a brilliant parable about prayer for the Holy Souls:

> You remember the fable about the lion which was caught in a net, and the mouse that helped it by eating through the net so that it could get out? You and I are like that when we pray for

> the souls of Christians departed.... We can help them, and it isn't presumptuous to think of ourselves as helping them, even splendid people who have fallen gloriously in battle—we are the mice nibbling away at the bonds which hold them, that is all.

Nor is it right to say that this is not "spiritual writing" in the strict sense of the term. The great quality that he possessed was that of being able to blend ascetic exhortation with straight instruction. Often the exhortation is implied rather than stated; but it is almost invariably there. At times, he becomes quite explicit, as when, talking about the Holy Ghost, he gives advice on prayer.

> I think we sometimes make a mistake about that when our prayers aren't going too well. We try to make a tremendous effort at concentration, try to pump up more energy from somewhere inside ourselves, and reduce ourselves to a better state of prayer by sheer will-power. Whereas I think really the right attitude for us is to fall back more on the Holy Spirit, and leave things more to Him. To say, "Go on praying in me, Holy Spirit; I can't do anything; I know I can't do anything by these frantic efforts of my own. Every time I really try to settle down to it, I find myself thinking about the holidays or about that girl I've quarrelled with, and nothing seems to come. But I *know* it's all right *really*, because it is *you* who do the praying; I am only a dumb instrument for you to make noises with. Since I find my own efforts make so little difference, let me keep still and leave room for you to go on praying, praying in me."

Are we mistaken in supposing that this sort of treatment is far more likely to encourage ordinary people to try to pray, or not to give up praying, than will many of the more formal treatises in the subject? Ronald Knox was not a man to water down the teaching of the Church; but he is insistent that, in this matter of prayer, we shall enjoy the freedom of the children of God. So, in his *Retreat for Lay People* he declares:

> When we are approaching him in the intimacy of our own private prayer, I think he likes it as well as anything else, because it shows more confidence in his understandingness, if we remain silent before him and let our silence do him honour. No need, even, that any special train of ideas should be passing through our minds, that we should be setting out, even in our silent

thoughts, any formula of petition. To keep quiet in his presence, letting our hearts go out to him in utter confidence, in appealing love, in a tender sense of our own unworthiness—that, no less than any formula of words, and perhaps more than any formula of words, is what is really meant by prayer. . . . He wants us to use the liberty of the spirit, and come to him boldly, as his children, choosing the prayer that suits us best.

Or, as he puts it in *The Priestly Life*:

Go through the motions of praying, if that is all you can do, and when you have finished, offer it up to God in a spirit of humility. Tell him he knows your fashioning, knows you are but dust; deplore that natural weakness which makes it so hard for you, his creature, to do the thing you were put into the world to do. Confess to him, at the same time, the habitual want of seriousness and purpose in your life, which prevents you attaining recollection when you want it. Tell him you wish your prayer had been one long peaceful aspiration to him; unite it with the prayer of our Blessed Lord while he was on earth, and ask to have it accepted with that mantle cast over it. . . .

Not that, as a spiritual counsellor, Ronald Knox was lax or easy-going. Occasionally, indeed, one seems to sense a touch of Puritanism in his attitude, as when he says:

There's this trouble about doing what God wants us to do—that it's so often, at the same time, the thing that *we* want to do. Even if it's the kind of thing that doesn't sound very attractive at the first go-off . . . it's extraordinary how people get to like it, and take a pride in doing it well, and want to go on doing it. That means, that we are never quite sure whether we are doing what is God's will because it is God's will or because it is ours.

The answer, of course, is that it is often because God's will coincides with our own that the service of God remains, basically, a reasonable and human activity. However, though in conversation on the topic of asceticism he sometimes revealed a strain bordering on the puritanical, his teaching was in the tradition of the great spiritual writers—the Fathers, St Thomas, St Francis de Sales, de Caussade, Newman, to mention but a few—it was vivified and made effective because of his own personal insight into human nature, its needs and its problems.

Here are a few samples of his shrewdness and his sanity:

Don't force yourself into an attitude of dramatized contrition about being the kind of person you are, so hardened, so frivolous, so insensitive. These pious rhodomontades don't really help us on.

There are a lot of Christians who do love God, but because they think they can't love God, never get on to the next thing—which is giving up their lives and their wills to him.

Our Lord said to St Thomas, "Blessed are those who have not seen, and yet have believed." I dare to hope that he will say to some of us, "Blessed are those who have not felt, and yet have loved."

You see, we men are very curious people. Each of us, in his heart of hearts, thinks he is right. We seldom take other people's advice, unless it chimes in pretty well with the decision we had already formed on our own account. Yet we care desperately what others think; we cannot be satisfied with the self-approval of our own conscience, we must be for ever justifying ourselves in the eyes of our fellow-men.

It is possible, no doubt, to take a strictly theological line about it; to fall down on your knees when the light goes out whilst you are shaving, and tell Almighty God that you have deserved this punishment by your sins, and that you are prepared if need be to go on in darkness all the rest of your life, to show your love for him. When I say that, you complain that I am making the whole thing sound silly and high-falutin' and exaggerated. Well, of course, I am; I'm just trying out a formula, and obviously it doesn't quite add up.

Largely because his spiritual writing took the form of sermons, retreat addresses or conferences to undergraduates, it is possible to overlook the massive theological structure underlying these *disjecta Membra*. What then were the basic theological topics discussed and illuminated in this corpus of writing? First and foremost, of course, it was the doctrine of the Incarnation which was at the heart of his teaching. This comes out most clearly in his two books of Oxford Conferences, developing the pattern of Christian thinking from the fundamentals of Natural Theology, through the traditional discussion of the *praeparatio evangelica* to the central theme of Christ's life and work, treated both historically or exegetically and also dogmatically. It was here above all that his immense scriptural learning came to bear most effectively and most movingly.

But the Incarnation was not left as a piece of theological antiquarianism; it was shown as fertilizing the life of the Church and her members in the sacramental system of which he was so brilliant an exponent, precisely because he could relate the theory of supernatural life to the realities of human experience. How many of us, reading his *Window in the Wall*, have been both thrilled at the mastery of his exposition of eucharistic doctrine and astonished at the fertility of a mind that, year after year, could find something not merely new but utterly penetrating to say on this subject! Most priests will have two or three sermons on the Blessed Sacrament. Here we have two score of them, each redolent of the preacher's own devotion and also holding a consoling or inspiring lesson for his congregation.

Perhaps more remarkable is his collection of wedding sermons, *Bridegroom and Bride*. Here again, the theological, sacramental, incarnational aspect of the occasion is beautifully blended with the tender humanity of a man who could enter, it would seem, into the minds and hearts of each couple, listening to him on this most solemn moment in their lives. Nowhere else, I believe, does he reveal so fully the secret of his success as a preacher and a spiritual writer. For him the platitudes of the textbook were living realities, because they referred to real men and women, genuine human situations.

So, too, was it with his sense of the priesthood. Alive as he was to the tremendous wealth at the disposal of Christ's priests, he was not less conscious, partly out of his own self-understanding, partly from his shrewd insight and wide experience of seminaries and presbyteries, that we do indeed keep this wealth in frail vessels. Aware of all this, he used the opportunities afforded him by the many retreats he was invited to give, not to exaggerate the burden, but to help to support it, not to depress but to console, not to criticize but to inspire. He did not gloss over the failures of too many priests; but by contrasting the reality with the glorious ideal he encouraged even the most disillusioned to renew their hope.

One of his conferences in *The Priestly Life* is "Our Lady". It concludes with these words: "She is something more to us than a theological symbol.... Rather, to each of us, she is a personal romance. Because a natural instinct makes us unwilling to discuss such things in public, I will leave it at that. The real secret of her influence on our lives is something undefined, something undefinable." Shy, undemonstrative and utterly unsentimental as he was, Ronald Knox has never from the beginning hidden or sought to hide his deep devotion to the Mother of God. We recall the footnote in *A Spiritual Aeneid* : "At the time of my ordination I took a private vow, which I always kept, never to preach without making some reference to our Lady, by way of satisfaction for the neglect of other preachers." This, of course, was in his Anglican days, but, if the occasion for such reference passed with his reception into the Church, the practice persisted.

Even at Eton, he "had a strong sense of the patronage of the Mother of God. Her name was part of our title; her lilies figured on our coat of arms; the blue of her robe you could see daily on the blazers of the Eight and the caps of the Eleven". True, but how many Etonians, one wonders, have appreciated these simple facts? Or again, who but Ronald Knox, at the time of his greatest need, when he was adrift from Anglicanism yet unable to accept Catholicism, would have read into a well-known line of Virgil the interpretation :

MARIA undique et undique CAELUM

In defending devotion to our Lady, he was, he knew, defending the central truth of Christianity. "Protestants have said that we deify her; that is not because we exaggerate the eminence of God's Mother, but because they belittle the eminence of God. . . . They refuse honour to the God-bearing Woman because their Christ is only a God-bearing Man." It was inevitable, then, precisely because his spirituality was essentially Christocentric, that it should include a marked emphasis on devotion to Mary. Not, as he confessed, that he cared to discuss her position in terms of theology. "For some reason, if there is one supposedly English word which annoys and depresses me, it is 'Mariology'." He did much more. He made her live in the minds and hearts of his listeners. As always, in his thought and utterance, theology was pointless unless it bore effectively and fruitfully on the life of the believer.

So was it in his treatment of the various Saints whom he was called upon from time to time to honour. If for example we look at the series of sermons on Saints, published in the volume entitled *Occasional Sermons*, we find the following typical passages. In a sermon on St Benedict:

> The founders of the great religious orders have picked up, each in his own characteristic way, that one life-giving message which Our Lord Jesus Christ brought to earth. St Francis seized upon his poverty, St Philip Neri on his simplicity, St Paul of the Cross on his love of suffering, St Ignatius on his untiring zeal to do the will of his Heavenly Father. But the great Saint whose memory we are celebrating today, the founder, directly or indirectly, of all our Western monastic institutions, caught up and preserved for ever, as the watchword of his Order, a single word from that interview in the Cenacle, the word "peace". In a world so full of unruly agitations and turbulent emotions, there should be cells —tombs if you will—where men should live consciously striving to attain the peace of Christ.

Nor was it any generalized lesson, so to say, which he drew from the example of the Saints. Again and again, he relates the lives of the Saints to the lives of his hearers, to their lives lived in the England of today.

> Man's happiness lies in devoting himself; his success is the offering he can make. And our Confessor was a successful man, yes, even in this world, because in his simple piety, in the unaffected generosity of his nature, he set himself to serve the men about him, by easing their burdens, by relieving their necessities, by confirming them in their allegiance to the Faith. Great opportunities passed him by and he never marked them; he might have altered the dynastic history of England, have left us different manners and a different political constitution, if he had been other than he was. Instead, he left all these things to God's Providence; and God's Providence, using the ambitions of human agents as its puppets, moulded our history beyond man's expectation. And what do they mean to us now, those human agents? Mere names in the history book, mere stiff, attitudinizing figures on the Bayeux Tapestry, they have become part of a past hardly less remote to us than legend.... The Conqueror, who diverted the stream of history, went to his grave disappointed, and lies there an historical memory. The Confessor, whose ambitions could be satisfied by

finding a poor man his dinner, saw no corruption in death, and lives the patron of his fellow-countrymen.

There is something Chestertonian in the following passage from a sermon on St Anselm.

It is not that the Saint has become unpractical, like the philosopher: the philosopher blinks because he has come out of the darkness of his study into the light of common things; the saint blinks because he has come out of the light of his oratory into the darkness of the world. He has been with God; and in seeing, as we do not see, the greatness of God, he has seen, as we do not see, his own smallness.... To the man who has once seen himself as he looks in comparison with God, all worldly preferment, not because it is too high or because it is too low a sphere for his attainments, not because others seem more competent to fill the post, not because it entails labour or responsibility, but simply because it must in some measure make him the recipient of worldly homage and give him honour in the sight of men, is an anomaly not to be thought of, a miscarriage of justice to be avoided at all costs.

And combined with the ascetic teaching is generally to be found the practical, apologetic lesson. Thus, in a sermon on St Albert the Great:

... This post-war world feels a different world to us elder people, and our juniors are not slow to rub it in. They talk, they write, as if the world of Einstein and Jeans and Rutherford and Eddington were a world re-born; as if every earlier guess at truth were not superseded or exploded; as if, for the first time, we had come to know. In such ears, what use to celebrate the praises of St Albert? The very name sounds worse than medieval; it sounds Victorian.

That is the secret of the modern world's attitude towards the Christian religion, and towards the Catholic Church in particular. They hate it not because it is something arrogant, not because it is something uncomfortable, not because it is something foreign, but because it is something out of date.... A hundred years back they hoped to dispose of the Church by disposing of the Bible; now their tactics have grown more subtle. They hope to dispose of the Church by disposing of Aristotle. It has become the fashion to

> gird at us because our whole thought is built up round a philosophical system which was fifteen hundred years old when we assimilated it, and has now ceased to hold the speculative allegiance of mankind. . . .
>
> The modern world lives on its intellectual capital, exploits the prevalent doctrine of the moment in the interest of its heresies; floodlights the universe with a gleam of partial illumination, or darkens the skies with doubt; the Church, who is wiser and older, stores new things and old alike in her treasure-house, and brings them out in their due relation to enrich, permanently, the experience of mankind.

Parallel to (and almost a corrective of) the foregoing is this passage from a sermon on Albert's more famous pupil, St Thomas Aquinas:

> St Thomas was a great saint and what we properly celebrate on the feast of a great saint are his virtues; his purity of soul, his humility, his easy converse with the other world. If he happened to be a philosopher as well, that does not really concern us; it was part of God's Providence that he should realise his sanctity in the life of a philosopher, just as it was part of God's Providence that St Benedict Joseph Labre should realise his sanctity in the life of a tramp covered with vermin. There is no more reason to talk about philosophy when you are celebrating the virtues of St Thomas than there is to talk about entomology when you are discussing the virtues of St Benedict Joseph Labre. . . . Sanctity is not a work done; it is a life lived.

Encouraging, consoling, inspiring at all times; yet there are occasions when he can speak with a devastating ruthlessness. Thus a sermon on the Church ends with the words: "A scandal carries further than a tale of sanctity; Our Blessed Lady loved and died unknown, but all Jerusalem knew when Judas hanged himself."

Or again, from a sermon on the Responsibility of Man:

> Prejudice is not carelessness, it is something deliberate; it means refusing to investigate the claims of the Church because you dislike it, the will driving the intellect, and driving it in blinkers.

One last quotation, from a broadcast sermon on the Assumption, may serve to exemplify the different aspects of his teaching and the peculiar felicity of his treatment.

When the Son of God came to earth, he came to turn our hearts away from earth, Godwards. And as the traveller, shading his eyes while he contemplates some long vista of scenery, searches about for some human figure that will give him the scale of those distant surroundings, so we, with dazzled eyes looking Godwards, identify and welcome one purely human figure, close to his throne. One ship has rounded the headland, one destiny is achieved, one human perfection exists. And as we watch it, we see God clearer, see God greater, through this masterpiece of his dealings with mankind.

XVII

SPIRITUAL READING FOR OUR TIMES

By Lancelot C. Sheppard

In many ways it is a pity that no one has attempted to do for English spiritual writers what Bremond did for the French. In his eleven volumes he is studying, he tells us, "the inner life of French Catholicism . . . the sources, main currents, and development of a religious renaissance treated by many historians but to the best of my belief only chronicled very summarily."[1] It is noteworthy that he decided to begin with the period of the wars of religion leaving untouched the previous centuries which saw the growth of the tradition to which his authors were the heirs. Such a method would hardly be suitable in a work about English spiritual writers for, as the present series of essays shows, there is a certain continuity to be discerned, tenuous though it is at times, through the whole series of writers down to our own days. Our medieval forebears, as Bremond said of his seventeenth-century mystics, "are much nearer to us than we think. Of that which we were formerly, 'something has remained in us, a fragment, a reminiscence, as it were'."[2]

The series of writers studied in this book presents us, then, in miniature, with a picture of the inner life of English Catholicism. After the medieval authors, Dame Julian, Walter Hilton, Richard Rolle, the author of the *Cloud*, what stands out most clearly is the comparative absence of mystical writers (in the technical sense) of whom we find only two, Fr Augustine Baker and Abbot Chapman. There are very good reasons for this. The sixteenth and seventeenth centuries, the period of the great mystical movement in France and Spain, was a time in this country of religious strife

[1] Henri Bremond, *Histoire Littéraire du sentiment religieux en France depuis les guerres de religion jusqu'à nos jours*, volume I, Paris 1916. English translation by K. L. Montgomery, *A Literary History of Religious Thought in France*, volume I, pp. v-vi, London 1928.

[2] Bremond, *op, cit.*, vol. I, p. vii.

and persecution when there was hardly any spiritual writing and mysticism found its living experience in martyrdom or else, as with Benet Canfield, was practised in exile. Catholics in England down to the beginning of the nineteenth century were a small body fighting for their very existence with the result that what they produced was either polemical or mere necessary material for the minimum religious life that was possible at the time.

With Emancipation, followed in less than a quarter of a century by the re-establishment of the hierarchy, a change occurred though other circumstances intervened to make this new situation less fruitful than might have been expected: the difficulties inherent in the re-establishment of the hierarchy, the increase of the Catholic population due to the influx of Irish as a consequence of the famine, the lack of financial resources necessary to provide the churches and schools that were needed, all combined to hamper very considerably the intellectual and cultural development of Catholics in the nineteenth century. As a result, there is little that is original to be found until the end of the century. Newman is the one exception, of course, towering head and shoulders above the rest, but it is significant that he was the product, not of a seminary in this country or of the English College in Rome, but of Oxford University. Faber, the writer who for his religious impact comes nearest to Newman, though in a very different class, had enjoyed similar advantages. As a result of Manning's mistaken policy to prevent English Catholics frequenting Oxford or Cambridge there was no provision for their higher education. If, in addition, it is recalled that the very large majority of them were poor it is hardly surprising that the nineteenth century has little of real importance to offer us save Newman.

Any appraisal of English religious writing must take account of the effects of the Reformation. Not only did it cut off Englishmen, the non-Catholics certainly and to a great extent the Catholics, from the continuing stream of religious thought on the Continent, but paradoxically it gave Catholics in this country a foreign *cachet* which they have been slow to lose. It could hardly have been otherwise. For something like two centuries their priests and leading laity were educated abroad, it was government policy to represent the Catholic Church as a foreign institution, Catholics were struggling for existence. Small wonder that they endeavoured to remain a compact body apart from their fellow-countrymen and appeared to shut themselves off from the main stream of national life and that even their speech and writings showed little mannerisms that could be termed un-English by their compatriots.[1]

Despite the fact that many of the Oxford Movement converts did their best to make as clean a break as possible with all aspects of their former religious allegiance they infused into the Catholic body some of the cultural heritage from which it had largely been cut off by the stern realities of penal days. In some ways it can be said that they brought back to English Catholics not so much the foreign devotions and lives of the saints that caused not a little trouble in the middle of the nineteenth century as some of the tradition of English religious writing that had been developed outside the Church on the basis of pre-reformation trends: Jeremy Taylor, Richard Hooker, Lancelot Andrewes, to mention but three, contributed something to our heritage having first absorbed something from it. Faber's "warmth", his liking for "hot" prayers, can be ascribed to his former evangelical background even if he found what he wanted in Italian sources. If an English Bremond were to write a history of English religious thought these are matters that he would have to take into account. Nor could he neglect the Anglican borrowings from Continental Catholic sources. Though this is too large a subject to be gone into here it may be worthwhile mentioning that in the seventeenth century Anglican editions of Francis de Sales, Louis of Granada and Lanspergius appeared and that among Bishop Ken's books (still preserved in the Bath Abbey Library) are the works of St John of the Cross, Fénelon, Francis de Sales, etc. Dean Granville of Durham in the eighteenth century recommends the Jesuit Fr Bartolomeo Ricci's *Ars cogitandi* and *Ars meditandi* and has a good word to say of Fr Augustine Baker, though he adds a warning against his "enthusiasm".

A further line needing lengthy exploration is the relationship

[1] Archbishop Ullathorne writing to Abbot, later Cardinal, Gasquet (25 January, 1888), says: "There is a phrase which you sometimes use, and which I take the liberty of pointing out, which the educated converts point out as limited to us old English Catholics, brought by us from France but not English, and refer to the phrase *in their regard*. . . . The English equivalent is *with respect to* or *with regard to*" (Shane Leslie, *Cardinal Gasquet*, London, 1953, p. 108). Then there is the difference in pronunciation by Catholics and non-Catholics of such words as *confessor*, *refectory*, etc., which continue to the present day.

between the Catholic mystical tradition and Donne, Herbert, Traherne and Vaughan (the metaphysical poets) or Whichcote, Culverwell, John Smith, Cudworth and Moore (the Cambridge Platonists). All these are so many influences that go to make up the complex of our religious tradition, signs of a mutual interpenetration that went on and indeed goes on imperceptibly despite barriers of religious allegiance and belief.

It is difficult to sum up the characteristics of the English spiritual writing that are mentioned in this book. A practical approach to problems, in general a plainness of statement, avoidance, within reason, of rhetorical artifice, a certain solidity, an absence of fireworks—all these qualities have been attributed to English spiritual writers in the past by foreign critics. And yet as we examine the writings of the men and the woman mentioned in this book nearly every one of them appears as an exception in some respect or other to the rather dull catalogue of qualities quoted above.

Reading such remarks one cannot escape the impression that the commentator really means that dullness is the outstanding characteristic of English spiritual writing. And yet as we examine the writings of those mentioned in this series it seems impossible to label any as dull or indeed to lump them together as belonging to one category, to make of them an English "school" of spirituality, all neatly docketed and subdivided.

Indeed it is better to avoid such terms unless we can be sure of making clear their entirely relative nature. In a recent book Fr Louis Bouyer writes of the practice of systematically cultivating

> a Benedictine spirituality, a Jesuit spirituality, a Carmelite spirituality etc. . . . There might be some justification for the practice if each Order or Congregation had confined itself to gathering together from its first Fathers those precepts and teaching applicable to its specific tasks. But it is hardly so when in each case an attempt is made to create a complete view of the spiritual world, systematically closed in upon itself and foreign, if not hostile, to other views formulated in a like manner. . . . Such attempts, whether overt or masked, contain an unavoidable contradiction. How, for example, can Ignatian spirituality and Carmelite spirituality be set up against one another like two opposing groups when it is obvious that St Teresa chose indiscriminately for directors Jesuits, Dominicans or Franciscans as well as Carmelites, provid-

> ing that they were men of God and good theologians? And even St Ignatius, despite the very definite structure of his spiritual edifice, neglected no source available to him in Catholic tradition, beginning with monastic sources whose ideal has sometimes been seen in radical opposition with his. . . . St Benedict, St Francis, St Ignatius never intended to do anything else than set before their contemporaries perennial Christian spirituality, Catholic spirituality, simply adapted in its presentation rather than in its fundamental principles to the immediate needs of their period.[1]

It seemed necessary to emphasize this at the end of a series like the present one. Dame Julian, Walter Hilton, Fr Persons, Bishop Challoner, Mgr Knox, to take a random selection, are all trying to set before their contemporaries Christian, Catholic spirituality, adapted to the needs of their period; because they write in our language, because their method of approach is one that we find sympathetic, because their manner of thought has affinities with ours, they strike a chord within us, we are attracted to them and read them more easily perhaps than we do a Frenchman or a German, but it would be wrong nonetheless to endeavour to set up an English school of spirituality, an English way of holiness.

It is the more necessary to point this out at the present time as since the beginning of this century, and especially since the last war, certain movements have arisen, or seem even to have come to maturity abroad, and are now beginning to have an effect in this country. Thinking of our past naturally leads us to think of the future, and a conclusion to a series of this kind seems to call for some sort of analysis, or at least of some indication, of probable trends in the same field in our own times together with some appreciation of advantages and dangers.

Since the beginning of the century there has been taking place in the Church a theological movement, a theological renaissance it might be called. It is characterized by a return to sources—to the Bible, regarded as containing God's message to mankind rather than as an anthology of snippets for quotation in support of a theological thesis, a polemical treasure chest; to the Fathers, also, as proclaiming and explaining the message; to the liturgy, in

[1] Louis Bouyer, *Introduction à la vie spirituelle*, Paris, 1960, p. 23.

which the proclamation of the message takes place, as the worship of the *Church*, one result of the deeper perception of the theology of the Church. All these aspects of the renewal of theology, thus briefly summarized, are the result of an immense effort of work by theologians, scripture scholars and liturgists. No one who examines attentively the theological work (in its broadest sense) being produced all over Europe at the present time can fail to observe the change that has taken place.

The results of all this are to be seen slowly emerging, even in this country, and it has exerted an influence on our religious writing, but not, perhaps, so great an influence as elsewhere. This is shown clearly enough in two matters that are really fundamental but which have not obtained here the prominence that they deserve. I refer to the liturgical movement and the Bible

It would take too long to go into the history of the liturgical movement and the reasons for the misunderstanding of it that was current for so long in this country. Here we must confine ourselves merely to a recent manifestation, the reform of the liturgy.

A reform of the liturgy is in progress because in it the Church expresses her unchanging belief and in the course of time certain aspects of that belief were seen to be given less emphasis than was required, their expression in the liturgy was overshadowed by other, less essential matters. For example, the restoration of the Easter Vigil emphasizing the centrality of the Resurrection in the Christian mystery, is a fundamental reform of obvious importance. Its relative failure in this country to make Easter night the high light of the whole of the Church's year, a pastoral occasion of immense importance, is indicative of our general lack of understanding of what the liturgical movement, now clearly encouraged by Rome, is all about.

Deepening of understanding of the nature of the Church's worship led to the need for fuller understanding of the Scriptures. Biblical theology and research have developed enormously in recent years, but it is significant that we do not yet possess a translation of the Bible into our own tongue from the original languages as do other parts of the world. This is not to decry Mgr Knox's great work which was truly a gigantic undertaking brought to a successful issue, but the fact that he translated from the Vulgate, that so far as can be seen nothing else was considered, has its significance.

The principal features of the theological renewal to which I have referred very shortly can perhaps be summed up by saying that it has resulted in a re-emphasis on the centrality of the passion, death and resurrection of our Lord—the paschal mystery—leading to a greater doctrinal insight, to an enriched eucharistic theology, a wider understanding of the theology of the sacraments and, in these apocalyptic times, a more integral eschatology.

In considering the religious writing of our day it is impossible not to be struck by the change that is taking place; new ideas, fundamental ideas that have previously very largely been lost sight of, are to the fore. But how much of all this is native to our country and how far are we lagging behind, following in the wake of others whom we seem content to allow to do our thinking for us? We have only to consider the amount of translated work, principally from the French and German, that is published annually to realize that our own contribution is not very large. There are advantages, of course, in having at our disposal the best religious thought of Europe in our own language. But there is a danger too. We are apt to adopt conclusions, to take up positions without perhaps doing the necessary preliminary thinking. Our practical approach sometimes leads us into difficulties. Translations of foreign works are very useful, but they do not dispense us from the original thought and hard effort needed to produce our own religious books.

The various movements of our times—Catholic Action, Young Christian Workers, secular institutes, and so on—that have largely come to us from abroad, have obviously contributed something to the impact of Catholicism in this country. And each of them, in one way or another, has led to a considerable specialized literature, even if most of it is to be found in booklets and periodicals. Yet in the sphere of religious writing of this sort again there lurks the danger alluded to above, of an *ad hoc* spirituality, an enclosed garden, so to say, specially thought out for a determined milieu or state of life.

In the book already quoted Fr Bouyer tells how an attempt was made to give the diocesan clergy a special spirituality so that they should not be indebted to the religious Orders. Following this came the idea of defining a lay spirituality in clear contrast with monastic and sacerdotal spirituality. It was forgotten that the first monks, the creators of monastic spirituality, desired on a last analysis to be no more than devout layfolk. From such ideas it was but a step in certain Catholic Action circles to propose a workers' spirituality, a student spirituality, even a spirituality of agricultural workers. "It looks as if there was some confusion between the proper concern to impregnate with the spirituality of the Gospel the problems belonging to each specialized milieu and a vague idea which, could it be defined, would amount to refashioning the Gospel according to the mentality, the professional distortions, the prejudices or fads current in different circles."[1] In this way would quickly arise a Christianity, or gather a whole host of Christianities, of classes and cliques, such as were envisaged by St Paul's exclamation : "Here is no more Gentile and Jew, no more circumcised and uncircumcised; no one is barbarian, or Scythian, no one is slave or free man; there is nothing but Christ in any of us" (Col. 3. 11).

Spiritual reading in most of the past centuries covered by this book, certainly in the last two or three, conjures up the idea of a regular exercise by the devout, by clergy and religious, undertaken for the particular purpose of personal progress towards perfection and confined to certain well defined matters—prayer, the virtues, eucharistic communion as a personal practice of devotion, the lives of the saints and so on—and very often confined to certain well-tried books.[2] Certainly nowadays we tend to cast our net wider and, if we do not follow von Hügel's advice to his niece to begin with the British Museum catalogue of Greek coins, we can appreciate to some extent the reasons that were behind his advice. Gradually the Bible is coming to occupy its proper place again and books about the Bible proliferate. Books also on the worship of the Church, on theology in all its aspects, biographies of the saints, the Fathers in English (two series are in course of publication) are abundant. All these are the elements of what should form the

[1] Bouyer, *op. cit.*, p. 24.
[2] Not so very long ago the only spiritual reading in one noviciate was Rodriguez on Christian perfection read aloud to the novices.

intellectual baggage, the religious culture of the Christian in the world today as in the past. Our greatest need in the modern world is for an adult Catholicism and to this our spiritual writers of the past in company with their modern counterparts can lead us, the older ones reminding us, perhaps, of much that we tend to overlook in our own times.

BIBLIOGRAPHY

General

KNOWLES, M.D.: *The English Mystical Tradition,* London, Burns & Oates, and New York, Harper, 1961.

POURRAT, Pierre: *Christian Spirituality,* volumes I-III, London, Burns & Oates 1922-24; volumes I-IV, Westminster, Md, Newman Press, 1953-8.

SITWELL, G.: *Medieval Spiritual Writers,* London, Burns & Oates, and New York, Hawthorn Books, 1961.

Aelfric

SKEAT, W. (Editor): *Aelfric's Lives of the Saints,* early English Text Society series lxxvi, lxxxii, cxiv (in two volumes), London and New York, Oxford Univ. Press, 1881-90.

WHITE, C.L.: *Aelfric: A New Study in his Life and Writings,* Yale Studies in English ii, Newhaven, Conn., Yale Univ. Press, 1898.

Rolle

ALLEN, Emily Hope: *The English Writings of Richard Rolle,* London and New York, Oxford Univ. Press, 1931.

COMPER, M.M. Frances: *The Fire of Love and the Mending of Life,* London, Methuen, 2nd edn, 1920.

HESELTINE, G.C.: *Selected Works of Richard Rolle,* London, Longmans, 1930.

Walter Hilton

UNDERHILL, E. (Editor): *The Scale of Perfection,* London, John Watkins, 1923, reprint, 1950.

SITWELL, G. (Editor): *The Scale of Perfection,* translated into modern English with Introduction and Notes, London, Burns & Oates, 1953, and Westminster, Md, Newman Press, 1954.

JONES, D. (Editor): *The Minor Works of Walter Hilton,* London, Burns & Oates, 1929.

The Cloud

HODGSON, P. : *The Cloud of Unknowing and the Book of Privy Counselling,* edited for E.E.T.S., London and New York, Oxford Univ. Press, 1944; reprint, 1954.

MCCANN, J. *The Cloud of Unknowing and Other Treatises,* London, Burns & Oates, and Westminster, Md, Newman Press, revised edn, 1952.

Julian of Norwich

HUDDLESTON, R. (Editor): *Revelations of Divine Love,* London, Burns & Oates, 1927 (reprint, 1952) and Westminster, Md, Newman Press, 1952.

MOLINARI, P. : *Julian of Norwich,* London and New York, Longmans 1959.

REYNOLDS, A.M. (Editor) : *A Shewing of God's Love,* London and New York, Longmans, 1958.

BUTLER BOWDEN, W. : *The Book of Margery Kempe, A Modern Version, London, Cape, and New York, Devin,* 1936.

St John Fisher

REYNOLDS, E.E. : *St John Fisher,* London, Burns & Oates, and New York, Kenedy, 1956.

The English Works of John Fisher, E.E.T.S. Oxford, Oxford Univ. Press, 1876; with additions, London and New York, Oxford Univ. Press, 1935.

St Thomas More

CAMPBELL, W.E. : *The English Works of St. Thomas More,* two volumes only published, London, Eyre & Spottiswoode, and New York, Lincoln MacVeagh, 1931.

CHAMBERS, R.W. : *Thomas More,* London, Cape, 1935 and Westminster, Md, Newman Press, 1949.

REYNOLDS, E.E. : *St Thomas More,* London, Burns & Oates, and New York, Kenedy, 1953.

Robert Persons, S.J.

Memoirs, London, privately printed for the Catholic Records Society, 1906.

Augustine Baker, O.S.B.

MCCANN, J. and CONNOLLY, H. (Editors) : *Memorials of Father Augustine Baker and other documents relating to the English Benedictines,* privately printed for the Catholic Record Society, London, 1933.

SWEENEY, N. (Editor): *Holy Wisdom or Directions for the Prayer of Contemplation,* London, Burns & Oates, 1933.

Bishop Challoner

BURTON, E.H.: *The Life and Times of Bishop Challoner, 1691-1781,* two volumes, London, Longmans, 1909.

POLLEN, J.H. (Editor): *Memoirs of Missionary Priests,* London, Burns & Oates, 1924.

Cardinal Newman

BOUYER, L.: *Newman, His Life and Spirituality,* London, Burns & Oates, and New York, Kenedy, 1958.

WARD, Wilfrid: *The Life of John Henry, Cardinal Newman,* two volumes, London and New York, Longmans, 1912.

TRISTRAM, H. (Editor): *John Henry Newman, Autobiographical Writings,* London, 1956, and New York, 1957, Sheed & Ward.

Meditations and Devotions, London and New York, Longmans, revised edn, 1953.

The collected edn of the *Works of Cardinal Newman* London and New York, Longmans, 1901-8.

MOZLEY, A. (Editor): *Letters and Correspondence of J.H. Newman,* London, Longmans, 1891.

DESSAIN, C.S. (Editor): *Letters and Diaries of John Henry Newman,* volume XI, London and New York, Nelson, 1961.

Cardinal Manning

FITZSIMONS, J. (Editor): *Manning: Anglican and Catholic,* London, Burns & Oates, 1951.

Father Faber

CHAPMAN, Ronald: *Father Faber,* London, Burns & Oates and Westminster, Md, Newman Press, 1961.

All for Jesus, revised edn, Westminster, Md, Newman Press 1956.

Bethlehem, Foot of the Cross, Spiritual Conferences, Philadelphia, Peter Reilly, n.d.

Growth in Holiness, London, Burns & Oates, and Westminster, Md, Newman Press, 1961.

Abbot Chapman

HUDDLESTON, Roger (Editor): *The Spiritual Letters of Dom John Chapman* with Introductory Memoir, London and New York, Sheed & Ward, 2nd enlarged edn, 1946.

Monsignor Knox

WAUGH, Evelyn : *The Life of the Right Reverend Ronald Knox,* London, Chapman and Hall, 1959.

The Belief of Catholics, London, Benn, 1927; reprint, New York, Sheed & Ward.

The Church on Earth, London, Burns & Oates, 1929.

Heaven and Charing Cross, Sermons on the Holy Eucharist, London, Burns & Oates, 1935.

In Soft Garments. A Collection of Oxford Conferences. London, Burns & Oates, 1942.

A Retreat for Priests, London and New York, Sheed & Ward, 1946.

Enthusiasm. A chapter in the history of religion with special reference to the seventeenth and eighteenth centuries, Oxford, Clarendon Press and New York, Oxford Univ. Press, 1950.

Stimuli, London and New York, Sheed & Ward, 1951.

The Hidden Stream, London, Burns & Oates, and New York, Sheed & Ward, 1952.

A Retreat for Lay People, London and New York, Sheed & Ward, 1955.

Commentary on the New Testament, London, Burns & Oates, and New York, Sheed & Ward, 1952-6.

The Window in the Wall and other sermons on the Holy Eucharist, London, Burns & Oates, 1956, and New York, Sheed & Ward, 1957.

The Priestly Life, London and New York, Sheed & Ward.

The Pastoral Sermons of Ronald A. Knox (ed. by Philip Caraman, S.J.), London, Burns & Oates, and New York, Sheed & Ward, 1960.

Occasional Sermons of Ronald A. Knox (ed. by Philip Caraman, S.J.), London, Burns & Oates, and New York, Sheed & Ward, 1960.

INDEX